Modellers' Guide to
MODERN BR
MOTIVE POWER

Modellers´ Guide to MODERN BR MOTIVE POWER

by

Peter Kazmierczak

PATRICK STEPHENS LIMITED
Wellingborough, Northamptonshire

Dedicated to my father for his patience and understanding, and to my late mother for her love.

First published in 1988

British Library Cataloguing in Publication Data

Kazmierczak, Peter
Modeller's guide to modern BR motive power.
1. Diesel locomotives—Great Britain—Models
I. Title
625.2'662'0941   TJ619.4.G7

ISBN 0-85059-843-5

*Patrick Stephens Limited is part of the
Thorsons Publishing Group, Wellingborough,
Northamptonshire, NN8 2RQ, England*

Printed in Great Britain by
Oxford University Press Printing House, Oxford

1 3 5 7 9 10 8 6 4 2

Contents

Acknowledgements

It is always a pleasure to thank people for their help when writing a work of this kind. Often just a single snippet of information can be of great help in completing the overall picture and so to those who, perhaps without knowing it, contributed to this book I convey my thanks.

Dr F.G.R. Zobel, Head of the Coatings, Polymers and Corrosion Unit at the Railway Technical Centre, was kind enough to explain to me the ins and outs of painting railway vehicles, and also to supply information about BR's current paint specifications. Mr A.C. MacLeod, on behalf of the Management Committee of 'The Railway Correspondence and Travel Society', allowed me to use material from their monthly magazine *The Railway Observer*. I am not a member of many societies but I can thoroughly recommend joining the RCTS, if only for the magazine which is a joy to receive each month and contains consistently reliable information about the current BR scene.

Introduction

The last ten years have seen a great upsurge in the interest shown towards modern forms of rail traction. Diesel locomotives in particular have attracted a wide following. The large crowds and enthusiasm apparent when the last of the 'Westerns' was withdrawn in 1977 surprised many people. Scenes of near hysteria accompanied the arrival of the final 'Deltic'-hauled train into London's Kings Cross station in January 1982.

Whilst the end of steam on Britain's railways signalled to some the end of a life-long hobby, others took up the challenge presented by the new diesels and electrics. Hence today trainspotting is still alive and well, as can be witnessed on any large station at weekends and during the school holidays. Locomotive numbers are not the only thing collected; nowadays coach and even wagon numbers are all meticulously jotted down. Many also delight in travelling over little used lines and freight-only routes, or being hauled by particular classes of locomotive.

On the modelling side of things however, the contemporary scene is rather neglected. The majority of layouts one sees at exhibitions are based on small branch termini set either in pre-war days or the 1950s. When diesels and electrics do appear they are seldom detailed to the same degree as their steam counter-parts. Until recently there seems to have been less enthusiasm for modelling the present scene. Nostalgia for the past may be one reason: perhaps it is thought that today's railways are boring and dull, lacking the colour and romance of bygone days. In this book I hope to show that Britain's modern locomotives have as much interest and individual character as their steam forebears and are equally worth modelling.

Without doubt, railways are the best chronicled of all the modes of transport. Each week a handful of new books is published on the subject whilst there is a tremendous choice of magazines to buy every month. The books can be broadly divided into two groups: the 'picture album' type, largely composed of photographs illustrating diesel and electric locomotives in various locations, with perhaps a short introductory text and then there are the modern technical books which delve into the engineering side of locomotives, looking in depth at their engines and transmissions and other features of their design. I want to steer a middle way between these two extremes by concentrating on the main features which are of interest to modellers: namely the liveries and external differences both between and within individual classes of locomotive. Also I hope to show how to add details to proprietary models to make them more accurate and that bit different from everyone else's.

In many ways a book is a personal statement as to how one views a particular subject and something of a compromise in terms of what to include and what to leave out. I hope that this book will introduce many newcomers to the variety of types of modern motive power on British Rail but inevitably in such limited space some classes must be covered in less depth than others. Having said that however, there should be something of interest and hopefully of lasting value here for everybody modelling the current scene on our railway system and the more enthusiasts there are who buy this book, the greater chance there is that I can persuade the publishers to produce a sequel going in to greater detail on specific classes. Just one final point: if one is really keen to model the prototype accurately, one should not rely upon any one source and although this book is designed to complement other books about modern British Railways (there being little point in duplicating what is already in print), there is really no substitute for going out there and seeing for oneself. Indeed, the ease with which this may be done is a great advantage in modelling the current scene. Such is the pace of change, however, that what may be true today, will not necessarily be so tomorrow. History, it seems, begins now.

Peter Kazmierczak
Alvaston
Derby

SECTION 1
Setting the scene

ONE
A pause for thought: modelling 'modern' railways

Railway modelling is a fascinating hobby which involves a number of diverse skills, embracing many different disciplines: woodwork, metalwork, design, engineering, electronics, sculpture and painting are only some of its facets. At times the hobby can be frustrating, but it can also be a lot of fun. It can tax one's patience to the limit yet give an immense amount of pleasure and sense of achievement. We are often accused of escapism, but what matter if it is? Creating a miniature world without any violence or discrimination, poverty or want and disputes or bigotry is no bad thing.

Before getting down in earnest to looking at the various types of diesel and electric locomotive which have run in Britain and before attempting to recreate these different classes in model form, it is worthwhile pausing for a moment to reflect on what is meant by the word 'modelling' and the term 'modern motive power'.

Read the model railway magazines to keep abreast of new developments in the hobby.

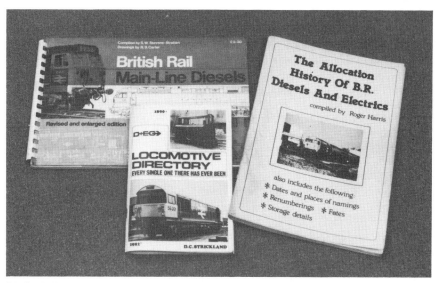

No book should be read in isolation. There are plenty on the market packed with information about the prototype which are of great value to us as modellers.

Models

There are models and there are models. We have all drooled over superb examples of exquisitely constructed locomotives displayed in glass cases and wished that we could build to such a high standard. Looking at such perfect examples of model engineering will probably spur us on to better things but it could also slightly depress us, realizing that we might never achieve such excellence. On the other hand we have all seen kits or proprietary models bodged-up by being badly painted or assembled and thought that we could do better. Whilst we can aspire to a very high standard we should not be put off because we feel that we cannot achieve a sufficiently high one. By the same token, can one criticise somebody for altering a ready-to-run model, trying to give it more character and individuality, and making a mess of it? After all, a model is only a representation or a caricature of part of the real world. Whilst a show-case model looks very nice it seldom turns a wheel or hauls a train. The proprietary model, though having its faults and inaccuracies, can pull coaches and wagons, which, all said and done, is what the real thing was designed to do.

A model can be defined, rather grandly, as a 'simplified structuring of reality'. This definition may sound somewhat pretentious, but these four words provide one of the keys to what railway modelling is all about. We are dealing with *reality*; something which actually exists or existed at one time. Thus we have to study the real thing and try to recreate it in miniature. But it is impossible to reproduce an exact scaled-down version of a full-size locomotive. If we did, the body would be paper thin and fall to pieces the moment we picked it up. We have to compromise by making parts thicker and more robust than if they were a precise reproduction. However, the question of compromise goes further than this. It also implies that we need to use our imaginations when modelling. Since every little detail of a locomotive cannot be included on our model, we have to *simplify* what we see. This is where imagination plays a great part in whether the completed model looks like the real thing. We have to decide which elements to simplify and yet retain the essential *structures* which go to make up the prototype. It does not really matter if all the dimensions of our model are not absolutely spot-on. It does not matter if we do not include every last nut and bolt or rivet. It even does not matter if some mistakes are made, so long as the errors are not too glaring. But what is important is that we capture the *character* of the locomotive, that we recapture the atmosphere and 'feel' of the full-size locomotive in model form.

There are many different materials and techniques in which to model. A set of low-melt white metal cast parts can be assembled to form the locomotive. More recently, etched brass kits have come into vogue. Away from metal, a one-piece fibreglass casting can be obtained to make up the body. Perhaps most popular of all is the plastic ready-to-run model. All these materials have their advantages and disadvantages. The cast metal kit builds into a nice heavy model with plenty of pulling power, but it can be difficult to obtain a really good finish to the bodywork. Etched brass enables a lot of sharp and intricate detail to be included, though care and a certain degree of skill is needed in assembly. The fibreglass shell forms a strong body but again, like the metal kit, requires a fair amount of work to produce an acceptable result. With the plastic model the quality of the mouldings can be excellent. It is also fairly easy to hack away at the body to alter its appearance and to add extra details. However it is equally easy to create a model with a horrid plastic-looking finish to it, totally unlike the real thing. Each medium has its pros and cons: there may be a certain snob appeal in saying that the model is made up from etched brass rather than a cheap plastic moulding, yet so long as the completed model resembles the prototype and captures its 'feel' then it has achieved its objective regardless of the material used in construction.

Modern motive power

'Modern' is a very subjective word. It is rather like asking somebody that old chestnut, 'How long is a piece of string?' The term is transient: what is regarded as modern today is not necessarily so tomorrow. A phrase which often crops up in modelling circles is 'modern image'. People will say that their layout is 'modern image' or that they only model 'modern image locomotives'. What they really mean is that they model diesels and electrics rather than steam locomotives but one never hears the term 'ancient image' applied to those whose layouts are based in steam days!

One could speak of being a modeller of the 'current' or 'contemporary' scene. However this presents us with the problem that a number of attractive types of locomotive are no longer in service and so could not strictly be run on a layout depicting present day practice. Perhaps the best method is to define the period being modelled rather than use such vague phrases at all. Hence one can talk of setting the model in the 1960s, '70s or '80s, rather as other enthusiasts describe their modelling of the 1920s and '30s.

The term 'motive power' is more objective than 'modern', but can also give rise to problems. It can be defined as having the power to cause motion. From a railway viewpoint, therefore, anything which has the strength to move itself or move another vehicle can be considered as 'motive power'. This definition is very broad — perhaps too broad. At many locations gravity is still used to move wagons from one siding to another and into the second half of this century horses were still being used in many goods yards on Britain's railways to shunt wagons. But locomotives, self-propelled machines running on rails, are what we usually think of as 'motive power'.

A locomotive is specifically designed to haul a train. There have been many different types of diesel and electric locomotives run in Britain; from small shunters to large mainline classes. The multiple unit comprising sets of coaches, usually two, three or four in number, with one or more powered, permanently or semi-permanently coupled together and run as one unit can also be considered a form of 'motive power'. Whilst these are an increasingly important part of the modern railway scene they have so far been neglected by the model trade. Only a couple of manufacturers produce any kits of these vehicles and assembling them is not really a task for the beginner. Ready-to-run models are equally sparse on the ground, just a handful of types having appeared over the years. Maybe in the future manufacturers will mend their ways and market a representative collection of diesel and electric multiple units. For this reason it is, perhaps, better to look at the field of multiple units at a later date when more ready-to-run examples have been produced. In that the High Speed Train and the Advanced Passenger Train can be defined as multiple units, I will give these types some attention in due course but there's plenty of interest in the variety of locomotive types. It would be folly indeed not to include the High Speed Train as this, above all the other types of motive power currently in service, epitomizes the modern railway scene in Britain.

Thought is a vital ingredient of modelling. It is important to have clear in one's own mind how one is to proceed, what parameters to work to and to what end. Knowing what one wants to achieve from modelling is half the battle.

TWO
Gone and almost forgotten - the early diesels and electrics

Many types of locomotive which were once an integral part of the railway scene have now passed into history. Classes typical of a particular area are now no more. Something that was an everyday sight is now just a blurred memory. Time marches on and designs which were considered, not too many years ago, to be the height of innovation and the 'state of the art' have been consigned ignominiously to the scrapheap. Such is progress or politics, or both.

Up until the late 1960s, there was no unified method to describe the various types of motive power seen on British Railways (BR). Each region had its own way to classify the different designs of locomotive. Take, for example, the type we now know as the Class '37'. On the London Midland Region (LMR) they were referred to as 'E.E. Type 3 1,750hp' — rather a mouthful and not very concise. The 'E.E.' was an abbreviation for English Electric, the makers of the machine; 'Type 3' was the broad power category, whilst the final figures gave the engine's power rating.

The Eastern Region (ER) devised a very neat numerical identification code which it applied to diesel locomotives. Under this system a Class '37' would be called '17/3'; the first figures representing the horsepower and the last being a code number for the manufacturers. Of course the Western Region (WR) had to be different. In true Great Western style they were known as the 'D66XX' Class, this relating to the number series then applied to the locomotives.

As a prelude to the computerization of its rolling stock records, BR set about devising a new classification system for its locomotive fleet. This appeared in 1968 and was extended in the early 1970s to encompass the multiple unit stock. The broad divisions of this numerical classification can be summarized as follows:

Classes	Broad categories
01-13	Diesel shunters
14-60	Mainline diesel locomotives
70-77	DC electric locomotives
80-91	AC electric locomotives
97	Departmental locomotives

Classes	Broad categories
98	Steam locomotives
100-156	Diesel-hydraulic and diesel-mechanical multiple units
201-210	Diesel-electric multiple units
250-254	Blue Pullman and High Speed Train
301-321	AC electric multiple units
370	Advanced Passenger Train
401-499	Southern Region DC electric multiple units
501-508	Other regions DC electric multiple units
920	Departmental AC electric multiple units
930-935	Departmental DC electric multiple units

The diesel multiple unit range originally extended up to Class '190' as the power cars and trailers were given separate class numbers. However at the beginning of 1979 the trailers were re-classified so as to have the same code as their associated power cars. There have been some other changes over the years as classes have disappeared and new ones introduced, but the broad categories remain. There were some locomotives, though, that did not survive long enough to be included in this system of classification and it is these early diesels and electrics that we will concentrate on in this chapter.

Diesel shunters

Nationalization of the British railway network took place as a result of the 1947 Transport Act. On 1 January 1948, the first day of the new national system, BR inherited twelve different types of diesel shunter. Not all of the designs were yet in service; only 52 locomotives had actually been completed. Many were under construction in various workshops or still at the planning stage on the order books.

The London Midland & Scottish Railway (LMS) provided four of the designs and the lion's share of those locomotives actually in service; 44 out of the 52 in fact. The four types, with their BR number series, were:

13000	Armstrong Whitworth	250hp 0-6-0 diesel-electric
12000-12002	Hawthorn Leslie	350hp 0-6-0 diesel-electric
12003-12032	LMS (Derby)	350hp 0-6-0 diesel-electric
12033-12138	LMS (Derby)	350hp 0-6-0 diesel-electric

Two designs of diesel shunter came from the London & North Eastern Railway (LNER):

15000-15003	LNER (Doncaster)	350hp 0-6-0 diesel-electric
15004	Brush	360hp 0-6-0 diesel-electric

Just one complete diesel shunter passed from the Great Western Railway (GWR) into BR hands, though others were at an advanced stage of construction:

15100	Hawthorn Leslie	350hp 0-6-0 diesel-electric
15101-15106	GWR (Swindon)	350hp 0-6-0 diesel-electric
15107	GWR (Swindon)	360hp 0-6-0 diesel-electric

Finally, the Southern Railway (SR) had three types:

15201-15203	SR (Ashford)	350hp 0-6-0 diesel-electric
15211-15236	SR (Ashford)	350hp 0-6-0 diesel-electric
11001	SR (Ashford)	500hp 0-6-0 diesel-mechanical

Of these twelve different types only two survived long enough to be included in BR's numerical classification system; the ex-LMS 12033-12138 becoming Class '11' and the ex-SR 15211-15236 being Class '12'.

LMS/Armstrong Whitworth 250hp 0-6-0 diesel-electric (13000)
This was one of the pioneer LMS diesel shunters. Introduced in 1934 it did not last very long under BR auspices, being withdrawn towards the end of 1949. It spent its final few years shunting in the yards around Willesden in north-west London and at Toton between Nottingham and Derby. At nationalization it was allocated the number 13000 but it retained its former LMS number, 7058, right to the end. Livery was plain black with red bufferbeams.

LMS/Hawthorn Leslie 350hp 0-6-0 diesel-electric (12000-12002)
Eleven of this type entered service on the LMS in 1936 but most were requisitioned by the War Department, never to return. Hence only three became BR property; the former LMS numbered 7074 becoming 12000, 7076 being 12001 and 7079 being 12002. Throughout the BR period they were based at Crewe, usually shunting in the large Basford Hall yard south of the station. Adorned in a plain black livery with red bufferbeams, the locomotives carried the first style of BR emblem (the 'cycling lion') on the body side. 'Overhead live wire' flashes were applied to 12001 shortly before it was withdrawn.

There were a number of differences between 12002 and the other two. Number 12002 had actually been built in 1934 by Hawthorn Leslie as a demonstration locomotive. On the footplate it had its fuel tanks mounted in front of its battery boxes whilst on the others they were reversed, with the fuel tanks next to the cab. The offside cab door on 12002 was in a different position; it also had much smaller front footsteps, fluted coupling rods (as against rectangular-section rods on 12000 and 12001) and vacuum brakes. Not surprisingly it was 12002 that was withdrawn first, going in the middle of 1956. Next to go was 12000 during 1961, whilst 12001 lasted until the early part of 1962.

LMS 350hp 0-6-0 diesel-electric (12003-12032)
These thirty locomotives were built by the LMS at Derby between 1939 and 1942, numbered 7080-7099 and 7110-7119. By early BR days they were largely divided between three sheds; Willesden, Speke (half way between Liverpool and

Runcorn) and Carlisle. Carlisle lost its allocation by the end of 1950 whilst those at Willesden were moved to Crewe during 1954 and 1955. Thus in the late 1950s these locomotives were concentrated at two sheds: Crewe and Speke. During the early 1960s a few moved down to the West Midlands, based at Bescot near Walsall, but the rest remained in their North-west stronghold. All had been taken out of service by the end of 1967.

Originally the class were painted plain black with red bufferbeams. After nationalization, the BR emblem was eventually applied to the body side. Prior to this, however, some locomotives (for example 12026 and 12028) had 'BRITISH RAILWAYS' painted in full on the engine compartment doors. At least one had this lettering whilst still retaining its former LMS number, this being 7117, albeit with an 'M' prefix. In 1956 it was decided to paint diesel locomotives in a green livery rather than the hitherto uninspiring black. At the same time a new design of BR crest was introduced. Gradually then these shunters were repainted in unlined Brunswick green and the new crest applied. The underframe, though, was still black and the bufferbeams red; the coupling and connecting rods were however also painted red. Some of the class appear to have had the top of the engine bonnet and the cab roof painted black, whilst D12016 was incorrectly given the 'D' prefix after overhaul in the late 1950s. It retained this prefix until it was withdrawn. Black and yellow warning stripes were applied to each end from around 1960 to make the locomotives more conspicuous to railway staff on the ground. Also in the early 1960s 'overhead live wire' flashes were added to most, if not all, of the class. None were ever painted in blue livery as the class was being withdrawn just as the new style was introduced.

There were a number of variations between individual members of the class, stemming from the fact that they were built in two batches:

12003-12022 had a raised casing between the windows on the back of the cab. The steps leading up to the cab had only two rungs initially but soon they were altered to three. To reach the battery boxes situated on the footplate, an additional set of footsteps was provided towards the middle of the locomotive by the jackshaft drive.

12023-12032 had a flat shape to the rear of the cab. They also lacked the middle pair of footsteps as the battery boxes were redesigned to open outwards rather than upwards as on the earlier examples. The locomotives were over a foot longer than the first batch since the cab was slightly longer and there was a larger radiator casing at the front. Of these ten diesels, the first six (12023-12028) also differed in having vertical bodyside louvres as against a horizontal type on all the others. They also had a small rectangular casing on the rear of the cab beneath the offside window. Numbers 12023-12028 were slightly different because they were originally used by the War Department for a short while.

Modifications applied to the class whilst in service included the provision of electric marker lights, front and rear, during the 1950s. By the early '60s most of the locomotives were working in areas close to 25kV AC overhead wires so, in the interests of safety, the ladders were removed from each side of the radiator at the front end.

LNER 350hp 0-6-0 diesel-electric (15000-15003)

Originally numbered 8000-8003, these were built by the LNER at Doncaster in 1944 and 1945. Almost all their time was spent shunting in the large Whitemoor marshalling yard at March in Cambridgeshire. However at the beginning of 1966 they were all transferred to the LMR for use in the Crewe area. As they were equipped with vacuum brakes, unlike their former LMS counterparts, they could work on more varied duties such as permanent-way trains. Their reign at Crewe did not last long as they were all withdrawn during 1967.

Like the previous diesel shunters we have looked at, they had a plain black livery with red bufferbeams. Unlike the others though, the BR emblem was positioned on the side of the cab with the locomotive's number on the engine compartment doors. Later, the new style crest was applied to the centre of the battery boxes on the footplate and the number put on the cab side. Number 15003 was subsequently repainted in green livery. There were a couple of external differences between these four diesels; 15000 and 15001 had straight rainstrips on the cab roof whilst they were curved on the other two. 15002 and 15003 also differed in having grab-holes in the engine compartment doors rather than the more usual handrails.

Brush 360hp 0-6-0 diesel-electric (15004)

Although completed at the Loughborough works of Brush, many of the mechanical parts of 15004 were built by the LNER at Doncaster and so this locomotive looked very much like 15000-15003. The main visual difference was the lack of battery boxes on the footplate. Entering BR stock in 1949 it was duly painted in plain black, but with the emblem on the cab side and the number on the engine compartment doors just like the other LNER-designed shunters.

Initially it worked alongside 15000-15003 at Whitemoor yard before moving to New England shed in Peterborough at the beginning of 1957. Here it remained until withdrawn in 1962.

GWR/Hawthorn Leslie 350hp 0-6-0 diesel-electric (15100)

Originally introduced on the GWR in 1936 and given the number 2 on their stock list, this locomotive was quickly renumbered 15100 by BR after nationalization. The former GWR green livery was soon submerged beneath a coat of black paint but a nice touch was the addition of the locomotive's number on each bufferbeam. There were no numbers on the cab side; instead they were applied, in slightly larger than normal figures, to the fuel tanks on the footplate. From the appearance viewpoint this locomotive was virtually identical to 12000 and 12001 (mentioned above) which was not surprising as they were built by the same firm at the same time.

Throughout the 1950s 15100 spent most of its time shunting in the Bristol area. Its last few years were, however, at Swindon from where it was withdrawn in 1965.

GWR 350hp 0-6-0 diesel-electric (15101-15106)

Built at Swindon, these six locomotives entered service during 1948 based at Old

Oak Common shed in west London. Towards the end of 1958 they were transferred to the Cardiff area where they remained until 1966. In that year they were moved to the West Midlands and ended up at Bescot. Their stay here, though, was rather shortlived as they were all withdrawn in the middle of 1967.

As a gesture to the Great Western, the class was turned out of Swindon in Brunswick green livery with brass cab side numberplates and 'BRITISH RAILWAYS' in GWR style lettering on the engine compartment doors. Each locomotive's number was also painted on each bufferbeam, above the couplings. However, during the 1950s they were repainted plain black like the other diesel shunters and the brass numberplates were removed. Later, electric marker lights were fitted and the ends painted black and yellow. At least one (15106) was subsequently painted green again, though by this time it lacked the numberplates and carried the BR crest on the body side.

GWR 360hp 0-6-0 diesel-electric (15107)
Externally almost identical to 15101-15106, number 15107 had a rather short life of less than ten years. Built in 1949 at Swindon it spent all its time working in the Bristol area until withdrawal in 1958. Livery was plain black with a large-sized BR emblem on the engine compartment doors. It too, had a brass numberplate fixed on the side of the cab, though it was in a slightly higher position than the previous class.

SR 350hp 0-6-0 diesel-electric (15201-15203)
Although largely built by the Southern Railway at Ashford during 1937, these three locomotives resembled the Hawthorn Leslie examples constructed for the LMS and GWR that we looked at earlier. However there were differences; notably the larger diameter wheels giving rise to a two-level footplate, and a different design of cab.

Numbered 1-3 on the SR, their early BR livery was plain black with cab side numbers and BR emblem on the engine doors. Bufferbeams were red and, like the GWR diesel shunters, the locomotive's number was painted above the coupling. Six-position electric marker lights were later fitted, whilst the ends were painted with black and yellow stripes and 'overhead live wire' flashes were applied to the body side. The final livery carried by the class was green, with the BR crest positioned on the side of the fuel tanks.

For most of their lives they were to be seen shunting in the yards at Norwood Junction near Croydon. However, 15202 moved to Hither Green in south-east London in the mid-1950s whilst 15201 spent its final months working from Eastleigh shed in Hampshire. All were withdrawn at the end of 1964.

SR 500hp 0-6-0 diesel-mechanical (11001)
The final pre-nationalization design of diesel shunter to appear was 11001 which was built at Ashford in Kent and entered service during 1950. Although designed not just for shunting work but for more varied duties such as hauling trains between different marshalling yards, surprisingly it was not fitted with

vacuum brakes. The 'Bulleid-Firth Brown' cast steel wheels, typically seen on all of Bulleid's designs, and a notable innovation of the last Chief Mechanical Engineer of the SR, were a notable feature of the locomotive.

In a plain black livery with red bufferbeams and BR emblem, 11001 was initially based at Norwood Junction and generally worked in the south and south-western suburbs of London. In the middle of 1952 it moved northwards to Yorkshire where it was tried on former Midland Railway lines in the Leeds area. It went to the ER for a short spell during 1956, allocated to Hornsey shed in north London. Back south of the Thames towards the end of that year it was again based at Norwood Junction, from where it was withdrawn in 1959.

Modelling possibilities

Unfortunately no models, either in ready-to-run or kit form, have been produced of these types of diesel shunter. This is not altogether surprising as these locomotives, it must be admitted, do not have quite the same attraction or marketing appeal as the larger mainline classes. It is doubtful if any will ever be made commercially. The SR 500hp diesel-mechanical, for example, was in every sense a one-off prototype. From the manufacturers' viewpoint the one with the most potential would be the Hawthorn Leslie diesel shunter because it could be used on LMS, GWR and, with a little modification, SR layouts, but for the present, short of scratchbuilding, what can be done?

Whilst there are no models of these specific classes, there are many of the Class '08' which was derived from these earlier designs. The following table compares the early diesels with the Class '08'.

BR numbers	Wheelbase	Diameter	Notes
13000	4ft 6in + 8ft 6in	3ft 6in	Jackshaft drive
12000-12002	5ft 9in + 5ft 9in	4ft ½in	Hawthorn Leslie body
12003-12032	6ft 0in + 9ft 3in	4ft 3in	Jackshaft drive
15000-15003	5ft 9in + 6ft 0in	4ft 0in	Class '08' type body
15004	5ft 9in + 6ft 0in	4ft 0in	Class '08' type body
15100	5ft 9in + 5ft 9in	4ft 1in	Hawthorn Leslie body
15101-15106	5ft 9in + 5ft 9in	4ft ½in	Class '08' type body
15107	5ft 9in + 5ft 9in	4ft ½in	Class '08' type body
15201-15203	5ft 9in + 5ft 9in	4ft 6in	Hawthorn Leslie body
Class '08'	5ft 9in + 5ft 9in	4ft 6in	—

Figure 1 shows the basic outlines of some of the early LMS diesel shunters. Though it might be difficult to model the two classes with a jackshaft drive, the others could be modified from the Class '08'. The easiest to do would be 15101-15106 and 15107 and in the smaller scales one could probably get away with simply repainting a Class '08'. With a little work around the cab it should not be too difficult to create 15000-15003 or 15004 either. On the other hand, those shunters with the Hawthorn Leslie body design would require more attention. The Class '08' chassis could form the basis for the model but the body would have to be scratchbuilt out of plastic card. Scale drawings of most of these

Figure 1 Early LMS diesel shunters

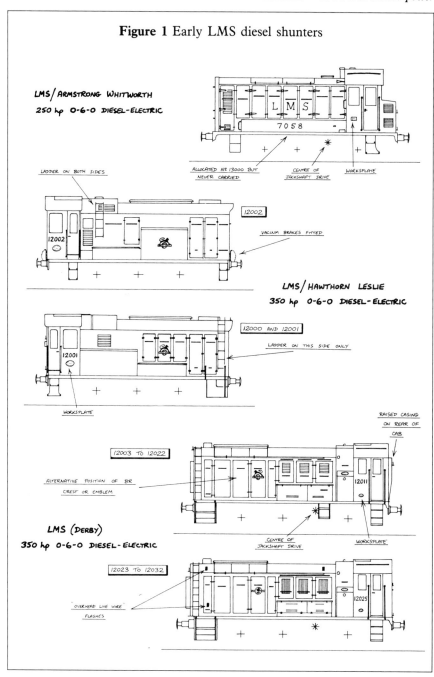

LMS/ARMSTRONG WHITWORTH
250 hp 0-6-0 DIESEL-ELECTRIC

L M S
7058

LADDER ON BOTH SIDES

ALLOCATED Nº 13000 BUT
NEVER CARRIED

CENTRE OF
JACKSHAFT DRIVE

WORKSPLATE

12002

12002

VACUUM BRAKES FITTED

LMS/HAWTHORN LESLIE
350 hp 0-6-0 DIESEL-ELECTRIC

12000 AND 12001

12001

LADDER ON THIS SIDE ONLY

WORKSPLATE

RAISED CASING
ON REAR OF
CAB

12003 TO 12022

ALTERNATIVE POSITION OF BR
CREST OR EMBLEM

12011

LMS (DERBY)
350 hp 0-6-0 DIESEL-ELECTRIC

CENTRE OF
JACKSHAFT DRIVE

WORKSPLATE

12023 TO 12032

OVERHEAD LIVE WIRE
FLASHES

12025

early types have been published in the model magazines; details are included in
the bibliography at the rear.

These pre-nationalization designs were not the only diesel shunters withdrawn
by BR prior to the introduction of their numerical classification system. There
were other types, ordered by BR themselves, that had all been withdrawn by the
late 1960s:

11104	Hibberd	52hp 0-4-0 diesel-mechanical
D2500-D2519	Hudswell Clarke	204hp 0-6-0 diesel-mechanical
D2700-D2707	North British	200hp 0-4-0 diesel-hydraulic
D2708-D2780	North British	225hp 0-4-0 diesel-hydraulic
D2900-D2913	North British	330hp 0-4-0 diesel-hydraulic
D2950-D2952	Hunslet	153hp 0-4-0 diesel-mechanical
D2957-D2958	Ruston & Hornsby	165hp 0-4-0 diesel-mechanical
D2999	Brush	200hp 0-4-0 diesel-electric

Hibberd 52hp 0-4-0 diesel-mechanical (11104)
Originally the smaller diesel shunters were numbered by BR from 11100
upwards. However in 1957 the decision was made to renumber these locomotives in the D2000-D2999 series. Eventually all received their allotted new
numbers with one exception, this being 11104. Introduced in 1950, this small
four-wheel shunter spent almost all of its time working at West Hartlepool.
Number 11104 was rather camera shy but its initial livery was probably black
with red bufferbeams. During 1953 it was renumbered into the Departmental
Stock List as number 52, coincidentally perhaps the same number as its horsepower rating. Final withdrawal was in 1967.

Hudswell Clarke 204hp 0-6-0 diesel-mechanical (D2500-D2519)
This class was built in two distinct batches; D2500-D2509 (originally numbered
11116-11120 and 11144-11148) appearing in 1955/56 and D2510-D2519 some
years later in 1961. With their short wheelbase (5in less than most of the other
types of 0-6-0 diesel shunters) they were particularly suited to areas with tightly-
curved tracks. This was reflected in their actual allocations in that the first of ten
were based at Birkenhead for shunting in the docks, whilst most of the second
batch were at Barrow-in-Furness, again working on the dock lines. The end for
the class came quickly as all twenty were withdrawn during the same year, 1967.
Appearance-wise one could easily be forgiven for thinking that D2500-D2509
and D2510-D2519 were built by two completely different firms. The first batch
could, at a glance, be mistaken for steam engines as their outline hardly
resembled a typical diesel profile at all. On the other hand the second batch of ten
locomotives appeared quite stylish and modern, yet all were constructed at the
same factory in Leeds. The early locomotives were turned out in plain black with
red bufferbeams and coupling rods. The BR emblem was on the cab side above

the number. All of the second batch were delivered new in green livery with black and yellow ends, and the BR crest. The early examples in black were eventually repainted green whilst 'overhead live wire' flashes were applied to many of the class. A couple of the class have been preserved and details of their location is given in one of the appendices to this book.

North British 200hp 0-4-0 diesel-hydraulic (D2700-D2707)
Another small class consisting of only eight members, there were nevertheless a number of differences between the first three and the other five. D2700-D2702 (originally 11700-11702) were built in 1953/4 with large round-headed buffers and no vacuum brakes. D2703-D2707 (initially 11703-11707) appeared during 1955/6 and had a larger cab, modified front radiator design, oval buffers and vacuum brakes.

The livery was plain black at first with the BR emblem and number on the cab side. Later they were painted green with the black and yellow stripes on the ends. The first three locomotives initially worked at West Hartlepool before moving to Goole in 1960. The others were all based in Scotland, mostly in the Edinburgh and Dunfermline areas. D2700 was the first to be withdrawn, as early as 1963. The remainder went during 1967 except for D2703 which lasted until the following year.

North British 225hp 0-4-0 diesel-hydraulic (D2708-D2780)
Construction of these locomotives was spread over the period from 1957 to 1961. The class spent the majority of their time shunting in yards and sidings of central Scotland, largely in the area bounded by Glasgow, Edinburgh and Dundee. In the mid 1960s about a dozen moved south for employment as works shunters at Crewe and at Wolverton in Buckinghamshire. Most of the class were withdrawn during 1967 but a few lingered on into 1968.

At first glance all the class appeared to be similar, but as they were built in three batches there were differences between them:
D2708-D2719 (originally numbered 11708-11719) were delivered in plain black livery with cab side numbers and the emblem on the engine compartment doors. The driving wheels had a diameter of 3ft 6in.
D2720-D2744 were over a foot longer than the earlier batch and had 3ft 9in diameter wheels. Green livery was applied with the BR crest and number on the cab side.
D2745-D2780 wore green livery with 3ft 9in wheels. They had a modified design of radiator grille and a raised bonnet section in front of the cab.

North British 330hp 0-4-0 diesel-hydraulic (D2900-D2913)
The last on the trio of North British 0-4-0s were these 330hp locomotives, though some sources suggest that their original engine rating may have been only 300hp. Throughout, their livery was green with cab side numbers and BR crest. However, the locomotive's number was above the crest rather than below as on most of the other diesel shunters. Black and yellow stripes were later applied to

the ends, and 'overhead live wire' flashes added to most, if not all, of them. Initially small round-headed buffers were fitted but these were later changed for larger-headed round ones.

Built in 1958 and 1959, the class worked at first in two distinct areas. D2900-D2907 were in east London shunting in the Bow and Poplar districts near to the Docks, whilst the remainder were sent to work in the Rugby area. During the middle of the 1960s most migrated further north to Crewe where they stayed until withdrawal in 1967.

Hunslet 153hp 0-4-0 diesel-mechanical (D2950-D2952)

This small class of but three locomotives appeared in 1954/5. They were built to replace former Great Eastern 0-6-0 tram engines working on the dock lines and quayside at Ipswich. These diesels, like the steam trams before them, had to be fitted with cow-catchers front and rear and side plates to conceal the wheels and coupling rods because they used lines running alongside public roads and unfenced from them. Their reign at Ipswich ended towards the latter part of 1966. D2952 was withdrawn whilst the other two were transferred to Goole. They were withdrawn in 1967.

Initially in plain black with red bufferbeams, cab side numbers and BR emblem, they were at first numbered 11500-11502. Later they were all repainted in the green livery, though the side plates remained black. The BR crest was applied and the ends given a coat of black and yellow stripes.

Ruston & Hornsby 165hp 0-4-0 diesel-mechanical (D2957-D2958)

An even smaller class consisting of just two locomotives built in 1956. At first based at Immingham near Grimsby for use in the docks there, they were soon moved south to Stratford shed in east London. Withdrawal came, like so many of these diesel shunters, during 1967/68. Originally numbered 11507 and 11508, the livery was again plain black with cab side numbers and BR emblem. One at least, D2958, was repainted green with black and yellow ends and given 'overhead live wire' flashes.

Brush 200hp 0-4-0 diesel-electric (D2999)

This was another locomotive based at Stratford in east London for shunting in that area. Actually built in 1959 by Beyer-Peacock in association with Brush, it was bought by BR during 1960. It only lasted until 1967, withdrawn in the general purge of shunters that year. Delivered to BR in a rather striking light orange shade with the top of the engine compartment in green, it was soon repainted in the standard green livery with black and yellow ends. The BR crest was on the engine compartment doors and 'overhead live wire' flashes were also applied.

Modelling possibilities

Like the earlier types of diesel shunter, these locomotives have been largely ignored by the model trade. Whilst it is true that manufacturers' catalogues

One of the few ready-to-run examples of a small 0-4-0 diesel shunter was this one from Tri-ang, *in either electric or clockwork power.*

have, over the years, included in their pages some small diesels, they were often of freelance design or even of continental origin with a fictitious BR number and livery applied. For example, in the mid 1960s *Tri-ang* had in their 00 gauge range an 0-4-0 diesel locomotive. Available in both electric and clockwork versions, it vaguely resembled one of the North British diesel-hydraulics but was really just a 'typical' diesel outline shape to fit on to a chassis that the firm already had in production. Having said that, an evening's work with a little plastic card, wire and paint can make it a little more presentable, albeit still a fictitious design.

The Hibberd four-wheel shunter (11104) could be built around one of the available motor bogies. For the other types, recourse would have to be made to stratchbuilding, though perhaps using a proprietary chassis as the basis. The wheelbase and wheel diameter of these diesel shunters is as follows:

BR numbers	Wheelbase	Diameter
D2500-D2519	4ft 3½in + 4ft 3½in	3ft 6in
D2700-D2707	6ft 0in	3ft 6in
D2708-D2719	6ft 0in	3ft 6in
D2720-D2780	6ft 0in	3ft 9in
D2900-D2913	6ft 0in	3ft 9in
D2950-D2952	5ft 6in	3ft 4in
D2957-D2958	5ft 9in	3ft 4in
D2999	6ft 0in	3ft 6in

These early types of diesel shunter, whilst not being to everyone's taste, have been included for the sake of completeness. Perhaps not quite in the 'modern image' mould, they were nevertheless an interesting bunch of locomotives. *Figure 2* shows the year in which they were introduced on BR and when the last was withdrawn.

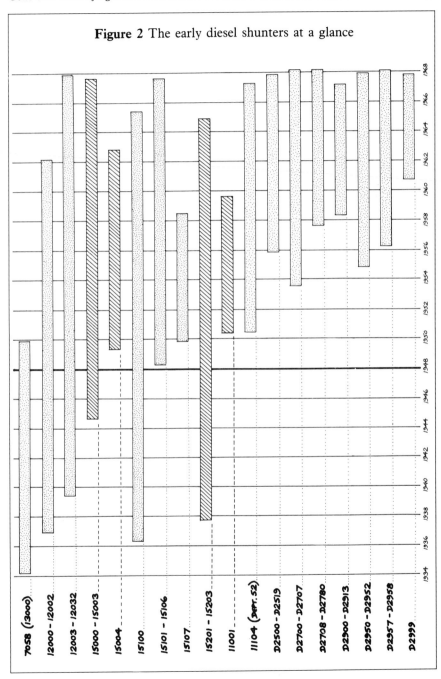

Figure 2 The early diesel shunters at a glance

Mainline diesel and gas turbine locomotives

Compared to the diesel shunter, mainline motive power was in its infancy at nationalization. Only one locomotive had actually been completed, though each of the four companies had plans to introduce new forms of traction. In 1947 the LNER had approved a scheme to buy 25 diesel-electrics for use on the East Coast route between London and Edinburgh. Unfortunately none was ordered before nationalization and BR was very quick to scrap the project after 1948.

Most tangible progress had been made by the LMS. One locomotive had been completed and another nearly so, whilst a different type was also under construction and a further design on the drawing board:

10000-10001	LMS (Derby)	1,600hp Co-Co diesel-electric
10100	LMS (Derby)/Fell	2,000hp 2-D-2 diesel-mechanical
10800	North British	827hp Bo-Bo diesel-electric

On the Southern Railway there were three diesels on order at the time of nationalization:

10201-10202	SR (Ashford)	1,750hp 1Co-Col diesel-electric
10203	SR (Brighton)	2,000hp 1Co-Col diesel-electric

The GWR went down a different road altogether and tried their hand at gas turbine rather than diesel power:

18000	Brown-Boveri	2,500hp A1A-A1A gas turbine
18100	Metropolitan-Vickers	3,000hp Co-Co gas turbine

LMS 1,600hp Co-Co diesel-electric (10000-10001)

Number 10000 was completed at Derby by the LMS just a few weeks before nationalization whilst 10001 appeared some months later in the middle of 1948. After initial trials, largely on the Midland line between Derby and London St Pancras, the two locomotives began working together on the West Coast route. Autumn 1948 saw them operating in multiple on passenger turns between London Euston and Carlisle, whilst the following summer they were on Anglo-Scottish trains. During the early 1950s the locomotives continued with their work on the West Coast main line, sometimes in multiple on the services to Glasgow, or singly on trains from Euston to Liverpool or Blackpool. However problems with their train heating equipment caused them to be relegated to fitted freight workings during the winter months.

The spring of 1953 saw the two locomotives transferred to the Southern Region. Here they hauled express passenger trains on two of the principal routes from London Waterloo; to Exeter and to Weymouth. Their stay down south only lasted a couple of years as they were back on the LMR by the summer of 1955. Here they began to appear more frequently on trains between Euston and Wolverhampton, and on other duties such as parcels trains.

After 1958 they were seen less on express passenger trains and more on suburban work from Euston to Bletchley and Northampton. Their appearance at the head of passenger trains gradually decreased in the early 1960s as they became increasingly assigned to freight work. The end came for number 10000 in December 1963 whilst 10001 lasted a few more years until the spring of 1966.

10000 and 10001 were not quite identical twins as there was one slight external difference between the pair. 10000 originally had an oval aperture on both sides of the body at the number two end (ie, the end furthest away from the circular roof fan). Close by these apertures on the body side were a couple of inset footsteps and hand grabholes. Possibly the intention was to fill the train heating boiler with water from lineside water columns. By the middle of 1949 the apertures had been plated over, but the footsteps and grabholes remained on this locomotive right up to its withdrawal. One other small difference was that 10000 did not initially have any rain strips above the cab side windows, but these were quickly added. Just before moving to the Southern Region in 1953 an additional pair of lamp irons and marker lights were fitted to each end of 10000 and 10001, the SR using a six-position system of train classification rather than the other regions' four. Finally, 10001 had four grabrails fitted on each end in the early 1960s.

The liveries carried by these locomotives are outlined in *Figure 3*. A combination of black and aluminium was applied initially, 10001 without the 'LMS' lettering of course as it was completed after nationalization. The 'LMS' initials were removed from 10000 during 1951 to be replaced by a large BR emblem, as had also been applied to 10001. By the autumn of 1956 both of the locomotives had been repainted green with orange and black lining. The roof was painted in a shade variously described as primrose yellow, cream, or lemon yellow. Within a couple of years the roof was painted in a more durable colour, namely grey. The orange and black lining was also abandoned in favour of an eggshell blue band. 'Overhead live wire' flashes were added to both the locomotives in the early 1960s whilst 10001 later received yellow warning panels on each end.

LMS/Fell 2,000hp 2-D-2 diesel-mechanical (10100)

Plans for this locomotive were made before nationalization but it was not actually constructed until 1950 at Derby. It was a joint venture between Fell Developments Ltd and BR to test the suitability of mechanical transmission for a high-powered locomotive. Although not initially owned outright by BR, it was nevertheless painted black with BR style numbering and emblem on the body side, but without any lining bands. By the spring of 1957 it had been repainted green with orange and black lining.

For the majority of its rather chequered career, 10100 worked on the Midland line between St Pancras, Derby and Manchester. Mostly its duties covered passenger trains on the route, both of the express and stopping variety. After being purchased by BR in 1955 it was tried out over the Settle and Carlisle line, and also the West Coast route between Preston and Carlisle before resuming its

Figure 3 The livery styles of 10000 and 10001

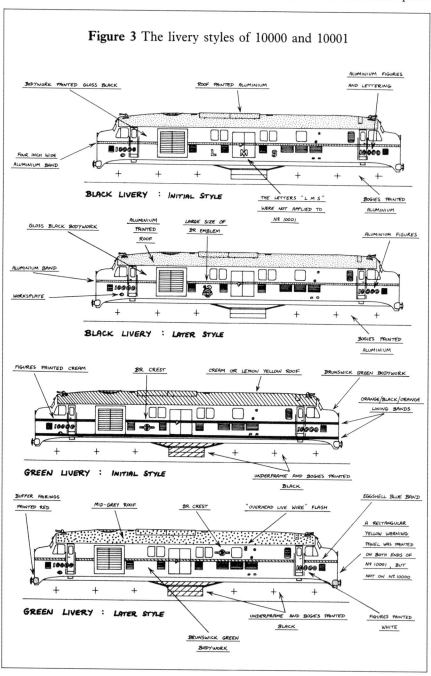

duties based at Derby. It was withdrawn towards the end of 1958 after its train heating boiler caught fire.

Number 10100 had proved to be a rather awkward locomotive to maintain, though whether the story that a great cheer went up in Derby Works when the news came that it was to be scrapped is true or not, I cannot say.

North British 827hp Bo-Bo diesel-electric (10800)

This small diesel locomotive was designed for both passenger and freight duties on secondary routes. Completed in 1950 it was at first used on the LMR based in the Bletchley area. The middle of 1952 saw it transferred to Norwood Junction on the SR for work on a variety of duties. After a brief trial on the London, Tilbury and Southend line at the beginning of 1955, it moved north to Rugby where it remained until withdrawn during the summer of 1959.

Throughout its time on BR, 10800 was painted plain black. In its early days though, its bogies were painted aluminium and for a very short period in 1950 the top of the engine compartment was also that colour. Prior to its move to the SR in 1952, an additional pair of lamp irons (but no extra marker lights) were fitted to each end. The mid-1950s also saw another modification as an extra row of ventilation louvres was cut into the engine compartment doors. After withdrawal 10800 was sold to Brush for research use, being dubbed *Hawk*.

SR 1,750hp 1Co-Co1 diesel-electric (10201-10202)

These two locomotives did much the same type of work as 10000 and 10001 considered earlier. Built at Ashford in 1950/1, they spent the first half of the 1950s on the Waterloo to Exeter and Weymouth routes. The pair were transferred to the LMR in 1955 and used on express trains out of Euston, more usually on services to Wolverhampton and Manchester. At the start of 1957 they began operating in multiple on Anglo-Scottish trains. Derated to 1,600hp in their final years, they became less common on top-link duties and appeared more often on suburban passenger and freight work. Withdrawal came at the end of 1963, though the two locomotives had been out of use for much of that year.

The pair were not quite identical as there was a vertical strengthening bar on each of the two main body side ventilation grilles on 10202, but not on 10201. A minor point perhaps, but something to look out for. Around the early part of 1958 what appears to be a gangway shield was fitted in front of the doors on each end of 10202.

Initially the liveries applied to these locomotives were gloss black with aluminium painted roof and bogie sideframes. The front of each bogie was painted red between the buffers and black below, whilst an aluminium-coloured band encircled the body at waist height. In 1956 they were repainted green with a cream or lemon yellow roof and a pair of orange/black/orange lining bands. Later the roof was painted grey and, in the early 1960s, 'overhead live wire' flashes were affixed to the sides and ends.

SR 2,000hp 1Co-Col diesel-electric (10203)

Outwardly very similar to 10201 and 10202, there were nevertheless a couple of external differences. Number 10203 was not fitted with gangway doors at each end at it was not intended to work in multiple with the other pair. On the body side the ventilation grilles were all the same depth, giving a neater appearance to the locomotive.

The livery styles applied were the same: originally black and aluminium, later giving way to lined green. However a year or so before withdrawal, yellow warning panels were painted on both ends and the chime whistles on each cab roof replaced with two-tone air horns.

Completed at Brighton in 1954 its main duties covered the Waterloo to Exeter and, to a lesser extent, the Waterloo to Weymouth lines of the SR. Like 10202 before it, it was tried for a week in the spring of 1955 on the 'Golden Arrow' and the 'Night Ferry', prior to moving on to the LMR. By the end of the 1950s its days at the head of the principal express trains such as the Royal Scot on the West Coast line were over and it appeared on more mundane tasks. Along with the other two Southern-designed diesels, it was officially withdrawn at the end of 1963 after less than ten years' service.

Brown-Boveri 2,500hp A1A-A1A gas turbine (18000)

This, the first of the two gas turbine locomotives ordered by the GWR, was built in Switzerland during 1949 and arrived in Britain early the following year. On this and the following locomotive, the gas turbine did not drive the axles directly. Rather it drove a generator which supplied electricity to traction motors and it was these that powered the wheels. Thus strictly speaking these are gas turbine-electric locomotives and in this way not dissimilar to diesel-electric machines.

Entering service on the WR in May 1950 it initially worked between London Paddington and Plymouth via the Westbury route. Regularly employed on expresses on the line from Paddington to Bristol, problems with its train steam-heating boiler over the winter of 1950/1 caused it to be relegated to hauling milk trains between London and Swindon for a while. After a spell working on the Bristol route again, the locomotive broke down there in the middle of 1951.

During the first half of 1952 it again appeared on the Paddington to Plymouth route, but this was to be the last time it regularly worked down to Devon. 1953 saw it on its usual Bristol diagram, when it was not in Swindon works for repair. Towards the end of 1955 it entered Swindon works yet again, not to reappear in service until the spring of 1957.

During this lengthy stay in the works, 18000 was repainted green. Originally in gloss black with aluminium painted roof, waistband and bogies, it was now in Brunswick green with a grey roof, red bufferbeams and orange lining. In the summer of 1959 it went into Swindon works for the final time and it never emerged to haul a train in Britain again. Its official withdrawal date was December 1960; the locomotive eventually returning to Switzerland for research purposes.

Metropolitan-Vickers 3,000hp Co-Co gas turbine (18100)
The second gas turbine locomotive was built in Manchester and began service on
the WR in April 1952. The livery was again a combination of black and aluminium, the then-standard BR colour scheme for non-steam mainline locomotives.
Initially it worked between Paddington and Bristol. Later in the summer of 1952
it started working on a regular basis down to Plymouth.

By the middle of 1953 it was back working from Paddington to Bristol but not
for long, as it disappeared from the scene by the autumn. It returned to the
manufacturers and it is doubtful if it ever ran in gas turbine form again. However
it was not officially withdrawn from BR stock until 1 January 1958.

1958 was not the end for 18100 though, as it reappeared later that year
converted into at 25kV AC electric locomotive. It survived just long enough to
become Class '80', so we will look at it again in the next chapter.

Modelling possibilities
Honour of producing the first ready-to-run model of a British mainline diesel fell
to *Kirdon Electric Ltd* who, in 1955, introduced an 00 gauge version of the LMS
10000. Available as either a two or a three-rail model, the body was of polystyrene whilst the bogie sideframes were of cast metal. At £5 15s 3d it was not a
particularly cheap model for the period, being more expensive than *Hornby
Dublo* and *Tri-ang*. Nevertheless it was a bold move to bring out a diesel model
at that time with so few real ones in service. It was to be another twenty years
before more models of these early mainline classes appeared, though none were
in ready-to-run form. In the mid 1970s *Q kits* came on the market with their
fibreglass bodyshell kits for 00 gauge. The Metropolitan-Vickers gas turbine
locomotive (18100) was soon in their range, to be followed by the LMS 10000 and
later the SR 10201 diesel types. The two diesel kits are still available but that for
the gas turbine is no longer included in their advertising.

Still in 00 gauge and still available are kits in a different medium for the 10000
and 10201 diesels. These are produced by *Modern Traction Kits* and consist of
pre-formed etched brass and cast metal parts. The motor bogies have to be
purchased separately or one could use a proprietary chassis. Moving up in size
to 0 gauge, *Post-War Prototypes* have the LMS 10000 in their range. Again
comprising a selection of pre-formed etched and cast parts, the wheels, motor
and gears also need to be bought to complete the model. In the much smaller size
of N gauge, *Langley Miniature Models* produced a white metal body kit of the
Brown-Boveri gas turbine locomotive (18000) to fit a proprietary underframe.

Finally, back in 00 gauge, a recent firm to appear on the scene is *d.c. kits*.
Amongst their range ia a fine scale resin body kit for the LMS 10000 locomotive.
A ready-to-run chassis is also available to complete the model.

Electric locomotives
BR inherited a total of sixteen electric locomotives at nationalization, but of this
total, the majority were in storage out of use, whilst one was not even in this
country, being on loan abroad. Most of the designs were of LNER or indeed pre-

LNER origin as follows:

26500-26501	Brush	640hp Bo-Bo 630V DC electric
26502-26511	NER (Darlington)	1,100hp Bo + Bo 1,500V DC electric
26600	NER (Darlington)	1,800hp 2-Co-2 1,500V DC electric
26000-26057	LNER (Doncaster)	1,868hp Bo + Bo 1,500V DC electric

Although there were no LMS or GWR electrics in the pipeline, there was one design from the SR:

20001-20003	SR (Ashford)	1,470hp Co-Co 660V DC electric

The SR electrics lasted long enough to become Class '70' whilst 26000-26057 became Class '76' in due course.

Brush 640hp Bo-Bo 630V DC electric (26500-26501)

Built in 1904 for the North Eastern Railway (NER), these two locomotives spent their entire lives working on the short Quayside branch. Situated on the north bank of the River Tyne just to the east of the centre of Newcastle, the branch linked the quay with sidings alongside the East Coast main line. The major portion of the line was electrified on the third rail principle, but the yards at each end were equipped with overhead wires so as not to endanger staff working in the sidings.

Renumbered by BR from 6480 and 6481 respectively, their livery during the 1950s was black. During 1961 the pair received a bright coat of NER green with black and white lining. On the cab side, in addition to the locomotive's number, were the BR crest and the NER coat of arms. Withdrawal came in the autumn of 1964: diesels had begun working over the branch in the spring of that year.

NER 1,100hp Bo + Bo 1,500V DC electric (26502-26511)

Introduced in 1914 for use on the seventeen miles of electrified line between Shildon, in County Durham, and Newport marshalling yard near Middlesbrough, these locomotives remained at work until 1935. In that year the 1,500V DC overhead system on the route was abandoned and the trains reverted to steam haulage. These ten locomotives were put into storage in the North-east until being officially withdrawn in the summer of 1950. Thus they never turned a wheel in revenue-earning service for BR, though they were all renumbered into the 26502-26511 series. Their livery during the BR period was black with red bufferbeams. They still had the letters 'LNER' on the cab sides but number 26504 went one better in retaining its original NER green livery with 'NORTH EASTERN' in full on the side of the body.

All the class were quickly cut up for scrap with one exception: in the 1940s 26510 had been rebuilt for possible use on the Manchester, Sheffield and Wath line then in the process of being electrified. When this did not work out, it went instead to Ilford carriage sidings in east London as a shunter. Renumbered 100, it ceased work in 1963.

NER 1,800hp 2-Co-2 1,500V DC electric (26600)

Finally in this review of electric locomotives inherited by BR comes this unfortunate engine, its original number (13), perhaps, being rather prophetic. The NER had great plans to electrify the main line from York to Newcastle but these came to nought and it was to be nearly seventy years before electric trains were running on this route. Built in 1922 it only ran intermittently on trials between long periods in store. Like the previous class it was withdrawn during 1950: probably the only time it moved in BR days was when it was hauled by a steam engine to the scrapyard. Renumbered from 6999 by BR, it was still in NER green livery at withdrawal, though with 'LNER' on the body side.

Modelling possibilities

No models of these three types of early electric locomotive have been produced commercially. Since they are rather angular in appearance however, scratch-building should not prove to be too difficult. Whilst none of these early diesel and electric types represent the height of modernity, they do illustrate the diversity of designs that once operated on BR and are now no more. Perhaps it is stretching things somewhat to include these classes in a book on modern motive power. However one sees so few models of these locomotives that it is good to be reminded of the variety that once existed. So why not have a go at recreating some of these designs in model form? Maybe one of the large and impressive gas turbines, or perhaps one of the range of small diesel shunters.

SECTION 2
A class-by-class survey of BR's locomotive fleet

One criticism often expressed against diesel and electric locomotives which is used as an excuse for not modelling them is that they are cold, lifeless machines. They have no character so it is said; they are dirty and smelly, and are not a patch on their steam predecessors. This is nonsense! Watch a Class '50' at it slowly winds its way out of Paddington at the head of a long train of air-conditioned coaches and accelerates into the distance past Royal Oak. Listen to a Class '58' as it hustles its rake of marching merry-go-round hoppers past Toton yard. Remember the 'Deltics' reverberating beneath the great sweep of York's station roof, or the 'Westerns' running alongside the coast where the red sandstone cliffs meet the sea at Teignmouth? There's interest too in a wet winter evening at Leicester as a Class '08' potters around with some parcels vans, or a hot summer afternoon somewhere on the West Coast main line as electrics belt through from Euston to the north. Those with an eye to see, an ear to hear and a heart to feel can appreciate that modern forms of traction are every bit as varied and fascinating as the steam engines of the past.

Over the next few pages is a summary of each of the classes of locomotive that have existed on BR from the time of the introduction of the numerical classification system up until the present day. For each of the different types there are five main aspects of interest to modellers:

1 The number series of the class (for accuracy in numbering models).
2 When the first was introduced into service and when the last was withdrawn (important in ensuring authentic 'period' layouts).
3 Main variations between different batches of the class.
4 The liveries applied to the locomotives.
5 The areas in which the class generally worked (again, this is a factor which must be considered when modelling a specific line during the 'modern' period).

THREE
The diesel shunters

Class '01': Barclay 153hp 0-4-0 diesel-mechanical

Five of these locomotives were owned by BR. Initially they were numbered 11503 to 11506, with the fifth in departmental stock as number 81. Around 1960 the first four were renumbered D2953 to D2956. After D2956 was withdrawn, the departmental member of the class was given that number in 1967. Hence two of this small class carried the same number, albeit not at the same time. D2954 and D2955 survived long enough to become 01001 and 01002 in the general renumbering of the locomotive stock in 1973/4 prior to computerization of the records.

The first of the class entered service in January 1956 whilst the last was withdrawn in March 1981.

Departmental number 81 was built some two years after the other members of the class and differed in a few details. The larger cab side windows and steel cab doors were particularly noticeable against the wooden ones of the earlier locomotives. Towards the end of its career, 01002 was fitted with oval buffers: the remainder retained round-headed buffers.

The livery applied was plain black with cab side numbers and emblems. In the early 1960s 'overhead live wire' flashes were applied and later black and yellow stripes were painted on each end. Number 81 sported green livery and, as D2956, carried the BR logo at the end. 01001 and 01002 were unique amongst BR's locomotive fleet in retaining their original black livery with the emblem, while at the same time carrying the new five-digit numbering style.

Initially the first four were allocated to Stratford shed in east London, whilst the fifth worked in Cambridge at the engineers depot there. During 1965 most were moved to Newton Heath on the north side of Manchester. A couple of years later two of these went to Holyhead for use on an isolated section of line by a breakwater.

Class '02': Yorkshire Engine Co 170hp 0-4-0 diesel-hydraulic

Originally numbered D2850 to D2869, most of the class were withdrawn around 1970 so only three came to be renumbered: D2851 became 02001; D2853 became 02003 and D2856 altered to 02004.

The first of this class of twenty entered service during September 1960 and last was withdrawn in June 1975.

Although built in two batches of ten each there were no differences between individual members of this class. However one modification applied to many, but not all of the class, was the addition of a horizontal handrail above the front radiator grille.

All the locomotives were delivered in green livery with red bufferbeams, black and yellow striped ends, cab side numbers and BR crest. All were soon fitted with 'overhead live wire' flashes. None was repainted into the later blue livery.

Designed for working on sharply curved tracks and in restricted locations, they took over many of the shunting duties previously handled by the famous Lancashire & Yorkshire 'Pug' engines. Many of us, I am sure, have at some time or other encountered the *Airfix* kit of this particular little 0-4-0ST. All the Class '02's were at first based on the LMR, working in the docks at Liverpool and Fleetwood, and in goods yards around Manchester and Salford. One was also allocated to Burton-upon-Trent for shunting in the complex of brewery sidings in the town. However in 1967 a couple crossed over the Pennines to work in the docks at Goole. As we saw in the previous chapter, Goole became something of a repository for small diesel shunters in the 1960s.

Class '03': BR 204hp 0-6-0 diesel-mechanical

This large class of 230 locomotives was an attempt by BR to standardize its range of low-powered diesel shunters. Initially they were numbered D2000 to D2199 and D2379 to D2399. Two were in departmental stock as numbers 91 and 92 but in 1967 they were renumbered into the main series as D2370 and D2371 respectively. With the general renumbering of 1973/4, just over half carried the new five-digit numbers in the series between 03004 and 03399.

The first entered service in December 1957 and there are now only a handful left in use on BR.

Built at Swindon and Doncaster over a period of some five years, there were differences between some of the batches. Because the class was built simultaneously at two works, and also due to the fact that some were completed out of sequence, the detail variations are not in strict numerical order. *Figure 4* outlines the main variants and it is worth looking at these in a little more detail.

Exhaust stack: There were two types, a conical design and a larger flared style. The early batches built in 1957/8 had the conical design, that is numbers D2000 to D2032 and the pair in departmental stock (later numbered D2370 and D2371). All the rest of the class had the flared stack. However over the years a few of the later members did have the conical type fitted in lieu of the flared style. These include 03129 and 03162.

Air horns: Initially two air horns were fitted to the front of the cab on D2000 up to about D2052, plus D2082 to D2085. The remainder had only a single air horn.

Lamp brackets: Most of the class had standard lamp irons on the front and rear on which to hang the lamps. However those destined to work in the WR, D2086 to D2088, D2114 to D2146 and D2181 to D2197, had the Great Western style of bracket which was set at ninety degrees to the normal type. Members of the

Figure 4 The main Class '03' variations

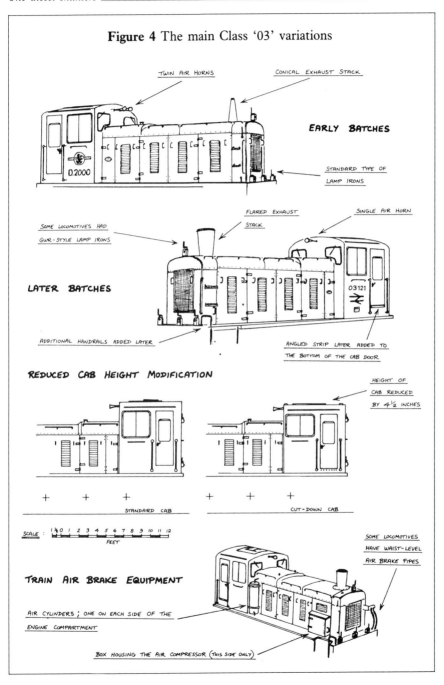

TWIN AIR HORNS

CONICAL EXHAUST STACK

EARLY BATCHES

D.2000

STANDARD TYPE OF
LAMP IRONS

FLARED EXHAUST
STACK

SINGLE AIR HORN

SOME LOCOMOTIVES HAD
GWR-STYLE LAMP IRONS

LATER BATCHES

03121

ADDITIONAL HANDRAILS ADDED LATER

ANGLED STRIP LATER ADDED TO
THE BOTTOM OF THE CAB DOOR

REDUCED CAB HEIGHT MODIFICATION

HEIGHT OF
CAB REDUCED
BY 4½ INCHES

STANDARD CAB

CUT-DOWN CAB

SCALE : ½ 0 1 2 3 4 5 6 7 8 9 10 11 12
FEET

TRAIN AIR BRAKE EQUIPMENT

SOME LOCOMOTIVES
HAVE WAIST-LEVEL
AIR BRAKE PIPES

AIR CYLINDERS ; ONE ON EACH SIDE OF THE
ENGINE COMPARTMENT

BOX HOUSING THE AIR COMPRESSOR (THIS SIDE ONLY)

class operating on the SR subsequently had an additional pair of marker lights and brackets fitted so as to accommodate that region's six-position headcode system.

Reduced cab height: In 1965 this class began working over the Burry Port & Gwendraeth Valley line to the north west of Llanelli in South Wales. Due to restricted clearances on the route the cabs on a number of these locomotives had to be reduced in height by 4½in. Initially six had their cabs cut down (D2141-D2146) with a further five altered later. The eleven so modified, with their five-digit numbers (if carried) were: D2119 (03119), D2120 (03120), D2141 (03141), D2142 (03142), D2143, D2144 (03144), D2145 (03145), D2146, 03151, 03152 and 03382.

In the autumn of 1984 another member of the class had its cab cut down but for another reason. This was number 03079 which had been transferred across to the Isle of Wight earlier in the year. To enable it to work through the tunnel at Ryde both its cab and exhaust stack had to be reduced in height.

Air brakes: In the late 1960s over twenty Class '03's were fitted with train air brake equipment. With air cylinders and compressor box on the running plate, these modifications made the locomotives quite distinctive from the rest of the class. The air-braked locomotives working on the SR were also equipped with waist-level brake pipes on each end so as to facilitate coupling up to the electric multiple units working on that region. Class '03's with air brakes were: D2059, D2063, D2066, D2073, D2078, D2089, D2094, D2112, D2158, D2162, D2170 and D2371. Those members with the additional waist-level pipes were: D2084, D2086, D2179, D2180, D2196, D2197, D2397, D2398 and D2399.

Initially all the class were finished in green. Most of the early batches up to around D2146 were delivered without black and yellow stripes on the ends, but had them painted on later.Early blue livery repaints had the BR logo above the locomotive's number on the cab side, such as on D2084. Soon this was altered to have the number above the logo, for example D2104. The 'D' prefix was also soon omitted from the number. Repainting into blue livery was not an overnight job and some, such as 03134 and 03382, carried the new five-digit numbers yet still wore the green.

The class worked on a wide range of duties, and was not restricted to shunting in goods yards. One advantage that they had over the larger Class '08' diesels was their higher maximum speed, so they often appeared on branch line freight workings and short distance mainline trip workings between different yards. Shunting in carriage sidings, station pilot duties and even hauling passenger trains at some locations came within their compass. The regional allocation of the class when the locomotives initially went into service was as follows:

Eastern Region — D2000 to D2043, D2370 to D2371
North Eastern Region — D2044 to D2081, D2089 to D2113, D2147 to D2174
Southern Region — D2082 to D2085, D2175 to D2180, D2397 to D2399
Western Region — D2086 to D2088, D2114 to D2146, D2181 to D2197
London Midland Region — D2198 to D2199, D2372 to D2396

Although over the years some of the class have been moved between the regions, most remained in their original base areas. None was allocated to sheds in Scotland and though there were some on the LMR, they were not particularly common there. Some worked in the docks at Birkenhead and others shunted in the carriage and wagon works at Derby, but that was about all. On the other regions however, they were more widespread and their duties more varied. Offering an interesting modelling possibility is the fact that on the SR they hauled passenger trains along the short Weymouth Harbour Tramway through the streets of the town linking the main line with the quay.

In North-east England they were often to be seen on station pilot work at such places as York and Newcastle. Here they would usually be coupled to a match wagon, often an old 'conflat' type. The locomotives were quite light and had a short wheelbase which meant that they sometimes became 'lost' on the track circuit diagram in the signalbox. With the addition of a wagon, however, they could activate the track circuits without any problems. From a modeller's viewpoint, the idea of a match wagon can be very handy. Permanently coupling such a wagon to our diesel shunter and fitting pick-ups from it to the locomotive's motor would help alleviate the problem of sticking on electrical dead spots on the layout.

Class '04': Drewry 204hp 0-6-0 diesel-mechanical

A total of 242 of these locomotives were built under the Drewry label. Eventually they all came to be numbered in the series D2200 to D2341 but at first things were a little more complex. The first sixty were initially in the 11100 number range:

> 11100-11103 became D2200-D2203
> 11105-11115 became D2204-D2214
> 11121-11135 became D2215-D2229
> 11149-11160 became D2230-D2241
> 11212-11229 became D2242-D2259

The final member of the class to enter service, D2341, entered departmental stock as number DS1173. None of the locomotives survived long enough to receive numbers in the 04XXX range.

The first of the class entered general service in May 1952 and the last was withdrawn twenty years later in May 1972.

Like the Class '03's, there were differences between the various batches of this type of locomotive. The diameter of the wheels varied from 3ft 3in on D2200 to D2214 and also on D2341, through 3ft 6in on D2215 to D2273 and D2340, up to 3ft 7in on the remainder. The size and shape of the cab windows also differed between individual locomotives as follows:

1   D2200-D2203, D2341: Small rectangular front cab windows and small cab side windows.
2   D2204-D2214: Larger front cab windows but still having only small cab side windows.

3 D2215-D2340: With the larger front cab windows and a new, more modern design of large sliding cab side window.

These cab variations are outlined in *Figure 5*, together with some other details to watch out for, notably the type of buffers and exhaust stack fitted. The early locomotives initially had round headed buffers but many were quickly changed to the semi-round type shown in the drawing. Later batches reverted to the round style but at least one member of the class, D2294, had oval buffers.

The first few built were not provided with exhaust stacks at all. Soon a rather rudimentary pipe was fitted on top of the engine bonnet, whilst later batches had a conical shaped exhaust. D2341 differed from the rest of the class in having two sets of ventilation louvres on each of its engine compartment doors and it also had a modified design of front radiator. The first four of the class, D2200 to D2203, were equipped with cowcatchers and side plates to enable them to work over three lines in East Anglia; the Wisbech & Upwell tramway, the Yarmouth tramway through the streets of the town to the fish market, and on the lines in Ipswich docks. Subsequently some other members of the class had skirting fitted to conceal their wheels and motion, namely D2210, D2212, D2280, D2281 and D2282.

The first sixty locomotives of the class, D2200 to D2259, were delivered in plain black livery with red bufferbeams and the BR emblem on the cab side. At this time, of course, they were numbered in the range between 11100 and 11229. The rest of the class were turned out in green livery, again with red bufferbeams, but with the later style of BR crest. Most, if not all, of those in the black livery were later repainted green. Some even managed to be painted in the later rail blue with the BR logo including D2211, D2258 and D2294.

The Class '04's worked largely down the eastern side of England and along the south coast. Areas with particular concentrations of these locomotives were Tyneside, Teesside and the Leeds/Bradford region, whilst many were based at Stratford in east London. South of the River Thames they were at many scattered locations such as Ashford in Kent, Brighton, Guildford, Southampton and Bournemouth.

Class '05': Barclay 204hp 0-6-0 diesel-mechanical and Hunslet 204hp 0-6-0 diesel-mechanical

The '05' classification actually covered two distinct types of locomotive, BR not allocating sufficient room to enable each to be given its own class number. The Barclay-built locomotives were originally numbered 11177 to 11186, later becoming D2400 to D2409. The Hunslet group of locomotives were much greater in number, a total of 69 being constructed as follows: D2550-D2557 (originally 11136-11143), D2558-D2573 (originally 11161-11176), D2574-D2618. D2612 and D2615 were subsequently renumbered into departmental stock as 88 and 89. D2554 was the only one of the class to carry a five-digit number, becoming 05001 in 1974 and later 97803 in departmental stock.

The first of the Barclay locomotives entered service in July 1956 and the last

Figure 5 Some Class '04' details

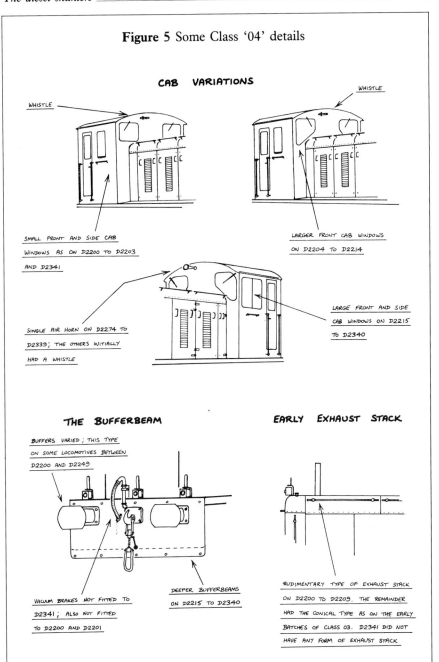

CAB VARIATIONS

WHISTLE

WHISTLE

WHISTLE

SMALL FRONT AND SIDE CAB
WINDOWS AS ON D2200 TO D2203
AND D2341

LARGER FRONT CAB WINDOWS
ON D2204 TO D2214

SINGLE AIR HORN ON D2274 TO
D2339; THE OTHERS INITIALLY
HAD A WHISTLE

LARGE FRONT AND SIDE
CAB WINDOWS ON D2215
TO D2340

THE BUFFERBEAM

BUFFERS VARIED; THIS TYPE
ON SOME LOCOMOTIVES BETWEEN
D2200 AND D2249

VACUUM BRAKES NOT FITTED TO
D2341; ALSO NOT FITTED
TO D2200 AND D2201

DEEPER BUFFERBEAMS
ON D2215 TO D2340

EARLY EXHAUST STACK

RUDIMENTARY TYPE OF EXHAUST STACK
ON D2200 TO D2209. THE REMAINDER
HAD THE CONICAL TYPE AS ON THE EARLY
BATCHES OF CLASS 03. D2341 DID NOT
HAVE ANY FORM OF EXHAUST STACK

was withdrawn in January 1969. The Hunslet-built Class '05's first appeared during October 1955. In June 1968 the last was withdrawn from general service but 97803 lingered on in departmental use until September 1983.

There were no differences between the ten Barclay Class '05's. It was a different matter, though, with those built by Hunslet. Three batches can be identified by the following means:

1   D2550-D2573: Overall height of 11ft with 3ft 4in diameter wheels. Fitted with round-headed buffers.
2   D2574-D2585: Overall height of 12ft with 3ft 9in diameter wheels. Fitted with oval buffers and larger cab windows: also a deeper bufferbeam, twin air horns and repositioned vacuum brake pipe.
3   D2586-D2618: As D2574 to D2585 but with modified radiator grille, slightly more rounded edges to the cab windows and the vacuum brake pipe moved back to the position occupied on the first batch.

All the Barclays and the first 24 Hunslet locomotives were delivered in plain black with red bufferbeams and BR emblem on the cab side. D2574 to D2618 were in green livery from the start with the BR crest. Only one Class '05' was repainted into rail blue livery, this being D2554.

D2400 to D2409 spent most of their careers working in Lincolnshire based at Boston, Immingham near Grimsby and at Lincoln itself. The Hunslet locomotives were allocated to different areas. D2550 to D2573 initially worked around Norwich, Ipswich and Harwich before moving across the country to Lancashire in the mid 1960s. D2574 to D2585 always worked in Scotland, mostly in Fife. The remainder were generally to be found in Yorkshire around Wakefield and in the docks at Goole, but some moved to Scotland later, especially to the Edinburgh area. The odd one out of all the class, D2554, was transferred across to the Isle of Wight in 1966 which accounts for its longevity.

Class '06': Barclay 204hp 0-4-0 diesel-mechanical
Essentially this class was an 0-4-0 version of the Barclay 0-6-0 considered above. A total of 35 were built, initially numbered D2410 to D2444. Ten survived to be renumbered in the 06XXX series between 06001 and 06010.

The first of the class went into service in June 1958 whilst the last was withdrawn from general service during September 1981. There were slight differences between the two batches built: D2410-D2424 had three windows in the rear of the cab. There was also a ladder, later removed, on the left side of the locomotive just in front of the cab which led to the fuel tank filler on top of the engine compartment. D2425-D2444 only had two rear cab windows, though they were larger than on the early batch. No ladder was fitted in front of the cab but there was one at the front end on the left side of the radiator. Again, this was subsequently removed.

All the class was delivered in green livery but the BR crest was not positioned on the side of the cab. Rather it was on one of the engine compartment doors, usually on the second or third from the front of the locomotive, but sometimes on the fourth just to confuse matters. Some were repainted blue but again the position of the BR logo varied: indeed a few did not carry the logo in their final years.

This class was very much a part of the Scottish scene, working in no other part of the country except for one which after withdrawal was sent to Reading for use in the signal works there. Initially D2410 to D2424 worked in the Aberdeen and Inverness districts whilst the rest were based on the south side of Glasgow and around Ayr. By the late 1960s there were more allocated to Edinburgh and Dundee at the expense of Aberdeen and Inverness. Dunfermline and Dundee were the last haunts for the handful which survived into the 1980s.

Class '07': Ruston & Hornsby 275hp 0-6-0 diesel-electric

One of the most distinctive and arguably one of the most attractive types of diesel shunter to have operated on BR, fourteen of this class were constructed and initially numbered D2985 to D2998. Most were later renumbered into the series between 07001 and 07013.

June 1962 saw the first of the class enter service whilst the last was withdrawn during July 1977.

As built, there were no differences between the individual members of the class. However between 1967 and 1969 air brake equipment was fitted to six locomotives, these being D2985, D2987, D2989, D2993, D2995 and D2997. This caused the addition of extra piping along the top of the engine compartment and down the right hand side of the locomotive. Equipment boxes for the air compressors and so forth were positioned on the running plate; a large one on the right hand side towards the front and a smaller one on the left side just in front of the cab. Finally waist-level brake pipes, like those fitted to some Class '03's, were provided at each end.

All the class was delivered in green livery but this was not the standard Brunswick green as applied to the other diesel shunters: rather it was a slightly lighter shade of Malachite green. With red bufferbeams and coupling rods, black and yellow stripes on each end, a grey cab roof, black wheels and underframe, and red and white lining the locomotives made quite a picture. Instead of the usual BR crest on the cab side, there was the circular coaching stock design of crest. All were later repainted into rail blue with yellow bufferbeams. Early repaints had the locomotive's number below the BR logo on the cab side but later the positions were reversed with the number above the logo.

These locomotives were designed for one purpose only, namely working on the complex of lines and sidings around the docks at Southampton. However with the decline of wagon load traffic to the docks and the rise of containerization, this class became surplus to needs. During 1976 a few were allocated to Bournemouth to replace the Class '03's there whilst others pottered around the Loco Works at Eastleigh. All had gone by the summer of 1977.

Class '08': BR 350hp 0-6-0 diesel-electric

Numerically, the largest class on BR are the standard 350hp diesel shunters. The

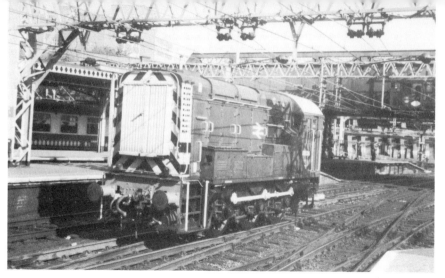

The standard BR 350hp diesel shunter, a familiar sight throughout much of the country.

vast majority are fitted with English Electric engines but there were some of different manufacture, produced by Blackstone and Crossley. The maximum speed of the various batches also differed and so it was these variations which led the 1,193 locomotives of this basic type '08' to be divided into three classes as follows:

Class '08': fitted with an English Electric engine. Maximum speed 15mph.
Class '09': fitted with an English Electric engine. Maximum speed 27½mph.
Class '10': fitted with either a Blackstone or Crossley engine. Maximum speed 20mph.

From the modelling viewpoint these internal differences are not really important. However there are detail variations between individual members which are of significance and so these shunters deserve separate mention later (see p. 48). Here then is just a brief summary, beginning with the Class '08's.

The Class '08's were numbered in the range from D3000 to D4192 as follows: D3000-D3116 (originally 13000-13116); D3127-D3136 (originally 13127-13136); D3167-D3356 (originally 13167-13356); D3357-D3361; D3362-D3366 (originally 13362-13366); D3367-D3438; D3454-D3472; D3503-D3611; D3652-D3664; D3672-D3718; D3722-D4048; D4095-D4098; D4115-D4192. Most of these locomotives were renumbered into the series from 08001 to 08958. In 1985 three of them had their cabs cut down and were further renumbered 08991 to 08993.

The first member of the class entered service in October 1952 and although many have been withdrawn, there will still be a large number of these at work well into the next century.

Detail and livery variations will be looked at later. Suffice to say that although at first sight all appear similar, there are subtle differences. The Class '08's have, and indeed still do, work in most corners of the BR system. To paraphrase some television advertisements: 'every layout should have one'.

Class '09': BR 350hp 0-6-0 diesel-electric

Initially numbered D3665 to D3671, D3719 to D3721 and D4099 to D4114. In 1973/4 they became 09001 to 09026 respectively.

The first entered service during February 1959 and so far none has been withdrawn.

This class is particularly associated with the Southern Region, though they have on occasion been allocated elsewhere. Liveries and other variations will be looked at later.

Class '10': BR 350hp 0-6-0 diesel-electric

The last in this trio of classes making up the standard BR 350hp shunter is the Class '10'. Strictly speaking the Crossley-engined examples were not given a class number as they were withdrawn prior to the implementation of the numerical classification system, but I have included them here. The locomotives were numbered as follows: Crossley engines, D3117-D3126 (originally 13117-13126); Blackstone-type engines, D3137-D3166 (originally 13137-13166), D3439-D3453, D3473-D3502, D3612-D3651, D4049-D4094. None were ever renumbered into the 10XXX series.

Those with the Crossley engine entered service from May 1955, with the last withdrawn in July 1967. The Blackstone Class '10's first appeared during February 1955 and were withdrawn by June 1972.

D3117 to D3126 spent most of their time based at Toton on the LMR, whilst the Blackstone ones were largely on the ER. Again, liveries and other details will be considered later.

Class '11': LMS 350hp 0-6-0 diesel-electric

Designed by the LMS, 106 of these diesel shunters were eventually constructed for use on Britain's railways. The majority were built at Derby but the final 36 came from Darlington. Numbered 12033 to 12138, the first ten were completed before nationalization and hence initially carried their LMS numbers 7120 and 7129. The first two built after nationalization, 12043 and 12044, also carried LMS numbers 7130 and 7131 at first, though with an 'M' prefix. The first of the class entered service on the LMS in May 1945 and the last was withdrawn from BR during November 1972.

Differences between individual members of the class were minimal.. The first six were originally destined for use by the War Department and so had a slightly different design of battery box from the others (the side of the boxes hinged outwards whilst the remainder had the top lid hinging upwards). Electric marker lights were not fitted to the early batches, but were from 12069. Subsequently the earlier locomotives had them fitted. The ladders on each side of the radiator were removed from many of the class prior to 1965.

Plain black livery was originally applied, with red bufferbeams, cab side numbers and the BR emblem on the middle engine compartment door. Repainting into Brunswick green, at first without the black and yellow ends, began in the late 1950s. Generally the BR crest was positioned on the engine compartment doors but on some, for example 12098 and 12102, it was applied to the front battery box on each side. A few of the class also received the later rail blue colour scheme with the number above the BR logo on the cab side. 12049 was one such example whilst 12062 was also in blue but with an incorrect 'D' prefix to its number.

Those locomotives built at Derby (ie, 12033 to 12102) worked on the LMR at numerous locations, from the north London sheds of Willesden and Cricklewood, through Birmingham and the Black Country, the Derby and Nottingham areas, past Cheshire and Lancashire almost up to the Scottish border at Carlisle.

Those constructed at Darlington stayed on the eastern side of the country; 12103 to 12138 being allocated to such sheds at Stratford in east London, March and Immingham, and also in the Hull area.

Class '12': SR 350hp 0-6-0 diesel-electric

Although ordered by the Southern Railway, this class did not make its appearance until after nationalization: 26 were built and numbered 15211 to 15236. These locomotives looked very similar to the Class '11' shunters and also those constructed by the GWR, numbers 15101 to 15107, considered in the last chapter. However they had larger 4ft 6in diameter wheels, as against the 4ft ½in of the others, and they were of the 'Bulleid-Firth Brown' type rather than the normal spoked variety of wheel.

The first entered service in April 1949 and the last member of the class was withdrawn in December 1971.

Differences between individual locomotives were negligible, though at first they were not fitted with the six-position marker lights at each end. Three of them were equipped with train air brakes in the late 1960s, these being 15230, 15231 and 15232. The remainder, like the Class '11's, had no train brakes. Unlike some other types of shunter, the Class '12's generally retained their ladders on each side of the radiator at the front end: the SR had less overhead wiring than other regions and hence there was less danger to staff climbing up them.

Livery was initially plain black with red bufferbeams. Later they were painted Brunswick green with the BR crest on the engine compartment door. One at least, number 15212, was subsequently to appear in rail blue with the BR logo on the side of the cab beneath its number.

At first the class was based in south London at either Hither Green or Norwood Junction. The early 1950s saw some move south-west to Eastleigh and later others moved east to Ashford. During the 1960s some were also working from Bournemouth shed.

Class '13': BR 700hp 0-6-0 + 0-6-0 diesel-electric

Finally we come to the last and most powerful class of diesel shunting locomotive that worked on BR. Three pairs of Class '08's were modified in 1965 to work as permanently-coupled twin-units for use in the large marshalling yard at Tinsley in Sheffield. For each of the units, one of the Class '08's retained its cab and was known as the 'master', the other had its cab removed and was the 'slave'. Deeper

13001 at Tinsley. These locomotives were modified from a pair of standard Class '08's.

and thicker bufferbeams were fitted to both the master and slave to improve adhesion. The locomotives were numbered as follows:

D4188 (master) + D3698 (slave) became D4500, later renumbered 13003
D4190 (master) + D4189 (slave) became D4501, later renumbered 13001
D4187 (master) + D3697 (slave) became D4502, later renumbered 13002

The first entered service in May 1965 and the last was withdrawn during January 1985.

When introduced into service the twin-units were marshalled with the driving cab towards the middle and the radiator ends outermost. However, within a couple of years the master units were turned round so that the driving cab was at the rear.

Initially the locomotives were painted in green with the BR crest on the battery boxes of the master unit only. Black and yellow stripes were only painted on each of the nose ends and not on the rear of the driving cab. After the master units had been turned round, the black and yellow stripes were applied to the rear of the cabs. All were subsequently repainted rail blue with the BR logo on the engine compartment door. With only three members in the class it might be imagined that with the standard blue livery applied they would all look alike: in fact subtle differences existed, as described below.

13001   Master unit: BR logo on engine compartment doors. Black and yellow stripes on cab end. Full yellow front on nose end.

Slave unit: BR logo on engine compartment doors. No stripes, just blue livery on rear end. Black and yellow stripes on nose end.

13002	Master unit:	BR logo on engine compartment doors. Black and yellow stripes on cab end. Black and yellow stripes on nose end.
	Slave unit:	No BR logo. No stripes, just blue livery on rear end. Black and yellow stripes on nose end.
13003	Master unit:	BR logo on engine compartment doors. Black and yellow stripes on cab end. Black and yellow stripes on nose end.
	Slave unit:	No BR logo. Black and yellow stripes on rear end. Black and yellow stripes on nose end.

I appreciate that not everyone is going to rush out to model the Class '13', but these variations do illustrate the need to check as many photographs as possible if one is modelling a specific locomotive. Even in a small class like this, which was based at the same shed and worked in the same location all of the time, differences did occur. If there are differences here, think what the permutations are for variations in other, much larger classes.

That concludes our summary of BR's diesel shunters — quite a varied bunch I think that you will agree. The following section examines in greater detail BR's standard shunter. *Figure 6* gives an overall view of when each of the classes were in service so you can compare which types were working at the same time. Although after withdrawal many were cut up for scrap, a fair number were sold for further use in industry. Hence some types now extinct on BR can still be seen at work today in various locations up and down the country.

The standard diesel shunter

The standard BR diesel shunter, a familiar sight in all parts of the country, is a 350hp 0-6-0 machine. Derived from the later designs of LMS/English Electric shunter, they are an essential ingredient of virtually any layout depicting the British railway scene over the past 35 years. These shunters lack the charisma of other types but despite the move to block-train working, with the consequent decline in remarshalling en route, the diesel shunters have a secure future well into the next century. With no successors on the horizon, they will be with us for a long time to come.

Liveries

These shunters have undergone a number of livery changes. Initially they appeared in plain black, then Brunswick green, next rail blue and finally Railfreight grey. It is worth looking at each of these colour schemes in a little more detail.

Plain black — 13000 to 13336 (remember that they were originally numbered in this series rather than D3000 to D3336) were initially painted plain black, with red bufferbeams, 8in high pale cream Gill Sans numerals on the cab sides and the medium size of BR emblem on the engine compartment doors. The handrails were also painted black whilst there were no diagonal yellow stripes

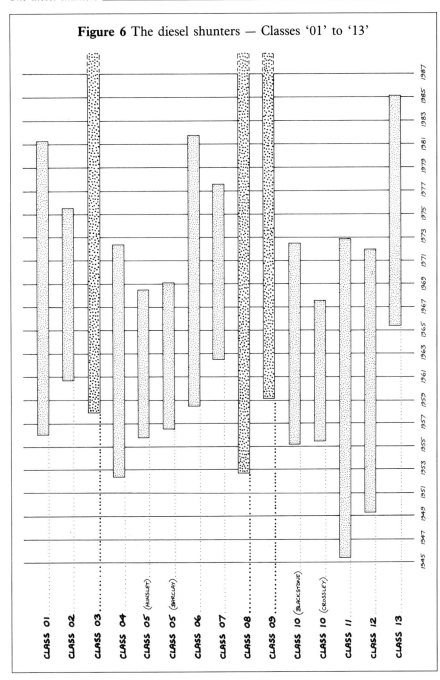

Figure 6 The diesel shunters — Classes '01' to '13'

on the ends and the coupling rods were left in their natural metal finish.

Brunswick green — Early in 1957 these 350hp shunters began to be turned out in Brunswick green. Hence the later built examples, that is those originally numbered 13337 to 13356, D3357 to D3361, 13362 to 13366 and D3367 to D4192, were delivered new in this colour. The bonnet and cab were painted Brunswick green with the underframe and wheels in black, and the bufferbeams and coupling rods in red. At first the numerals were still in Gill Sans, including some of those with the 'D' prefix to their number. Later examples had the 6in white block style numerals from the outset. A small-sized BR crest was applied to the body side, though its position varied. Some locomotives had it on the engine compartment doors whilst others had it located on the side of the battery boxes. Handrails, and the radiator ladder if fitted, were originally painted green. Later these features were picked out in white. Black and yellow diagonal warning stripes were applied to the ends from 1959 onwards, whilst 'overhead live wire' flashes appeared the following year.

Rail blue — 1966 saw the start of painting these shunters into the familiar rail blue livery, though it was not until 1980 that the Brunswick green was extinct. The wheels and underframe were again painted black, with the handrails in white and yellow/black end stripes. Like the BR crest before it, the BR logo had two alternative positions; either on the bonnet doors or on the battery boxes. The coupling rods were now painted yellow and the bufferbeams were generally this colour too, although they were sometimes to be seen in black.

Railfreight grey — Early in 1986, Railfreight grey began to be applied to some of these shunters. The body sides and cab roof were painted in this grey, the cab sides in yellow and the edges of the footplate in red. Bufferbeams and coupling rods are also red, with the obligatory yellow and black diagonal end stripes and white handrail. The BR logo is sited on the engine compartment doors with the Railfreight legend applied to the battery boxes. More recently, some one-off livery styles have been applied to these locomotives. Ranging from black, through green and various shades of blue, to the grey, white and red Inter-City colour scheme, nobody can now say that these shunters lack variety.

Detail variations and modifications

The standard BR diesel shunter, or Classes '08', '09' and '10' in later parlance, all have the same basic type of bodywork. Understandably though, with well over a thousand locomotives in this category there are some differences to look out for.

1 Footplate equipment The most obvious external variation amongst all the shunters is the arrangement of the various rectangular boxes located on the footplate on either side of the bonnet. Now a locomotive is often described by referring to its number one or number two end; the number one end being the radiator end of the machine. The sides of a locomotive also have labels; the 'A' and the 'B' sides. *Figure 7* sketches out the various pieces of equipment on the footplate on the 'A' and 'B' sides of these diesel shunters. All, without exception, have battery boxes on both sides. Those members fitted with train air brakes have an air compressor in a cubicle on the 'B' side footplate. Air brakes, and hence this cubicle, began to be fitted from 1968 onwards. Some locomotives have vacuum exhausters on both sides, whilst others only have one on the 'B' side. As a general guide, and I stress *general*, the following have exhausters on both sides — D3000 to D3244, D3709 to D3727, D3738 to D3762, D3773 to D3812 and D3823 to D4192. The remainder just have the single exhauster on the 'B' side. This gives a broad outline of the situation regarding the vacuum exhausters, but, as usual, if you are modelling a specific diesel shunter then check with photographs.

Figure 7 Main features of the standard diesel shunter

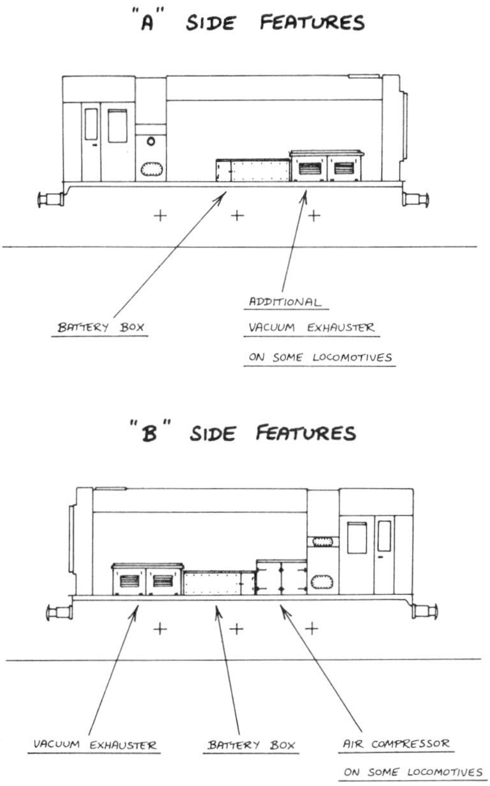

"A" SIDE FEATURES

BATTERY BOX

ADDITIONAL VACUUM EXHAUSTER ON SOME LOCOMOTIVES

"B" SIDE FEATURES

VACUUM EXHAUSTER   BATTERY BOX   AIR COMPRESSOR ON SOME LOCOMOTIVES

2 Waist-level air brake pipes The majority of the 350hp shunters based on the Southern Region have waist-level air brake pipes similar to those on the Class '03's and '07's. These enable the locomotives to couple and shunt electric multiple-unit stock.

3 Cab doors Two designs can be noted. Early batches have a panelled door with just a single handle, whilst later examples have a flush metal door with twin handles on each.

4 Cab side windows The very early examples of these shunters have a slightly smaller side cab window than on the later-built ones. The actual aperture in the cab side is the same size but the early locomotives have a noticeably thicker inset framing around the window.

5 Radiator ladder All the locomotives originally had a ladder on both sides extending up to the top of the radiator. With the spread of overhead electrified wiring, one could not have staff clambering up these ladders to fill the radiator. Revised filling arrangements enabled the radiators to be topped-up from ground level and hence the ladders were removed.

6 Marker lights Watch out for the variations in these. Most locomotives were built with four on each end, though some of the early batches only had two. Some shunters based on the Southern Region were equipped with six marker lights on the ends. In more recent times after overhaul, some of the shunters that originally had four marker lights have had the middle pair removed, just leaving the two outer ones on each end.

7 Cut-down cab To replace the Class '03's working over the Burry Port & Gwendraeth Valley line up to Cwm Mawr, north of Llanelli, three Class '08's have had their cabs reduced in height by about 9 in. 08259 was the first to be so altered in the middle of 1984. Following successful trials over the Cwm Maw branch, two others were similarly modified, these being 08203 and 08592. During April 1985 they were renumbered as follows: 08991 (ex 08203); 08992 (ex 08259); 08993 (ex 08592). In addition to the cut-down cabs, these locomotives have a square headlight positioned on each end.

The models

There is no shortage of ready-to-run models of the standard BR shunter, at least in the smaller scales. *Graham Farish* produce an N gauge example, whilst many years ago there was one in TT gauge from *Tri-ang*. The most varied selection, however, is in 00 gauge with models from three manufacturers: *Hornby*, *Wrenn* and *Lima*. The *Hornby* model derives from the original *Tri-ang* version and whilst it has been updated over the years it cannot really be considered as a scale model due to the totally inaccurate underframe. To me at least, it just does not capture the look of one of the standard BR shunters. The *Wrenn* diesel shunter is the same as that produced by *Hornby-Dublo* in the early 1960s. It is a very smooth and powerful runner that belies its age, though it is the most expensive of the various 00 gauge ready-to-run versions. Finally in this trio is the representative from *Lima*, and it is this model that I want to concentrate on here.

Like the majority of proprietary models, the *Lima* diesel shunter benefits from

The 'A' side of the Lima *diesel shunter, comparing an example taken straight from the box (above) with one that has been detailed (below). Note the improvement in the appearance by reducing the width of the coupling rods and painting the sides of the wheels black.*

a little detailing work to bring out some of the more subtle characteristics of the prototype. The first step in achieving this is to separate the body from the chassis by undoing the front screw on the underside of the model. Remove the large metal weight from the chassis and ease off the two couplings which are a push fit. The coupling rods on the model are much too wide and need to be filed down to finer proportions. Each of these rods is secured by three nuts: loosen them with pliers and then unscrew them with your fingers. On my model I filed down the rods by ½mm. More could be taken off but a compromise had to be made between appearance and strength for these rods have to be strong enough to transmit power from the driven axle at the rear to the middle and front ones. When reassembling the rods, remember that the dummy oil boxes are uppermost.

By their very nature, shunting locomotives generally operate at fairly slow speeds. Therefore on the model, current pick-up is particularly important if it is to work smoothly and not falter over points or uneven track. The *Lima* model only picks up the current from the front and rear pair of wheels so it is worth fitting additional pick-ups to the centre ones as well. Extra pick-ups made from strips of phosphor-bronze can be fitted to lead from the existing contacts to the middle wheels. Another way is to cut two pieces of springy wire, each about 2½in long, and slip them between the wheel treads and the main frame of the chassis.

As well as making the centre wheels live, it also makes them slightly sprung which further aids pick-up.

Turning now to the body shell, first consider the bufferbeams. On the model there are two square holes in the rear bufferbeam which help secure the body to the chassis. On the prototype these holes are used to accommodate lifting tackle to raise the locomotive. Similar holes are provided in the front bufferbeam so drill through the plastic to make the initial apertures, then enlarge to the correct shape with the blade of a sharp knife. Carve off the moulded handrails either side of the cab doors and replace with ones formed from wire. Also add wire handrails to the front steps of the locomotive as these are a prominent feature of the real thing. The *Lima* model is rather a hybrid in that it has the later pattern of flush metal door, yet also has the small cab side windows that were only to be found on the early batches. It is very easy to enlarge the windows by carving away the moulded framing with the blade of a sharp modelling knife. Flush glazing the

A side view of a detailed Lima *shunter. The moulded plastic cab door handrails have been replaced by ones made up from wire. Wire handrails have also been fitted to the front steps.*

An everyday sight as a Class '08' does a spot of shunting. The cab windows have been flush-glazed and windscreen wipers made from wire have been added.

windows really enhances the overall effect and remember to add windscreen wipers from pieces of wire. One feature I forgot to add to my model was the central rib on the front two bonnet sections on the roof. A thin strip of plastic card will suffice to represent this. It is oh-so-easy to be wise after the event!

Before reuniting the body and chassis, a crew can now be squeezed into the cab. By slitting a suitable figure down the middle, each of the halves can be secured to either side of the motor, thus helping to disguise it. Replace the metal weight in the chassis and glue it into position. The body can now be screwed back into place and the couplings snapped back into their holes. Finally the painting. My model is in rail blue and as *Lima*'s shade is quite good I did not repaint the bodywork. However I did touch up the black and yellow diagonal stripes on the ends and continued them round the front of the locomotive. The handrails were picked out in white, the coupling rods painted yellow and the sides of the wheels black.

FOUR
Mainline diesels: The Type '1's and '2's

The mainline diesel fleet of BR is divided into five broad divisions:

Type 1 = Up to 1,000hp
Type 2 = 1,000hp to 1,500hp
Type 3 = 1,500hp to 2,000hp
Type 4 = 2,000hp to 3,000hp
Type 5 = 3,000hp and upwards

Type '1's

At the bottom end of the horsepower range are the Type '1's. Primarily designed for freight duties of a more secondary nature, such as transfer workings between different yards in one district or on branch line goods trains, when two are coupled together and operated in multiple they become effective units for hauling heavier longer distance freights. Not being fitted with train heating equipment, their appearance at the head of passenger train is limited to the warmer summer months.

Class '14': BR 650hp 0-6-0 diesel-hydraulic

Fifty-six of these diesel-hydraulics were built by BR at Swindon. Numbered D9500 to D9555, their reign on BR metals was very short with a service of life of less than five years. Although not outstandingly successful, they were not an unmitigated disaster either for most were sold by BR for further use in industry.

The first Class '14' entered service in July 1964 and the last was withdrawn in April 1969.

Externally there were no differences between the individual members of the class. Only one livery style was applied to the locomotives during their BR days. Standard Brunswick green was the main colour, with black underframe and wheels, yellow bufferbeams and black and yellow stripes on the ends. Handrails and the edging around the top of the bonnets were picked out in white, whilst 'overhead live wire' flashes were carried from the outset. The cab towards the centre of the locomotive was painted a much lighter shade of green (Sherwood green) with a pale grey roof. The coaching stock crest was positioned on the cab side, with the locomotive's number below. These numerals were in a different type of face from that usually applied to green-liveried locomotives, but similar to the type that would later become standard on blue-painted locomotives. None of the Class '14's was repainted blue.

Initially the entire class was based on the WR. Most worked in South Wales, but over a dozen were allocated to the Bristol area and in their early days a few also operated in west London. At the end of 1966 and in the first half of 1967 over thirty of the class quit the WR for pastures new on Humberside. However their active life working in and around Hull was shortlived as they were withdrawn *en masse* in the spring of 1968. Those still on the WR lingered on in South Wales for another year.

Class '15': British Thomson-Houston 800hp Bo-Bo diesel-electric

A class of 44 members, numbered D8200 to D8243, four were retained in departmental stock as carriage heating units DB968000 to DB968003 after withdrawal.

Entering service during November 1957, the last of the class was withdrawn in March 1971. Although built in two batches, there were no variations between them.

All were delivered in Brunswick green with red bufferbeams, cab side numbers and crest. Each end of the cab was painted eggshell blue. Subsequently small yellow rectangular warning panels were painted on the ends and 'overhead live wire' flashes applied. None received the rail blue livery but many did have the whole of their ends painted yellow. Some, including D8213, D8226 and D8238, carried the BR logo on the cab side whilst still retaining the green livery.

These locomotives generally worked in the area between London, Chelmsford, Colchester and Ipswich. They appeared on cross-London freight workings, station pilot duties at Kings Cross and Liverpool Street stations, and on branch line goods trains throughout much of Essex and parts of Hertfordshire.

Class '16': North British 800hp Bo-Bo diesel-electric

Descended from the LMS inspired Bo-Bo diesel (10800), ten of these locomotives were built and numbered D8400 to D8409.

The first of the class entered service in May 1958 and the last was withdrawn during September 1968. Like the previous class, there were no variations between the ten members. However one point to note is that these locomotives were fitted with spoked wheels rather than the more usual disc type.

Livery style was similar to the Class '15's with green bodywork, black bogies and underframe, and red bufferbeams. The first three of the class did not initially have the ends of the cabs picked out in eggshell blue, but were soon to have them painted so to match the remaining seven. Small yellow warning panels appeared on the ends in the early 1960s and most had their ends painted entirely yellow by the end of 1967. None of the class survived long enough to receive the blue livery.

Their short life of but ten years was spent at one shed, Stratford in east London. As the class was withdrawn just at the time that steam power was finishing on BR, their demise went largely unnoticed.

Class '17': Clayton 900hp Bo-Bo diesel-electric

Visually, these locomotives were by far the most attractive of all the Type '1's on BR: mechanically they were something of a disaster. When they were introduced they were heralded as the standard Type '1' design, yet within ten years all had been withdrawn from service. Without even the saving grace of being sold for further use in industry, all, with a single exception, were cut up for scrap. The odd one out, D8568, did see some industrial use and is thankfully now preserved; the sole survivor of a class of over a hundred members numbered D8500 to D8616.

The first of the class appeared in September 1962 and the last was withdrawn during December 1971.

The only external variation within the Class '17's concerned D8586 and D8587. These were fitted with Rolls-Royce engines as against the Paxman-made power units on all the other locomotives. To accommodate this different design of engine, the centre portion of the top of the bonnet was slightly raised.

Initially the locomotives were painted in a two-tone green style as outlined in *Figure 8*. The whole class was delivered new with yellow warning panels on each end and 'overhead live wire' flashes. In the late 1960s some had the whole of their fronts painted yellow, whilst eventually about half of the class received rail blue livery with the BR logo on the cab side.

Although the majority worked in Scotland, their influence was more widespread than this. Initially the locomotives were based in four main areas as follows. D8500-D8553 were allocated to Polmadie shed on the south side of Glasgow and worked largely in Lanarkshire, Ayrshire and Dumfriesshire. D8554-D8587 were allocated to Haymarket shed in Edinburgh; they worked north of the Firth of Forth in Fife, and south through the Scottish Borders to Carlisle. D8588-D8603 were allocated to Thornaby and Gateshead sheds. They worked on Teesside and Tyneside. D8604-D8615 were initially allocated to Tinsley shed but soon moved to Staveley in Derbyshire. They worked around Sheffield and the North Derbyshire coalfield.

Those in Derbyshire moved to Scotland in 1966 and some of the class working in the North-east also moved north of the border just before they were withdrawn. Carlisle had an allocation of Class '17's in 1968 where they could be seen on the line between there and the Workington area of Cumberland. Scotland was, however, the final resting place for these distinctive locomotives.

Class '20': English Electric 1,000hp Bo-Bo diesel-electric

The only Type '1' locomotives now left in service on BR are the Class '20's. With around 200 in the fleet and with their future assured for many years to come, these locomotives are an important element in BR's freight motive power. They deserve to be looked at in more detail but for the moment here is a brief summary.

A total of 228 Class '20's were constructed, initially numbered D8000 to D8199 and D8300 to D8327. During 1973/4 all were renumbered into the series between 20001 and 20228.

Figure 8 Some features of the Clayton class '17's

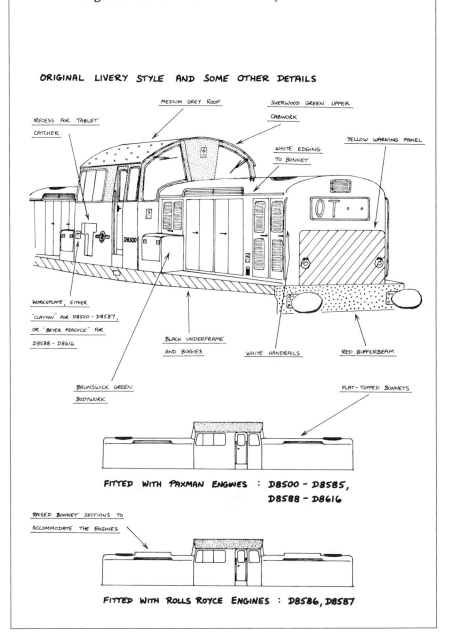

ORIGINAL LIVERY STYLE AND SOME OTHER DETAILS

MEDIUM GREY ROOF

SHERWOOD GREEN UPPER CABWORK

RECESS FOR TABLET CATCHER

YELLOW WARNING PANEL

WHITE EDGING TO BONNET

WORKSPLATE, EITHER "CLAYTON" FOR D8500 - D8587, OR "BEYER PEACOCK" FOR D8588 - D8616

BLACK UNDERFRAME AND BOGIES

WHITE HANDRAILS

RED BUFFERBEAM

BRUNSWICK GREEN BODYWORK

FLAT-TOPPED BONNETS

FITTED WITH PAXMAN ENGINES : D8500 - D8585, D8588 - D8616

RAISED BONNET SECTIONS TO ACCOMMODATE THE ENGINES

FITTED WITH ROLLS ROYCE ENGINES : D8586, D8587

Above *Beyond 20162, 20136 stands in the old roofless steam engine shed at Westhouses in the East Midlands. This is one from the later batch of Class '20's with four-digit headcode boxes on the ends.*

Below *A side view of a detailed Wrenn Class '20'. Headcode boxes and round-headed buffers have been fitted. Note how the flush-glazed cab windows improve the overall appearance of the model.*

The Wrenn *model lacks the front-facing cab window, a serious omission. Note here that these missing windows have been cut out of the spectacle plate, again improving the look of the model.*

The first of the class entered service in June 1957 and (as just mentioned) the great majority are still hard at work.

The most obvious variation between the different batches concerned the type of headcodes carried. D8000 to D8127 had four discs on each end to display the train classification whilst the other hundred were fitted with headcode boxes.

D8000 to D8175 and D8177 were delivered in Brunswick green. The remainder were painted in rail blue from the outset. Subsequently the earlier locomotives received a coat of the blue paint too. Currently the Class '20's are appearing in railfreight grey livery with a large BR logo on the body side. The highly capable Class '20's have worked over most of the BR network.

★　★　★

Although the BR Type '1's are an interesting group of locomotives, they are not really ideal as the basic form of motive power for a small layout. Without any form of train heating their use on passenger trains is limited, whilst today, coupled together in pairs, they haul heavy mainline freights. For a more general purpose machine we need to look at the next group of locomotives, the Type '2's.

The Type '2's

These locomotives are designed for both passenger and freight work on branch lines and cross-country routes, and secondary duties on major routes. They appear at the head of all manner of trains, from express passenger turns to local freight workings, intensive suburban usage to sleepy branch duties. Hence they are very useful and versatile locomotives, both from the prototype and the model viewpoint.

Class '21': North British 1,000hp/1,100hp Bo-Bo diesel-electric

In the days of steam the North British Locomotive Company was one of the 'greats' of the industry. Unfortunately the diesel era was not a happy time for the firm and in the end it went out of business. This unhappiness seems to have percolated down to the designs of diesel locomotive that they produced for none are now in service on BR. The Class '21's are a case in point, a troublesome type which never reached their full potential.

Between 1958 and 1960, 58 of these MAN-engined locomotives were built and numbered D6100 to D6157. The engines on D6100 to D6137 were rated at 1,000hp whilst on the remainder they were set at the higher 1,100hp rating. Plagued by problems, in the mid 1960s twenty were fitted with new Paxman engines in an attempt to improve their overall reliability. In this guise they became known as the Class '29's so we will return to them later in the chapter.

The first of these locomotives appeared during December 1958 and the last of those retaining their MAN engines were withdrawn from service in August 1968.

With the Class '21's there were a number of variations of interest to modellers and these are shown in *Figure 9*. The first difference to appear related to the design of the main body side grille. Initially this was in two rectangular sections but was soon altered to a less deep, more square style. The final twenty of the class were destined for use over former Great North of Scotland lines. As these routes were largely of single track, a tablet catcher recess was made into the cab side below the driver's side window. The cab side windows were of a modified design too, being of the sliding type rather than fitted with droplights. D6138 to D6157 also differed from the rest of the class in having electro-pneumatic control equipment. As a result of this the multiple-working jumper cable socket was situated on the front of the body above the nearside buffer. The earlier locomotives, which had electro-magnetic control, had this jumper socket actually on the bufferbeam.

Standard Brunswick green livery with a grey roof, red bufferbeams and black underframe was initially applied to all the class. In the early 1960s small yellow warning panels and 'overhead live wire' flashes appeared on the locomotives. Only one was repainted in rail blue, this being D6109.

Although all of the class was eventually based in Scotland, the first 38 were initially allocated to the ER. D6100 to D6109 worked out of Hornsey shed in north London, mainly on outer suburban passenger trains from Kings Cross to Hitchin and Royston, and further afield to Cambridge. In east London, D6110 to D6119 were at Stratford shed working mostly on freight turns to the large marshalling yards in the district at Ripple Lane and Temple Mills. The final

Figure 9 North British Class '21' details

ARRANGEMENT OF BODYSIDE GRILLES

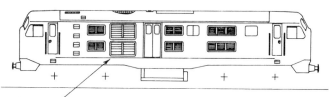

INITIAL STYLE OF MAIN RADIATOR
GRILLE ON D6100 TO D6109

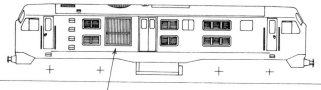

LATER DESIGN OF RADIATOR GRILLE ON D6110 TO D6157. THE
INITIAL TEN LOCOMOTIVES WITH THE EARLIER STYLE OF GRILLE
WERE SOON ALTERED TO CONFORM WITH THE REST OF THE CLASS.

SOME VARIATIONS

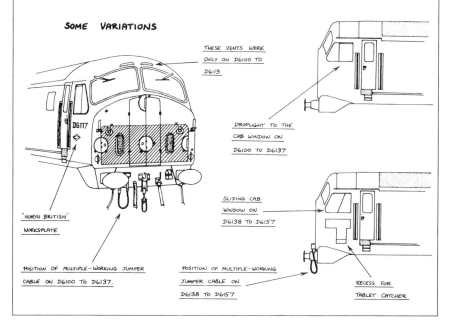

THESE VENTS WERE
ONLY ON D6100 TO
D6119

DROPLIGHT TO THE
CAB WINDOW ON
D6100 TO D6137

SLIDING CAB
WINDOW ON
D6138 TO D6157

"NORTH BRITISH"
WORKSPLATE

POSITION OF MULTIPLE-WORKING JUMPER
CABLE ON D6100 TO D6137.

POSITION OF MULTIPLE-WORKING
JUMPER CABLE ON
D6138 TO D6157

RECESS FOR
TABLET CATCHER

batch on the ER, D6120 to D6137, were allocated to Ipswich. The remaining twenty members of the class were based near Aberdeen, covering both passenger and freight duties.

In 1960, D6100 to D6137 moved north to Scotland and were put to work on three main routes: Glasgow Buchanan Street to Aberdeen (via Perth and Forfar); Glasgow Buchanan Street to Dundee West; Glasgow Buchanan Street to Oban (via Stirling and Callander). When working on passenger duties over these lines, they generally operated in multiple, coupled in pairs. After lengthy periods out of use or in storage, the Class '21's were withdrawn during 1967 and 1968.

Class '22': North British 1,000hp/1,100hp B-B diesel-hydraulic

Coming from the same stable as the Class '21's, this diesel-hydraulic class had many features in common with its diesel-electric brethren. Numbered D6300 to D6357 they could, at a glance, be easily mistaken for the previous class. However they were nearly 4ft shorter in length and had a different arrangement of body side grilles. Also they were another of the few diesel classes to have spoked wheels. The first six had 1,000hp engines whilst the rest of the class were uprated to 1,100hp.

The first of the class entered service during January 1959 and the last was withdrawn thirteen years later in January 1972.

The first six locomotives (D6300-D6305) had a different design of main radiator grille and a slightly altered arrangement of body side grilles. Unlike the Class '21's however, the early batch of locomotives did not have their grilles subsequently changed to conform with the rest of the class.

Other variations largely concerned the front end details and these are outlined in *Figure 10*. D6300 to D6333 did not initially have headcode boxes on the ends,

A North British Class '22' at Worcester Shrub Hill. D6331 is in Brunswick green livery but with full yellow nose ends.

Figure 10 Class '22' front end variations

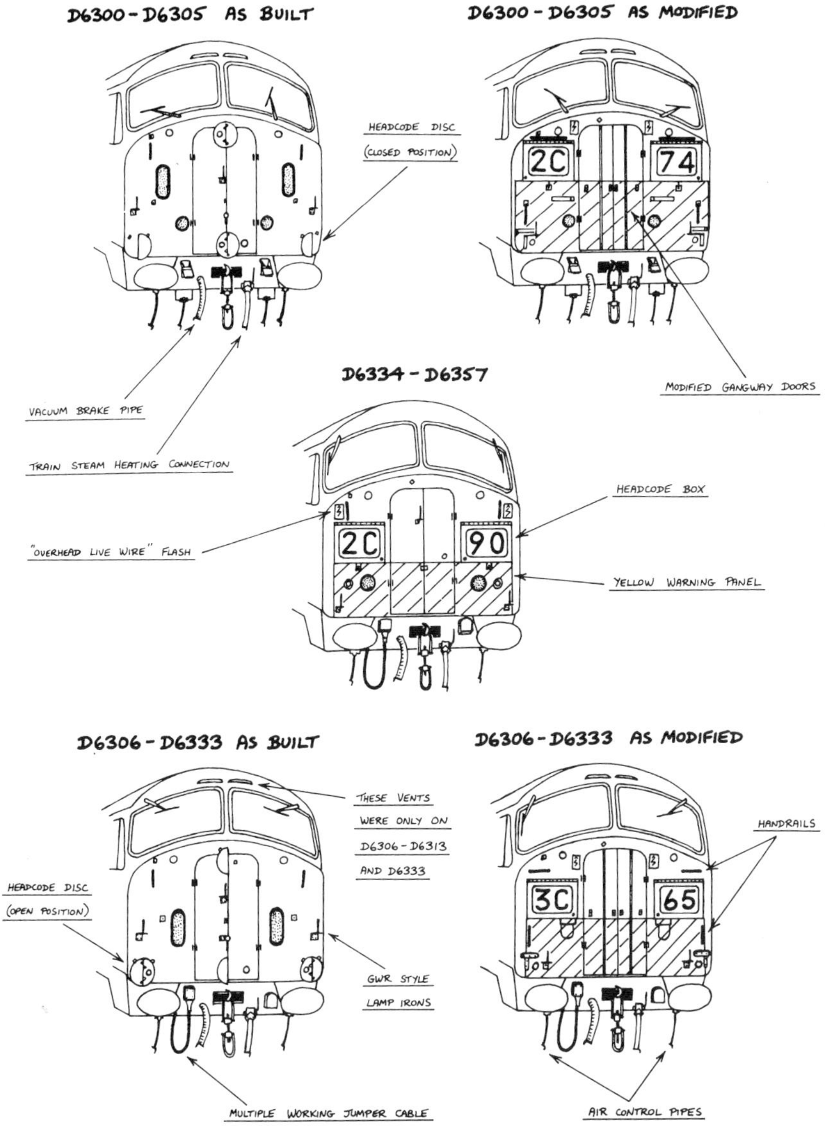
D6300-D6305 AS BUILT
D6300-D6305 AS MODIFIED
HEADCODE DISC (CLOSED POSITION)
2C
74
D6334-D6357
MODIFIED GANGWAY DOORS
VACUUM BRAKE PIPE
TRAIN STEAM HEATING CONNECTION
HEADCODE BOX
"OVERHEAD LIVE WIRE" FLASH
2C
90
YELLOW WARNING PANEL
D6306-D6333 AS BUILT
D6306-D6333 AS MODIFIED
THESE VENTS WERE ONLY ON D6306-D6313 AND D6333
HANDRAILS
HEADCODE DISC (OPEN POSITION)
3C
65
GWR STYLE LAMP IRONS
MULTIPLE WORKING JUMPER CABLE
AIR CONTROL PIPES

being fitted instead with headcode discs. Eventually, with the exception of D6301, all these early members of the class were equipped with headcode boxes. Because these headcode boxes slightly protruded from the front of the locomotive, the central gangway doors also had to be modified so that they could swing open easily. Other differences within the class to watch out for are a modified radiator grille on D6303, variations in the design of the jumper cable sockets on the bufferbeam and the style of end footsteps.

All the class originally carried Brunswick green livery with a grey roof and a light grey waist band. Yellow warning panels were applied to D6337 onwards from new, whilst the others soon received them too. Just under half of the Class '22's were subsequently repainted in rail blue. The position of the BR logo varied at first; some (eg, D6314 and D6327) carried it on the body side. Early repaints like these retained their small yellow warning panels. Later locomotives had full yellow ends with logos on the cab sides; initially the logo was below the number but was subsequently revised to carry the logo above the number.

The Class '22's were once a common sight on most of the lines in Cornwall, Devon and Somerset, working both passenger and freight duties. During the middle of the 1960s some were based at Old Oak Common shed in London for use on empty coaching stock trains in and out of Paddington station. Also around this time, with the closure of many branch lines in the West of England, they appeared more frequently in Gloucestershire and occasionally worked as far north as Worcester.

Class '23': English Electric 1,100hp Bo-Bo diesel-electric

With a nine-cylinder Napier Deltic engine, this class became known as the 'Baby Deltics'. A total of ten were constructed, numbered D5900 to D5909.

Entering service in April 1959, the last was withdrawn in March 1971. However, D5901 remained in departmental use until 1976.

There were no variations as such between the individual members of this class. Their appearance was altered though, after a long period in storage between 1962 and 1965. During this time they were refurbished and the end gangway doors and headcode discs were removed to be replaced by a headcode box.

The original livery was Brunswick green with a medium grey roof and black underframe. Along the bottom edge of the body side was a broad band of light grey, this changing to red on the nose ends. After refurbishment the main colour was still green, but the waist band running round the length of the body was now light green. Yellow warning panels were also applied on each end. Only one Class '23' received rail blue livery (D5909),though many of the others were given full yellow ends whilst still retaining the green colour scheme.

The locomotives spent most their time on suburban and outer suburban passenger trains from Kings Cross to Hitchin and Cambridge. On occasions they appeared on freight turns and often at weekends worked permanent way trains. Broad Street station in London also saw this class and from time to time they appeared at Moorgate on suburban trains.

Class '24': BR 1,160hp Bo-Bo diesel-electric

This class eventually totalled 151 members, numbered D5000 to D5150 at first. Most subsequently carried numbers in the series between 24001 and 24150. Though not the most stylish of the diesel designs, the Class '24's were the forerunners of BR's standard Type '2'.

Appearing in August 1958, the last was withdrawn from revenue earning service during October 1980. One is still in use: 97201 (originally D5061) is based at the Railway Technical Centre in Derby.

The most noticeable variation within the class concerned the headcode fitments. D5000 to D5113 had headcode discs whilst the remainder had a roof-mounted indicator box on each end. The locomotives also had a fairing around the bottom of the body side but in later years this was removed. Some of the more subtle differences between individual members of the class are outlined in *Figure 11*. One alteration made to the majority of the class was the welding up or plating over of the front gangway doors. They were seldom used and were a notorious creator of draughts within the cab.

Brunswick green with a medium grey roof and black underframe was the initial livery applied to the locomotives. This was relieved by a light grey band running along the bottom edge of the body. A small number, including D5037, later appeared in two-tone green in the style that later became standard on the Class '25's. The great majority of the class ended their days in rail blue with full yellow ends.

Over the years Class '24's have worked in many parts of the country: from the island of Anglesey to the Isle of Thanet, from the Highlands of Scotland to the Fenlands of East Anglia. Reallocations over the years, however, saw more and more of the class based on the LMR. They became almost synonymous with the

Class '24' 5025 in early blue livery with cabside BR logos. Note the fairing along the bottom edge of the bodywork.

Figure 11 BR Class '24' details

RADIATOR GRILLE DESIGN

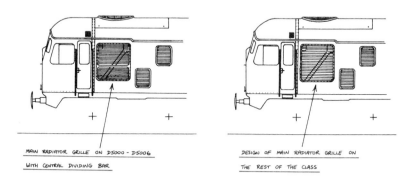

MAIN RADIATOR GRILLE ON D5000 - D5006
WITH CENTRAL DIVIDING BAR

DESIGN OF MAIN RADIATOR GRILLE ON
THE REST OF THE CLASS

"SCOTTISH" CLASS 24's

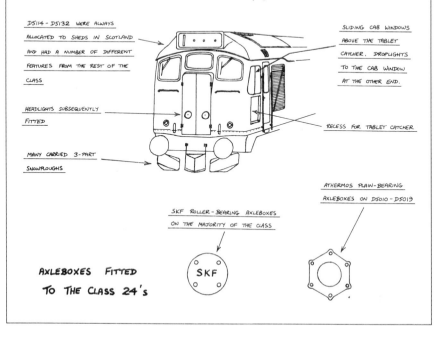

D5114 - D5132 WERE ALWAYS
ALLOCATED TO SHEDS IN SCOTLAND
AND HAD A NUMBER OF DIFFERENT
FEATURES FROM THE REST OF THE
CLASS

HEADLIGHTS SUBSEQUENTLY
FITTED

MANY CARRIED 3-PART
SNOWPLOUGHS

SLIDING CAB WINDOWS
ABOVE THE TABLET
CATCHER. DROPLIGHTS
TO THE CAB WINDOW
AT THE OTHER END.

RECESS FOR TABLET CATCHER

ATHERMOS PLAIN-BEARING
AXLEBOXES ON D5010 - D5019

SKF ROLLER-BEARING AXLEBOXES
ON THE MAJORITY OF THE CLASS

SKF

AXLEBOXES FITTED
TO THE CLASS 24's

North Wales coast line to Llandudno and Holyhead, and the former Cambrian lines in Mid Wales to Aberystywth and Pwllheli. Often during the summer months they appeared at the head of holiday trains, working in multiple, carrying visitors from the West Midlands to the seaside resorts there.

Class '25': BR 1,250hp Bo-Bo diesel-electric

Derived from the previous class, with the engine uprated to 1,250hp, these machines eventually totalled over 300, becoming the largest class of Type '2's on BR. Initialy numbered D5151 to D5299 and D7500 to D7677, they subsequently became 25001 to 25327 respectively. Towards the end of 1985, twelve were renumbered 25901 to 25912 for a slightly extended life span. The first Class '25' appeared in April 1961 and the last members of this once large group of locomotives were withdrawn in March 1987.

Visually the locomotives can be divided into two groups: D5151 to D5232 and D7568 to D7597 have end gangway doors; D5233 to D5299, D7500 to D7567 and D7598 to D7677 are without gangway doors and with a redesigned body side.

Early batches were in Brunswick green livery in the same style as applied to the Class '24's. From D5233, a two-tone green livery was adopted. The final few members of the class were delivered new in rail blue.

With the exception of the SR, all regions of BR have had an allocation of these locomotives at some time or another. As befits their Type '2' designation, the work they have performed has been wide and varied in many parts of the country.

St Pancras before the erection of the overhead catenary. One of the final batch of Class '25's built, 25323, arrives with some Mark 1 stock.

Above left *The windows have been flush-glazed, windscreen wipers added and details on the gangway doors filed off.*

Above right *Another view of the detailed* Hornby *Class '25'.*

Class '26': Birmingham Railway Carriage & Wagon 1,160hp Bo-Bo diesel-electric

These chunky looking Type '2's, along with the similar Class '27's, will forever be associated with the Scottish Region of BR. Any model layout portraying the Scottish scene over the past 25 years will need at least one of these locomotives if it is to be authentic. Initially numbered D5300 to D5346, they later became 26001 to 26046. Most retained the same last two digits, for example D5301 becoming 26001, but the following were exceptions: D5300 became 26007; D5307 became 26020; D5320 became 26028. D5328 was withdrawn before the introduction of the new numbering.

The first of the class appeared during August 1958. The class have a reasonably bright future — at least into the first half of the 1990s.

There are a number of variations between individual members of the Class '26's, especially concerning differences on D5300 to D5319 and the remainder of the class. *Figure 12* and *Figure 13* outline the main differences and also show changes which have been made to the locomotives over the years. Not every locomotive has gone through all the alterations so if modelling a specific member of the class at a particular period it is as well to check with photographs to see if it carried a snowplough or was fitted with headlights.

The original livery applied to these locomotives was one of the most attractive on any of the Type '2's. The Brunswick green bodywork, grey roof and black

Figure 12 The Class '26's: D5300-D5319

D5300-D5319 : EARLY STYLE

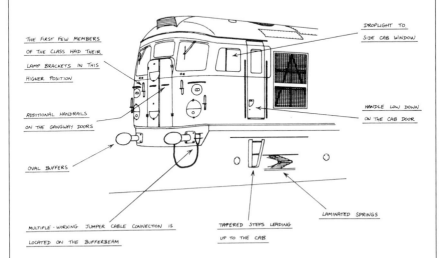

DROPLIGHT TO
SIDE CAB WINDOW

THE FIRST FEW MEMBERS
OF THE CLASS HAD THEIR
LAMP BRACKETS IN THIS
HIGHER POSITION

ADDITIONAL HANDRAILS
ON THE GANGWAY DOORS

HANDLE LOW DOWN
ON THE CAB DOOR

OVAL BUFFERS

LAMINATED SPRINGS

MULTIPLE-WORKING JUMPER CABLE CONNECTION IS
LOCATED ON THE BUFFERBEAM

TAPERED STEPS LEADING
UP TO THE CAB

26001-26020 : CURRENT STYLE

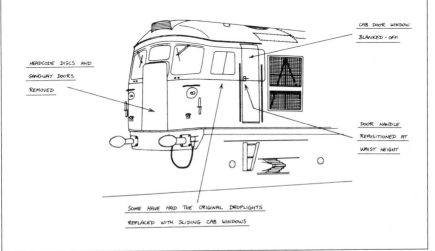

CAB DOOR WINDOW
BLANKED-OFF

HEADCODE DISCS AND
GANGWAY DOORS
REMOVED

DOOR HANDLE
REPOSITIONED AT
WAIST HEIGHT

SOME HAVE HAD THE ORIGINAL DROPLIGHTS
REPLACED WITH SLIDING CAB WINDOWS

Figure 13 The Class '26's: D5320-D5346

D5320 - D5346 : EARLY STYLE

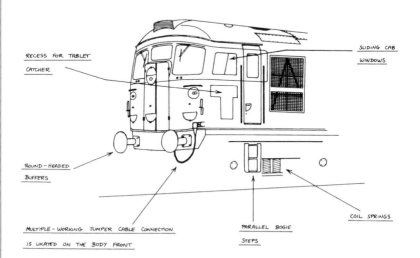

SLIDING CAB
WINDOWS

RECESS FOR TABLET
CATCHER

ROUND - HEADED
BUFFERS

COIL SPRINGS

MULTIPLE - WORKING JUMPER CABLE CONNECTION
IS LOCATED ON THE BODY FRONT

PARALLEL BOGIE
STEPS

26021 - 26046 : CURRENT STYLE

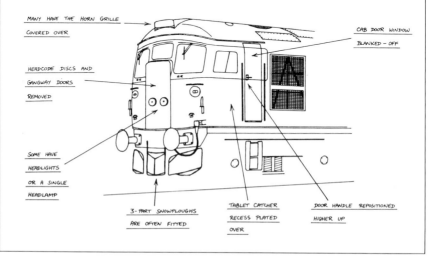

MANY HAVE THE HORN GRILLE
COVERED OVER

CAB DOOR WINDOW
BLANKED - OFF

HEADCODE DISCS AND
GANGWAY DOORS
REMOVED

SOME HAVE
HEADLIGHTS
OR A SINGLE
HEADLAMP

3- PART SNOWPLOUGHS
ARE OFTEN FITTED

TABLET CATCHER
RECESS PLATED
OVER

DOOR HANDLE REPOSITIONED
HIGHER UP

underframe was enlivened by the cab window surrounds picked out in off-white, together with a waist band of the same colour running round the locomotive. Subsequently they were all repainted in rail blue with the BR logo towards the centre of the body. Currently the class is appearing in railfreight grey, with the fronts, including the cab doors, in yellow. The window surrounds are in black with the bufferbeams and solebars in red.

Potters Bar rather than Plockton, Stevenage instead of Strathcarron. Yes, the Class '26's began their working life on suburban trains out of London Kings Cross. D5300 to D5319, together with D5330 to D5335, were based in the Metropolis for a period before moving up to Scotland. By the autumn of 1960, all the class were north of the Border where they were divided between Haymarket shed in Edinburgh, and the depot at Inverness.

Throughout the 1960s, '70s and into the '80s the class could be seen on both passenger and freight duties in the Highlands, the eastern side of the country and down into the Borders. In the late 1960s D5300 to D5306 had their train steam heating boilers removed and air brakes fitted so they could work merry-go-round coal trains in the Edinburgh district. With more powerful Class '37's and '47's now working in the Highlands, the Class '26's have been concentrated on Eastfield shed in Glasgow largely relegated to freight duties. The first seven of the class, however, are still based in Edinburgh.

Class '27': Birmingham Railway Carriage & Wagon 1,250hp Bo-Bo diesel-electric

In the same way that the Class '25's were a development of the Class '24's, these locomotives stemmed from the Class '26's: 69 of these 1,250hp machines were constructed, numbered D5347 to D5415. Using the same bodyshell as that employed on the Class '26's, the two types looked very similar, the main distinguishing feature between the two being that the Class '27's had a roof-mounted headcode box instead of the discs of the earlier design. During 1970/71, 24 of the class were fitted with air brakes and push-pull equipment for working trains between Glasgow and Edinburgh. Thus when the locomotives came to be renumbered into the five-digit scheme, they were divided into two groups: 27001-27044 were to the standard design; 27101-27124 were fitted for push-pull operations.

You will note that this only adds up to 68; one of the class, D5383, was withdrawn in 1966 long before the renumbering of BR's diesel fleet. In the mid 1970s, half of the push-pull fitted batch were given electric train heating equipment and renumbered 27201 to 27212. After being displaced from their push-pull duties by Class '47's, in the early '80s this equipment was removed, along with the electric train heating, and the whole class was numbered in one series from 27001 up to 27066.

The class entered service during June 1961. The last Class '27' was withdrawn from service in August 1987.

Initially the class was split between three regions and this gave rise to a number of variations. The first batch, D5347 to D5369, went to Scotland. They had

In August 1971, when Class '27's worked on the Edinburgh to Glasgow push-pull service, 5412 stands at Glasgow Queen Street. Note that the front gangway doors have been removed.

sliding cab side windows and recesses for tablet catchers like those on later Class '26' locomotives. D5370 to D5378 were allocated to the North Eastern Region and had droplights to the side cab windows. They were not fitted with a train heating boiler and so lacked the water tank slung beneath the body between the bogies. The remaining members of the class went new to the London Midland Region. These also had droplights to the cab windows, and were fitted with a train steam heating boiler. In their later days the gangway doors were welded up and many had the tablet catcher recess plated over. Number 27007 became something of a celebrity to enthusiasts in the early 1980s after the centre window on the cab front was also plated over.

The initial livery style of these locomotives was the same as the previous class: Brunswick green with off-white cab surrounds and waist band. One Class '27' engine, D5380, appeared in two-tone green livery with small yellow warning panels during the mid 1960s. Soon rail blue became standard for the class though there were initially some variations in the position of the numbers and BR logo. For example, one of the early repaints, D5389, only had small yellow warning panels with the logo situated on one of the cab sides. Full yellow ends soon became the norm with the BR logo towards the middle of the body side.

D5347 to D5369 were delivered new to the ScR. They were based at Eastfield shed on the north side of Glasgow, working over the West Highland line to Fort William and Mallaig amongst other duties. D5370 to D5378 initially operated on freight traffic around Teesside. However by the beginning of 1966 they had moved south to join D5379 to D5415 on the LMR. Here the class worked the former Midland line from London St Pancras as far north as Nottingham. Although they did appear on passenger trains, most of their time was spent on freight haulage, particularly in Bedfordshire, the Wellingborough area and in Leicestershire. By the spring of 1970 all the class was concentrated in Scotland. The following year they began operating Edinburgh-Glasgow push-pulls, with a locomotive at each end of the train. Relegated to less onerous duties by the arrival of Class '37's and '47's in the region, the locomotives that were once quite a common sight over much of Scotland are now just a memory.

Class '28': Metropolitan-Vickers 1,200hp Co-Bo diesel-electric

These locomotives, numbered D5700 to D5719, form another of the less successful types of diesel that worked on BR. Although on occasions they put up a spirited performance, the class will best be remembered for their unusual Co-Bo wheel arrangement and pyrotechnic engine exhaust.

Entering service in July 1958, the last were withdrawn during September 1968. D5705, renumbered as TDB968006, remained in departmental stock until the late 1970s.

In appearance terms the main alteration came in the mid 1960s, when the original wrap-round front cab windows in aluminium surrounds were replaced with flat panes of glass set in thick rubber mountings.

Standard Brunswick green was the initial livery, with the side grilles picked out in eggshell blue and a body side band of the same colour. Rather surprisingly the bogie sideframes were also painted eggshell blue, evoking memories of the aluminium painted bogies on the early designs of diesel locomotives. Later the bogies were given a coat of black paint, the grilles and lining band now being off-white, and small yellow warning panels applied to each end. As far as is known, only D5701 received the rail blue livery, possibly at the end of 1967 after a visit to Crewe Works.

The Class '28's spent all their lives allocated to the LMR. At first they worked on the Midland main line out of St Pancras, usually in multiple, on expresses to Manchester Central. They also hauled, again in multiple, the crack 'Condor' freight from Hendon (London) via the Settle and Carlisle line to Glasgow. Working singly, the locomotives appeared regularly on stopping trains between Derby and Manchester, and sometimes on suburban duties in the London area.

Problems with the class saw them being put into store during 1960/61. After refurbishment they were all reallocated to Barrow-in-Furness, being employed on both passenger and freight duties in the area. The coastal route from Lancaster through Barrow, Whitehaven and Workington to Carlisle became their home until withdrawal.

Class '29': North British 1,350hp Bo-Bo diesel-electric

As I mentioned earlier in the chapter, twenty of the Class '21's were equipped with new 1,350hp Paxman engines to improve their performance. In this guise they became known as the Class '29's. The locomotives involved were: D6100, D6101, D6102, D6103, D6106, D6107, D6108, D6112, D6113, D6114,

Figure 14 Features of the Class '29'

FRONT END DETAILS

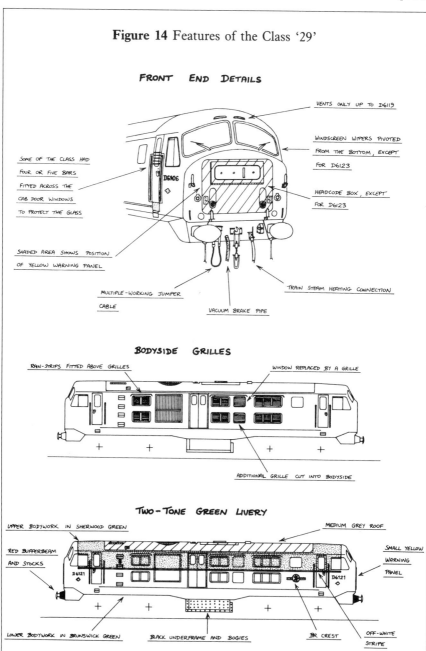

VENTS ONLY UP TO D6119

WINDSCREEN WIPERS PIVOTED FROM THE BOTTOM, EXCEPT FOR D6123

SOME OF THE CLASS HAD FOUR OR FIVE BARS FITTED ACROSS THE CAB DOOR WINDOWS TO PROTECT THE GLASS

HEADCODE BOX, EXCEPT FOR D6123

D6106

SHADED AREA SHOWS POSITION OF YELLOW WARNING PANEL

MULTIPLE-WORKING JUMPER CABLE

VACUUM BRAKE PIPE

TRAIN STEAM HEATING CONNECTION

BODYSIDE GRILLES

RAIN-STRIPS FITTED ABOVE GRILLES

WINDOW REPLACED BY A GRILLE

ADDITIONAL GRILLE CUT INTO BODYSIDE

TWO-TONE GREEN LIVERY

UPPER BODYWORK IN SHERWOOD GREEN

MEDIUM GREY ROOF

RED BUFFERBEAM AND STOCKS

SMALL YELLOW WARNING PANEL

D6121

D6121

LOWER BODYWORK IN BRUNSWICK GREEN

BLACK UNDERFRAME AND BOGIES

BR CREST

OFF-WHITE STRIPE

D6116, D6119, D6121, D6123, D6124, D6129, D6130, D6132, D6133, D6137.

The first Class '29' (re-engined Class '21') appeared in June 1963, with the remainder being modified between 1965 and 1967. All had been withdrawn by the end of December 1971.

Rebuilding the Class '21's into Class '29's caused some structural alterations to be made to the bodywork and also some slight modifications made to the roof details. Front end changes involved the original headcode discs and gangway doors being removed, to be replaced with a headcode box. However on D6123, the first to be re-engined, the headcode discs were retained and it had other detail differences from the remainder. *Figure 14* shows the main features of the majority of the class.

Two-tone green was initially adopted as the standard livery for this class and the first thirteen re-engined members were so painted. On D6123, the two shades of green were separated by a black stripe along the middle of the body. The rest had the colours separated by an off-white band. By the time that the final seven Class '29's appeared in 1967, rail blue was the standard BR livery for locomotives. Hence D6100, D6107, D6108, D6119, D6124, D6129 and D6137 appeared in overall blue with full yellow ends. Whilst none of those in two-tone green were later repainted blue, some did receive full yellow ends before withdrawal, including D6106 and D6132, though by this time without the 'D' prefix to the number.

The Class '29's initially worked on the line between Glasgow and Aberdeen. Soon, however, they appeared on the West Highland line to Fort William and Mallaig, a route which they came to be particularly associated with up until the end of the class.

Class '30' and Class '31': Brush 1,470hp A1A-A1A diesel-electric

With the decline in the numbers of Class '25' locomotives in service and their eventual extinction, the Class '31's are now the largest and thus the 'standard' group in the Type '2' power range on BR. Initially they were fitted with Mirrlees engines, rated at either 1,250hp or 1,365hp. However a few had their engines set at 1,600hp whilst one of the class, D5835, was rated at 2,000hp making it, on paper at least, a Type '4'.

With these Mirrlees engines fitted, the locomotives were referred to as the Class '30's. Problems with the diesel engines led to the entire class being equipped with new English Electric 1,470hp units between 1964 and 1969, so becoming the Class '31's with which we are so familiar today. Originally numbered D5500 to D5699 and D5800 to D5862, following the 1973/74 renumbering they were divided into three sub-classes:

Class '31/0' were numbered 31001 to 31019, and had electro-magnetic control equipment. All had been withdrawn from service by the end of 1980.

Class '31/1' are numbered in the range between 31101 and 31327 and have the more usual electro-pneumatic control.

Class '31/4' numbered 31401 to 31469, these are like the Class '31/1' but are additionally fitted with electric train heating equipment.

The first of the class appeared during October 1957 and the great majority are still going strong. They have a secure future well into the 1990s, and it would not be surprising to see some at work during the early years of the next century.

Visually, the main variation within the class concerned those fitted with headcode discs, and those equipped with headcode boxes. These are shown in the table below.

Class '31' locomotives with headcode discs (and subsequent renumberings)

D5500 (31018)	D5514 (31014)	D5528 (31110)
D5501 (31001)	D5515 (31015)	D5529 (31111)
D5502 (31002)	D5516 (31016)	D5535 (31117)
D5503 (31003)	D5517 (31017)	D5539 (31121)
D5504 (31004)	D5518*	D5543 (31125)
D5505 (31005)	D5519 (31019)	D5547 (31129, 31461)
D5506 (31006)	D5520 (31102)	D5551 (31133, 31450)
D5507 (31007)	D5521 (31103)	D5552 (31134)
D5508 (31008)	D5522 (31418)	D5555 (31137, 31444)
D5509 (31009)	D5523 (31105)	D5556 (31138)
D5510 (31010)	D5524 (31106)	D5559 (31141)
D5511 (31011)	D5525 (31107)	D5562 (31144)
D5512 (31012)	D5526 (31108)	
D5513 (31013)	D5527 (31109)	

*Following an accident, D5518 was given new cabs in 1967 with headcode boxes. Thus in its renumbered form as 31101, it never carried the discs.

Figure 15 outlines the main features of those members of the class which have headcode discs and those with the later style of roof-mounted headcode box. Note that the first twenty of the class, D5500 to D5519, had electro-magnetic rather than electro-pneumatic control equipment. This change necessitated some alteration in the positions of the multiple-working connections on the bufferbeam. As a result of its accident damage, D5518 received, in addition to its new cabs, control gear of the more usual electro-pneumatic type. Some of the other changes which have been applied to the class are shown in *Figure 16*. The mid 1960s saw D5671 to D5676 fitted with tablet catchers for working over the single track branch lines serving ironstone quarries south of Grantham on the borders of Lincolnshire and Leicestershire. Although these lines have been closed for some ten years and the actual tablet catchers removed from the locomotives, some still retain the recesses beneath the driver's side cab door window.

Other modifications applied to the whole of the class over the years have included the plating over of the seldom-used gangway doors and, more recently, the headcode boxes as well. When electric train heating equipment was fitted to some of the locomotives, the socket was initially positioned on the front between the nearside buffer and the gangway doors. From 31425 the socket was located

Figure 15 Front end variations of the Class '31's

FITTED WITH HEADCODE DISCS AND ELECTRO-MAGNETIC
CONTROL EQUIPMENT

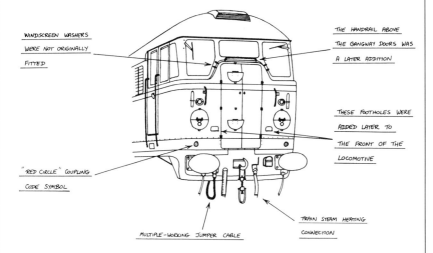

WINDSCREEN WASHERS
WERE NOT ORIGINALLY
FITTED

THE HANDRAIL ABOVE
THE GANGWAY DOORS WAS
A LATER ADDITION

THESE FOOTHOLES WERE
ADDED LATER TO
THE FRONT OF THE
LOCOMOTIVE

"RED CIRCLE" COUPLING
CODE SYMBOL

MULTIPLE-WORKING JUMPER CABLE

TRAIN STEAM HEATING
CONNECTION

FITTED WITH HEADCODE BOXES AND ELECTRO-PNEUMATIC
CONTROL EQUIPMENT

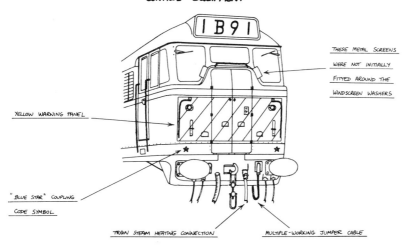

THESE METAL SCREENS
WERE NOT INITIALLY
FITTED AROUND THE
WINDSCREEN WASHERS

YELLOW WARNING PANEL

"BLUE STAR" COUPLING
CODE SYMBOL

TRAIN STEAM HEATING CONNECTION

MULTIPLE-WORKING JUMPER CABLE

Figure 16 Some features of the Class '31' diesels

CURRENT FRONT END DETAILS

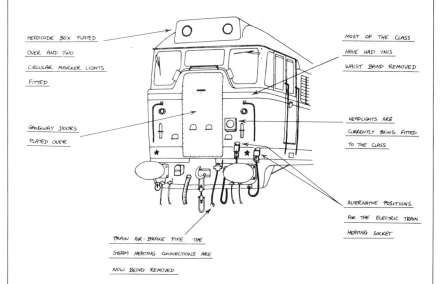

HEADCODE BOX PLATED
OVER AND TWO
CIRCULAR MARKER LIGHTS
FITTED.

GANGWAY DOORS
PLATED OVER

MOST OF THE CLASS
HAVE HAD THIS
WAIST BAND REMOVED

HEADLIGHTS ARE
CURRENTLY BEING FITTED
TO THE CLASS

ALTERNATIVE POSITIONS
FOR THE ELECTRIC TRAIN
HEATING SOCKET

TRAIN AIR-BRAKE PIPE. THE
STEAM HEATING CONNECTIONS ARE
NOW BEING REMOVED

TABLET CATCHERS

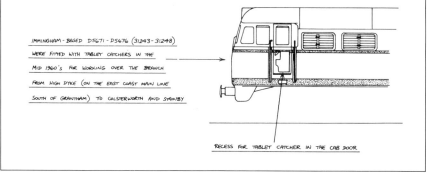

IMMINGHAM-BASED D5671-D5676 (31243-31248)
WERE FITTED WITH TABLET CATCHERS IN THE
MID 1960's FOR WORKING OVER THE BRANCH
FROM HIGH DYKE (ON THE EAST COAST MAIN LINE
SOUTH OF GRANTHAM) TO COLSTERWORTH AND STAINBY

RECESS FOR TABLET CATCHER IN THE CAB DOOR

slightly lower down on the front of the locomotive and on the other side of the nearside buffer. Headlights began to be fitted to the class during 1984, at first only to the Class '31/4's, but now they are to be a standard fitment.

Brunswick green with the usual medium grey roof, black underframe and red bufferbeams was the initial livery, but this was embellished with two broad off-white lining bands running round the length of the body. D5500 to D5519 originally had their cab window surrounds picked out in this colour as well.

Two exceptions to the standard green were D5578 and D5579 which were delivered new at the beginning of 1960 in experimental colours. D5578 appeared in 'electric blue' without the lining bands, this colour being the same as that originally used on the 25kV AC electric locomotives of the LMR. D5579 was painted in what was officially termed 'golden ochre', a shade similar to that which later appeared on one of the Class '52's. Unlike D5578, D5579 also had the off-white lining bands applied.

During 1966 the all-over rail blue colour scheme with full yellow ends began to appear on the class and by about 1974 all were in this style. During the late 1970s some of the larger sheds began to personalize their allocations with some individual touches. For example, Stratford gave some of their Class '31/0's light grey roofs and red bufferbeams, whilst Finsbury Park painted the centre lining band on the Class '31/4's in white. The spring of 1985 saw the start of repainting all the Class '31/1's in railfreight grey livery as, with the removal of their train heating boilers, they are now primarily used on freight work. The Class '31/4' variant, however, is still painted blue.

All the Class '31's were initially based on the ER. The first batches were used extensively throughout East Anglia on both passenger and freight duties. Deliveries during 1960 saw the locomotives working suburban trains out of Kings Cross, displacing Class '21' and '26' locomotives. During the early and middle part of the 1960s the class could be found in three main areas: East Anglia; the southern end of the East Coast main line; around Sheffield and in Lincolnshire. By the early 1970s their allocations were more widespread. With electrification on the ER and more recently the main routes in East Anglia, there has been a gradual drift of the class to the LMR. Here, replacing the Class '25's, they can be seen through the length of England from London to Carlisle.

★   ★   ★

That covers our broad look at the Type '2' locomotives on BR. Quite a varied range of motive power, to be seen on a wide variety of duties, they are a useful type to have on any layout, equally at home on passenger and freight work.

FIVE
Mainline diesels: The Type '3's

The Type '3's arrived quite late on the scene. None was ordered in the BR Modernization Plan of 1955 and it was not until the 1960s that they began to appear on the scene in any great numbers. Eventually just over 500 were built, to three different designs. All things considered, the Type '3's have probably been the least troublesome group of locomotives in BR's diesel fleet, proving to be really useful machines.

Class '33': Birmingham Railway Carriage & Wagon 1,550hp Bo-Bo diesel-electric

Coming from the same manufacturer as the Class '26' and '27', the Class '33's are very similar in appearance to their stablemates. A total of 98 were built and

A broadside view of 33116 standing in the sidings alongside Eastleigh station in Hampshire.

Above *Painting the edges of the front cab windows in black improves the appearance of the model. The windscreen wipers are each made from two small pieces of wire glued into position.*

Below *Larger round-headed buffers have been fitted, together with footsteps made from card which have been stuck above the buffer stocks. Small squares of paper cover over the body side openings that clip on to the underframe tabs.*

The model in action; 33021 at the head of a rake of cement wagons.

initially numbered D6500 to D6597. During 1973/74 they were renumbered into three series to reflect their detail differences: 33001 to 33065 were the standard design; 33101 to 33119 were fitted with push-pull equipment; 33201 to 33212 had narrower bodies.

The first of the class entered service in January 1960. Only a few have so far been withdrawn, and these largely as a result of accident damage.

Brunswick green bodywork with off-white cab surrounds and waist band was the original livery style. Later, rail blue with full yellow ends was applied, and this is still the standard for the class.

The Class '33's have always been based on the Southern Region except for brief periods on loan to other areas for driver training and the like. Although most of their duties have been performed in southern England, they have also worked further afield. In their early days they appeared, for example, on cement trains from Kent which they hauled across London and down the East Coast main line, and on oil trains from Southampton to the Midlands. More recently they have had regular workings into parts of Wales.

Class '35': Beyer Peacock 1,700hp B-B diesel-hydraulic 'Hymeks'

The 'Hymeks', as everyone called this class, are amongst the most attractive of all the diesel designs. Certainly they were the most visually pleasing of all the low and medium powered types in BR's diesel fleet. Appearance-wise, they were streets ahead of their contemporaries. Between 1961 and 1964 a total of 101 were constructed, numbered D7000 to D7100.

The first entered service during May 1961 whilst the final members of the class

Figure 17 Some features of the 'Hymeks'

FRONT END DETAILS

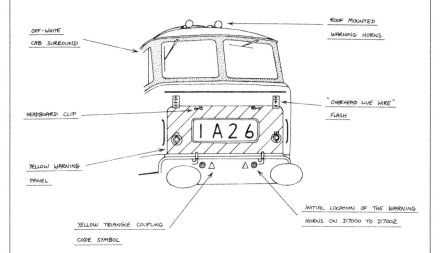

ROOF MOUNTED WARNING HORNS

OFF-WHITE CAB SURROUND

"OVERHEAD LIVE WIRE" FLASH

HEADBOARD CLIP

YELLOW WARNING PANEL

INITIAL LOCATION OF THE WARNING HORNS ON D7000 TO D7002

YELLOW TRIANGLE COUPLING CODE SYMBOL

CABSIDE DETAILS

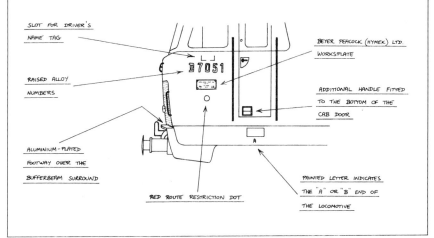

SLOT FOR DRIVER'S NAME TAG

BEYER PEACOCK (HYMEK) LTD WORKSPLATE

RAISED ALLOY NUMBERS

ADDITIONAL HANDLE FITTED TO THE BOTTOM OF THE CAB DOOR

ALUMINIUM-PLATED FOOTWAY OVER THE BUFFERBEAM SURROUND

RED ROUTE RESTRICTION DOT

PAINTED LETTER INDICATES THE "A" OR "B" END OF THE LOCOMOTIVE

Above *The* Tri-ang *OO gauge 'Hymek'. Scale couplings have been fitted and the bufferbeam hoses are made from pieces of wire. The windscreen wipers have also been fabricated out of pieces of wire whilst the tail lights are pin heads.*

Below *Another detailed* Tri-ang *'Hymek'. The livery is Brunswick green with a light green skirt.*

were withdrawn from revenue-earning use in March 1975.

Variations within the class, some of which are illustrated in *Figure 17*, tended to cover minor differences rather than major ones. Nevertheless, it is just these subtle differences which can make or mar a model. The most obvious variation concerned the position of the warning horns on the locomotive. On the first three, D7000 to D7002, horns were mounted at bufferbeam level. In this location they were not all that effective, so on the rest of the class they were put on the roof of the cab. Aesthetically, putting the horns on to the cab roof was a brilliant stroke and gave the locomotives a more balanced look. Around 1965, D7000 to D7002 also had their horns moved to the roof, so matching the remainder of the class.

Another feature which altered were the headboard clips on the front end. Initially the 'Hymeks' were not fitted with these but during 1962 it was decided to equip the class with these clips after all, so D7034 to D7100 were delivered with them from the start. Soon though, the idea of train nameboards fell out of favour and therefore the earlier members of the class were never fitted with them after all. From 1966 an additional door handle began to appear on the bottom corner of each of the cab doors: not strictly a handle, but rather a recess with a bar across to enable the door to be shut from ground level. Eventually the entire class received this rather useful modification.

The roof details on the 'Hymeks' are worthy of note and these are outlined in *Figure 18*. One point to watch out for is the design of the train-heating boiler exhaust outlet. Early batches of the class had a rectangular outlet covered with a grille whilst later members had a slightly different shape without the grille. Nos D7000 to D7044 had a different make of boiler from the rest, so perhaps this accounts for the change in design.

The liveries carried by the class are shown in *Figure 19*. Brunswick green was applied initially, relieved with off-white cab surrounds and a light green skirt. The first of the class, D7000, differed from the remainder in having its bufferbeam surround painted black. By 1965, however, it had been painted light green to match the others. Up to D7008 locomotives were delivered without the 'overhead live wire' flashes, but they were subsequently added.

The small yellow warning panels on each end of the locomotives did not appear until the spring of 1962 and so the early members of the class ran without them at first. The location of the live wire flashes on the locomotive's front varied according to the date of application. The usual position for these was a couple of feet directly above the tail lights but some, including D7000, D7004, D7005, D7007 and D7008, had them more widely spaced in line with the vertical handrails on the cab front. This probably arose because these locomotives were given live wire flashes prior to the application of their yellow warning panels. On the other hand, D7002 had its warning panel applied before its 'overhead live wire' flashes and so when they were fitted, they were correctly positioned.

The first repaints to the new rail blue livery appeared during 1966. Initially there was some confusion as to how this would be applied to the 'Hymeks'. A few, including D7004 and D7007, were turned out with the bodywork and cab

Figure 18 Roof details on the 'Hymeks'

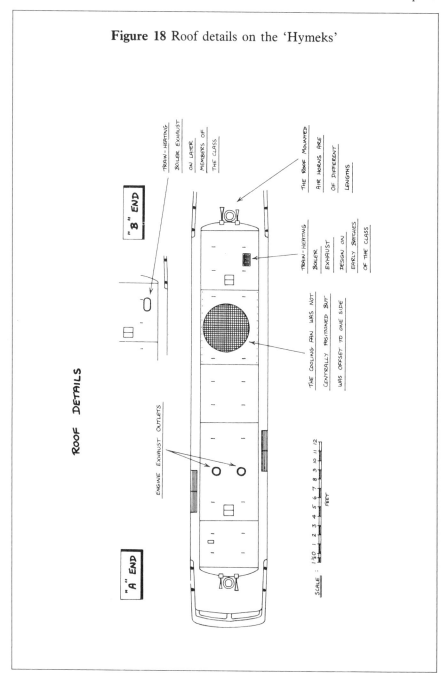

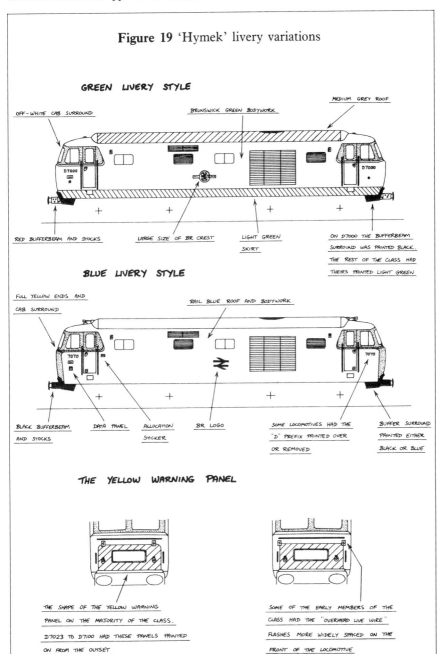

Figure 19 'Hymek' livery variations

GREEN LIVERY STYLE

OFF-WHITE CAB SURROUND

BRUNSWICK GREEN BODYWORK

MEDIUM GREY ROOF

RED BUFFERBEAM AND STOCKS

LARGE SIZE OF BR CREST

LIGHT GREEN SKIRT

ON D7000 THE BUFFERBEAM SURROUND WAS PAINTED BLACK. THE REST OF THE CLASS HAD THEIRS PAINTED LIGHT GREEN

BLUE LIVERY STYLE

FULL YELLOW ENDS AND CAB SURROUND

RAIL BLUE ROOF AND BODYWORK

BLACK BUFFERBEAM AND STOCKS

DATA PANEL

ALLOCATION STICKER

BR LOGO

SOME LOCOMOTIVES HAD THE "D" PREFIX PAINTED OVER OR REMOVED

BUFFER SURROUND PAINTED EITHER BLACK OR BLUE

THE YELLOW WARNING PANEL

THE SHAPE OF THE YELLOW WARNING PANEL ON THE MAJORITY OF THE CLASS. D7023 TO D7100 HAD THESE PANELS PAINTED ON FROM THE OUTSET

SOME OF THE EARLY MEMBERS OF THE CLASS HAD THE "OVERHEAD LIVE WIRE" FLASHES MORE WIDELY SPACED ON THE FRONT OF THE LOCOMOTIVE

surrounds in blue, yet still retaining small warning panels. Eventually two main styles emerged: the majority of the class wore the standard overall blue livery with full yellow ends and cab surrounds and D7033 was the first to appear in this style. However some other members of the class, whilst being repainted blue, kept their off-white cab surrounds and small yellow warning panels. About a dozen retained this non-standard livery until withdrawal, including D7010, D7036, D7040, D7047, D7056, D7057 and D7059.

Following the end of steam on BR in 1968, many of the class had their 'D' prefix to the number painted over or removed. One at least, D7017, had its metal numerals erased completely and replaced by transfers. Not every 'Hymek' survived long enough to receive the blue livery and over a dozen remained in green throughout their careers. Many retaining the green livery also kept the small yellow warning panels (eg, D7002, D7005, D7021, D7024 and D7054). However a small number, including D7020, had full yellow ends applied whilst still in green.

The 'Hymeks' were always based on the Western Region although on occasions they worked further afield. Most of the class were allocated to one of three sheds: Old Oak Common in London, Bath Road in Bristol or Canton in Cardiff, initial deliveries going to Bristol. Cardiff received its first members of the class early in 1962 and soon put them to work on expresses from South Wales to London.

Away from top-link duties, in West Wales the 'Hymeks' became an everyday sight on both passenger and freight trains. By the mid 1960s those based at Old Oak Common were working from London over the Cotswolds to Worcester and Hereford, a route with which they will long be remembered. Whilst regularly appearing in Devon, indeed a few were based at Plymouth for a short period, the class were a much less common sight in Cornwall. At the other end of the region, in the autumn of 1967 D7021 to D7025 took over banking duties on the famous Lickey incline near Bromsgrove. The early 1970s saw a rapid reduction in the numbers of 'Hymeks' in service and those that remained were concentrated in the London area until final withdrawal of the class in the spring of 1975.

Class '37': English Electric 1,750hp Co-Co diesel-electric
The largest of the Type '3's on BR, both numerically and in terms of their horsepower rating, are the Class '37's. These locomotives are amongst the most highly regarded of all the diesel fleet and are equally at home on passenger or freight work. A total of 309 were built and until quite recently their numbering was reasonably straightforward. The first 300 built were originally numbered D6700 to D6999. As the D7XXX series had by then been taken by the 'Hymeks', the final nine of the class appeared as D6600 to D6608. As a result of extensive accident damage, D6983 was withdrawn in 1966. Hence 308 of the class came to be renumbered into the five-digit series during 1973/74 as follows: D6700 became 37119; D6701-D6818 became 37001-37118 respectively; D6819 became 37283; D6820-D6982 became 37120-37282 respectively; D6984-D6999 became 37284-37299 respectively; D6600-D6608 became 37300-37308 respectively. So

A Class '37' at Nottingham. All these locomotives are carried on the standard English Electric three-axle bogie. The grille over the radiator shutters has been removed.

far so good, but in the mid 1980s things began to get more complex. As a result of a life extension programme to take the class into the next century, they are all being renumbered again into separate series to differentiate between those used on passenger duties and those employed on freight work. During 1985/86 the majority of those between 37265 and 37307 had their generators replaced by Brush alternators and electric train heating equipment fitted. Numbered 37401 to 37431, these are now the passenger version of the Class '37's. The remainder are having their steam heating boilers removed, that is if they still have them at present, and after a heavy general repair will be largely confined to freight work. Eventually they will be numbered in four series as follows:

1) **375XX series:** These are from the batch between 37001 and 37119. 37501 upwards are to have Brush alternators whilst 37599 downwards are being fitted with GEC alternators.

2) **376XX series:** These come from the later batch between 37120 and 37308. 37600 upwards have GEC alternators whilst 37699 downwards have alternators of Brush manufacture.

3) **377XX series:** To increase adhesion levels, some Class '37's are being weighted with extra ballast. Of those between 37001 and 37119, 37701 upwards are having Brush alternators and 37799 downwards are having alternators of the GEC variety.

4) **378XX series:** Likewise, of the batch between 37120 and 37308 provided with additional ballast weights, 37800 upwards are to have GEC alternators whilst 37899 downwards have alternators made by Brush.

Figure 20 Features of the Class '37's in their early days

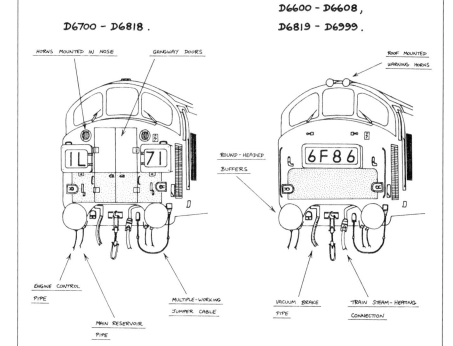

D6700 – D6818 .

D6600 – D6608,
D6819 – D6999 .

HORNS MOUNTED IN NOSE   GANGWAY DOORS

ROOF MOUNTED
WARNING HORNS

ROUND – HEADED
BUFFERS

ENGINE CONTROL
PIPE

MULTIPLE–WORKING
JUMPER CABLE

MAIN RESERVOIR
PIPE

VACUUM BRAKE
PIPE

TRAIN STEAM – HEATING
CONNECTION

BODYSIDE   DETAILS

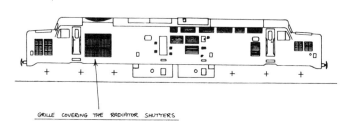

GRILLE COVERING THE RADIATOR SHUTTERS

Why this rather convoluted numbering scheme — is it a ploy to confuse railway enthusiasts? Well, not quite. It arose because BR initially had not decided how many of the class would receive new alternators and of which manufacture they would be. Hence the topsy-turvy renumbering. Just to cloud the picture a little more, half a dozen of the class have had their English Electric engines replaced by some of a different design. Numbered from 37901 to 37906 range, they will be the test-bed for a possible new Class '38' type of locomotive. In the meantime a further move in 1986 saw twelve of the class renumbered 37310 to 37314 and 37320 to 37326 for dedicated use on British Steel traffic.

The first of the Class '37's entered service in December 1960 and they have a secure future ahead of them.

Considering the size of the class, the number of external variations are quite few in number. The main one concerned whether the locomotives had central gangway doors with two-digit headcode boxes mounted on either side, as on D6700 to D6818 (37001-37119), or if they had the later four-digit headcode box and roof-mounted warning horns, as on D6819 to D6999 and D6600 to D6608 (37120-37308).

Figure 20 outlines the main features of the class during the 1960s and early 1970s. Points to watch out for include the design of lamp brackets. Most had the standard BR style, but those members of the class allocated to the WR had a different type derived from the GWR. Not every locomotive was fitted with a train steam-heating boiler, and hence lacked the relevant connection on the bufferbeam. By the 1980s changes were being made to the front end appearance with the gangway doors being welded up or plated over since they were seldom, if ever, used and tended to create draughts inside the cab. The headcode boxes, too, began to be plated over and marker lights were fitted. Some of these changes are shown in *Figure 21*, together with the more recent alterations applied to the class. As the positions of some of the lamp brackets and handrails vary between individual locomotives, be wary if modelling a specific member of the class.

All Class '37's were originally painted in Brunswick green with a medium grey roof and black bogies. The first thirty or so of the class initially lacked the small yellow warning panels on each end, but the rest had them on from the beginning. On the other hand, the 'overhead live wire' flashes were applied right from the start on all the locomotives. With the exception of the unfortunate D6983, all were eventually repainted in rail blue with full yellow ends. Apart from some 'one-off' liveries which appeared during the early 1980s, particularly on those which worked over the West Highland line in Scotland, the overall blue style remained the norm.

In 1985 it was decided that after refurbishing the Class '37's would be finished in two basic styles. Those in the '37/4' series were given rail blue body sides, a light grey roof, yellow ends and nose sides, and black window surrounds. Large numbers and BR logo added the finishing touch. Refurbished examples in the series between '37/5' and '37/9' have the roof and body sides in railfreight grey, yellow ends and nose sides, and black cab window surrounds. The large BR logo on the side of the body is complemented by standard sized numbers in black on

Figure 21 Some current features of the Class '37's

37001 – 37119 OR
37/5 AND 37/7 SERIES.

37120 – 37308 OR
37/4, 37/6, 37/8
AND 37/9 SERIES.

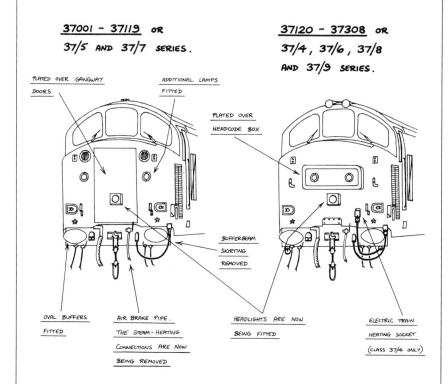

PLATED OVER GANGWAY DOORS

ADDITIONAL LAMPS FITTED

PLATED OVER HEADCODE BOX

BUFFERBEAM SKIRTING REMOVED

OVAL BUFFERS FITTED

AIR BRAKE PIPE. THE STEAM-HEATING CONNECTIONS ARE NOW BEING REMOVED

HEADLIGHTS ARE NOW BEING FITTED

ELECTRIC TRAIN HEATING SOCKET (CLASS 37/4 ONLY)

BODYSIDE DETAILS

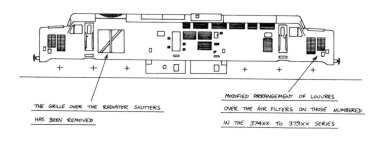

THE GRILLE OVER THE RADIATOR SHUTTERS HAS BEEN REMOVED

MODIFIED ARRANGEMENT OF LOUVRES OVER THE AIR FILTERS ON THOSE NUMBERED IN THE 374XX TO 379XX SERIES

one of the cab sides and 'Railfreight' lettering on the other. However prior to this a few unrefurbished members of the class were painted in the style that was subsequently used on the '37/4's. These were all Scottish-based examples as follows:

37004	37022	37043	37111	37183	37262	37320
37008	37025	37051	37114	37188	37264	(ex-37026)
37011	37026	37079	37117	37191	37310	37326
37012	37027	37081	37146	37260		(ex-37111)
37021	37035	37085	37175	37261	37311	

One ER example, 37116, has also been painted in a similar style with a large BR logo on the body side. In addition 37196, based in the West Country, appeared in railfreight grey livery, as have 37118, 37180 and 37255. Furthermore, although after refurbishment number 37501 was painted in railfreight grey, early in 1987 it appeared in a new British Steel Corporation light blue livery; possibly the start of a new trend towards more specialized livery styles.

Initially the Class '37's were based in the following areas: D6700 to D6729 worked in East Anglia becoming particularly associated with the line from London Liverpool Street via Cambridge to King's Lynn. D6730 to D6741 went to Hull, largely for freight duties. D6742 to D6754 worked around the Sheffield area, mostly on freight. D6755 to D6795 were mostly based in North-east England, hauling freight trains in the heavily industrialized regions of Teeside and Tyneside. D6796 to D6818 went to Sheffield for steel and coal haulage. D6819 to D6958 were allocated to the WR in South Wales primarily on freight trains. D6959 to D6968 were at Sheffield. D6969 to D6999 and D6600 to D6608 were also in South Wales.

The mid 1960s saw a large number of the class move to Scotland and in the early 1980s they began to be seen more frequently on passenger work. Nowadays they are the most commonly seen locomotives on the West Highland line and over the routes to the north and west of Inverness. At the other end of Britain, a handful are employed on the china clay traffic in Cornwall, whilst elsewhere on the WR they appear on some of the stone trains in the area around Westbury in Wiltshire. A more recent development for the class is on passenger work over the former Cambrian lines in central Wales. Electrification of the major routes in East Anglia has seen their passenger duties in that part of the country decline. Freight haulage is still their chief task in South Wales and the North-east, and will remain so for many years to come.

* * *

To end our review of the low and medium-powered diesels in the BR fleet, *Figure 22* outlines when each of the different classes was in service. One can see at a glance the variety of types that existed during the 1960s compared with the number of designs still with us today.

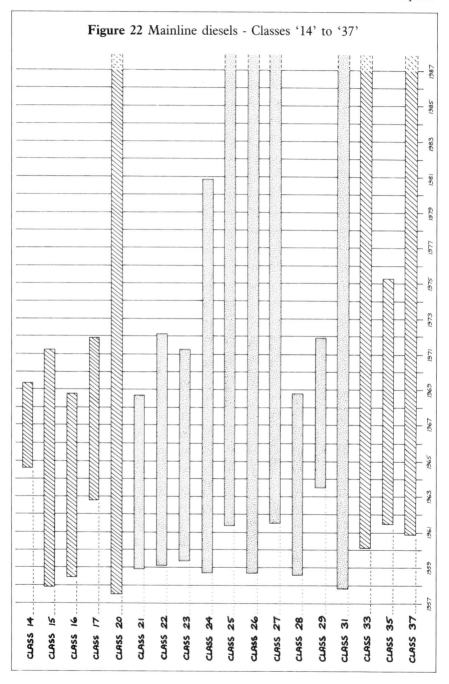

Figure 22 Mainline diesels - Classes '14' to '37'

SIX
Mainline diesels: The Type '4's

The Type '4's are one of the most interesting and diverse groups of diesels on BR. All manner of duties fall within their range, from front line express passenger work to heavy freight trains. Most modellers can justify at least one of these classes on the layout.

Class '40': English Electric 2,000hp 1Co-Col diesel-electric
Two hundred of these large locomotives were built between 1958 and 1962. Initially numbered D200 to D399 they later became 40001 to 40199. After withdrawal in 1985, four were retained for departmental use and renumbered in the 974XX series.

Over half of the Class '40's had headcode discs and gangway doors on the nose ends as illustrated by this example. The locomotives involved were D200 to D324, or in their later numbering 40122, 40001 to 40121, 40123 and 40124 respectively. D322 was not re-numbered into the 40XXX series as it had been withdrawn as early as 1967 following accident damage.

Above *D325 to D344 (40125 to 40144) also had gangway doors but no headcode discs. Instead they were fitted with a pair of two-digit headcode boxes, one on each side of the gangway door. For the remainder of the class, that is D345 to D399 (40145 to 40199), the gangway doors were abolished and a central four-digit headcode box fitted. This latter arrangement is shown here in the view of 40155.*

Below *In the mid-1960s, Scottish-based members of the class that originally had the headcode discs, that is D260 to D266, were fitted with headcode boxes and the gangway doors were removed. Here we see 40064 (originally D264) on the left with the headcode box whilst 40034 alongside still retains its headcode discs.*

The first Class '40' appeared in March 1958. With one exception, they were all withdrawn from revenue-earning service by February 1985. The oldest survivor, D200 (or, in its renumbered form, 40122), was, however, retained in stock after this date for use on railtours.

Variations centre on the provision of either headcode discs or headcode boxes on the front of the locomotives. D200 to D324 had the headcode discs, though they were later removed from D260 to D266 and replaced with a four-digit box. Of the rest of the class, D325 to D344 had a pair of two-digit boxes on each end whilst D345 to D399 had a central four-digit headcode box.

The original livery for the class was overall Brunswick green. The majority were later painted in rail blue, but a few kept their green colour throughout.

Allocated to all regions except the Southern and Western, their duties varied from top-link express work to heavy freight traffic. In their latter years they were concentrated on the LMR in North-west England.

Class '41': North British 2,000hp A1A-A1A diesel-hydraulic

The pioneer Class of 'Warship' diesel-hydraulics, numbered D600 to D604. They were the least successful of all the Type '4's, having an active life of less than ten years.

Appearing in January 1958, all were withdrawn during December 1967. The main modification applied to the class over their short life was the substitution of the front headcode discs for headcode boxes.

The initial livery on these early 'Warships' was Brunswick green. Somewhat surprisingly, a couple were later to be turned out in rail blue.

At first the locomotives worked over the West of England main line from Paddington to Penzance on some of the principal expresses. By the mid 1960s they were largely confined to Cornwall and seldom ventured further east than Plymouth.

Class '42': BR 2,200hp B-B diesel-hydraulic

A more compact form of 'Warship', the Class '42's were the best of the first generation of high-powered diesel-hydraulics. Numbered from D800 to D832 and D866 to D870, the first three were slightly less powerful than the rest at only 2,000hp. On the other hand, D830 was fitted with a different make of engine and was rated at 2,400hp.

The first of the class entered service during August 1958. The last members were withdrawn in December 1972.

Externally, the main variation again centres around the front end details. D800 to D812 initially had headcode discs, though later headcode boxes were fitted to match the rest of the class.

Brunswick green was the first livery style. In the mid 1960s about half were painted maroon whilst later most were given the overall rail blue shade.

Always based on the WR at either Laira shed in Plymouth or nearby Newton Abbot, their early years saw them handling expresses on both the Paddington to

Above *The final style of blue livery on the 'Warships' is shown in this view of 852 at Hereford. Note the position of the BR logo in the centre of the body.*

Left *Very little work is needed on the Mainline/Dapol model, as it is already of a very high standard. Sticking small rectangles of black card over the existing headcodes to make them larger, then applying new train codes, does make the front end look much more effective.*

Below *Fitting engraved or etched nameplates is always a good investment. They are glued into place with a contact adhesive.*

Bristol and Paddington to Penzance lines. By the middle of the 1960s they were also working over the former Southern route from Waterloo to Exeter.

Class '43': North British 2,200hp B-B diesel-hydraulic

Appearance-wise these locomotives were almost identical to the Class '42's. Coming under the same generic 'Warship' tag, they were numbered D833 to D865.

They were not in service as long as their BR-built brothers. The first appeared in July 1960 whilst the last were withdrawn in October 1971.

No real major variations existed within the class except that some had additional cab ventilation grilles fitted in later years.

Liveries followed the same pattern as the previous class. First Brunswick green, then to maroon and finally rail blue.

Duties, too, were similar to the Class '42's. However the Class '43's did not appear on the Waterloo to Exeter service, working instead over the Paddington to Worcester and Hereford line.

Class '44': BR 2,300hp 1Co-Co1 diesel-electric

Better known as the 'Peaks', ten of these rather lumbering machines were built in 1959/60. Initially numbered D1 to D10, they later became 44001 to 44010 respectively.

Entering service during August 1959, the last three members of the class were withdrawn in November 1980.

D9 and D10 differed from the rest in the design of their side grilles. On these two the grilles had a vertical mesh, whilst on the rest it was horizontal.

Liveries were fairly straightforward. Brunswick green was the initial standard but all later received the rail blue.

After a brief spell working passenger trains on the West Coast main line, the class settled down to heavy freight haulage in the East Midlands. Although there

Like the early batches of the Class '40's, these '44's had gangway doors in the nose ends and were fitted with headcode discs. However, following collision damaged in the mid-1960s, D9 (44009) received a new nose section at the number one end which contained a single four-digit headcode box.

The last two Class '44's, D9 and D10, had a different style of bodyside grille as compared to the earlier members. This later design of vertical mesh grille is illustrated here.

were only ten in the class they became almost synonymous with this part of the country.

Class '45': BR 2,500hp 1Co-Co1 diesel-electric

These were the production version of the original 'Peaks'. A total of 127 were constructed, numbered D11 to D137. In the mid 1970s fifty were fitted with electric train heating equipment, so with the general locomotive renumbering of that period, they were divided into two series: 45001-45077 retained their original train steam-heating boilers; 45101-45150 had their boilers removed and replaced with electric train heating equipment.

First appearing in September 1960, the days for these locomotives are now numbered. In particular, the writing is on the wall for the '45/0' variety, with many of them already withdrawn. Great inroads, too, have been made into the ranks of '45/1' series and their future is far from secure.

Yet again, it is the arrangement of headcode boxes on the front of the locomotives which gives rise to the main variations. As built, there were three styles: on D11-D15 a two-digit headcode box was positioned each side of the central gangway door; D16-D30 and D68-D107 sported two-digit boxes at the sides but did not have the gangway doors; D31-D67 and D108-D137 had a pair of two-digit headcode boxes positioned towards the centre of the locomotive's front. Over the years these distinctions have become blurred as new fronts were fitted to the class.

Above *D31 to D67 and D108 to D173 had a pair of two-digit headcode boxes located towards the centre of the nose ends.*

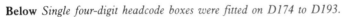

Below *Single four-digit headcode boxes were fitted on D174 to D193.*

Above *As the years progressed more loco-motives were retrospectively fitted with the single four-digit headcode box. From the mid-1970s, new nose sections were fitted that incorporated two small circular lamps in the ends and completely erased the former head-code boxes. This design is illustrated here. More recently, in the mid-1980s, larger head-lights in a square casing have been fitted to the Class '45/1' variant of these locomotives.*

Above *Cabside details of 45010, the former D112. Note the weathering of the bodyside running down from the rain strip over the cab door and the discolouration of the bogie side-frames.*

Below *The number one end roof details on 45064 (D105). Note the arrangement of the rain strips at cantrail level.*

From the mid-1960s, all of the Class '46's and some of the Class '45's had an additional grille cut into the lower bodyside, beneath the main side grille. One of the Class '45's so treated was 45105 (D86), seen here leaving Derby.

All the Class '45's were delivered in Brunswick green. Eventually they were repainted in rail blue with yellow nose ends.

The 'Peaks' were the mainstay of both passenger and freight trains on the former Midland line north from St Pancras to Nottingham, Derby, Sheffield, Leeds and Carlisle for twenty years. They were also a common sight on the main North-east to South-west corridor across the country. Today all the remaining members of the class are based at Tinsley, though they still wander far and wide over many parts of the BR system.

Class '46': BR 2,500hp 1Co-Co1 diesel-electric

With a different make of generator and traction motors, the Class '46's were none-the-less almost identical, from the point of view of appearance, to the Class '45's. Initially numbered D138 to D193 and later becoming 46001 to 46056 respectively, 56 were built.

Entering service during October 1961, the remaining members of the class were withdrawn in November 1984.

Like the Class '45's, it was the design of headcode boxes which created the main variations: D138-D173 had a pair of two-digit headcode boxes positioned towards the centre; on D174-D193 there was a single four-digit box in the centre of the locomotive's front. Eventually the early batches also received the four-digit style of headcode box.

Brunswick green was replaced by the standard rail blue livery on all these locomotives.

The Class '46's were initially divided between two regions, D138 to D165 on the London Midland, and D166 to D193 on the North Eastern. On the former they worked the same duties as the Class '45's, whilst on the latter they operated over the East Coast main line and on Newcastle to Liverpool services. The LMR batch later moved to the WR.

Class '47': Brush 2,580hp Co-Co diesel-electric

One of the best known of all BR locomotive types and a 'must' for any layout representing the current scene, over 500 Class '47' locomotives were built between 1962 and 1968, initially numbered D1500 to D1999 and D1100 to D1111. At first the class was rated at 2,750hp, but stress problems with the engines led them to be set permanently at 2,580hp.

Five of the class (D1702-D1706) originally had a different design of engine which produced 2,650hp. In this condition they were termed as Class '48', but around 1970 they had their engines changed to conform to the rest of the class. Whilst the numbering of the Class '47's in their early days was reasonably straightforward, today the situation is rather more complex:

Class '47/0': Numbered in the range between 47001 and 47299, these locomotives are the standard version of the class. Many have train steam-heating boilers but these are currently being removed.

Class '47/3': Numbered between 47301 and 47381, these are the freight version of the class without any form of train heating.

The ubiquitous Class '47'. These locomotives work over all regions of BR including the Southern, as shown here by 47440 leaving Basingstoke in Hampshire.

Above *Two-tone green livery was initially applied to the great majority of the Class '47's. Kings Cross has changed somewhat since this photograph of 1760 was taken.*

Below *D1953 to D1961 were delivered new in overall rail blue livery. These blue examples had the BR logo positioned on each of the four cabsides, as shown here by 47514 which was originally numbered D1960.*

Above *Later blue repaints had the BR logo located on the body side adjacent to the cab doors, with the locomotives number on the cabside.*

Below *Eventually only one BR logo was applied to each side of the locomotive and this was positioned towards the centre of the body side. 47184 shown here exhibits a light grey roof, typical of Stratford depot in East London and the locos allocated to it.*

Above right *The original style of headcode display of the Class '47's was the standard four-digit box on each end, displaying the train classification and code.*

Right *The Western Region was the first to name some of its Class '47's. For the shorter names it had cast alloy nameplates with serif style lettering. Longer names, like the one illustrated here, had fabricated nameplates.*

Below right *From 1976 onwards, the 'marker light' arrangement of two white circles on a black background became an increasingly common sight on the Class '47's.*

ISAMBARD KINGDOM BRUNEL

Above *Towards the end of 1976 the headcode boxes began to be plated over and two lenses fitted, illuminated from behind.*

Below *The Class '47/0' variant, fitted with steam-heating boilers.*

One other variation to look out for on the Class '47's is the design of the grilles on the side of the roof at the number one end. Early batches of the class had a fixed design as shown by D1532 in the photograph. Later examples had movable slats and eventually all the class was fitted with this type.

Class '47/4': Numbered in the 474XX, 475XX and 476XX series, the '47/4's are the passenger version of the class and they are equipped with electric train heating.

Class '47/7': Numbered 47701 to 47716 and used on internal Scottish Region services these engines have electric train heating and push-pull equipment.

Class '47/8': Numbered in the 478XX series, this sub-class is a recent development without train heating and specially ballasted for heavy freight work. However, at the time of writing none has yet appeared and it may well be that this project has been postponed.

Class '47/9': Consists of just one locomotive, numbered 47901, fitted with a Class '58' type engine which, as 47601, was previously used as the test bed for the Class '56's.

The first of the Class '47's appeared during September 1962. They will remain the mainstay of BR's Type '4' fleet into the next century, though some examples have been withdrawn, especially from the early batch of '47/4's between 47401 and 47420.

Major external variations within the class have been remarkable by their

Above *A comparison between two* Hornby Class '47's. *The top model is just as it was taken straight from the box, whilst that below has received some attention. Note how the bottom one looks more 'solid' and less toy-like.*

Below *Gently carving off the moulded bodyside lines to produce a smooth finish really improves the look of the model. Note that the engine exhaust outlet on the roof has been cut out to give it more depth.*

Another view of the detailed Hornby Class '47'. *The bogies and underframe tanks have been lightly weathered.*

absence. However there are numerous more subtle differences to be seen between individual members and so, once again, it is worth checking with photographs if one is modelling a specific member of the class.

The majority were delivered in a two-tone green livery style, whilst a few of the later-built ones carried rail blue from the start. Eventually the entire class, save for one or two that were withdrawn prematurely due to accident damage, received the overall blue livery with full yellow ends. The mid 1980s saw the class painted in several distinctive styles:

1 Classes '47/0', '47/3', '47/8' and '47/9' in railfreight grey.
2 Class '47/4' in either blue with large BR logo and numbers, or in two shades of grey with white and red body side stripes. A handful have also appeared in the 'Network SouthEast' livery.
3 Class '47/7' in two shades of grey with white and light blue body side stripes.

At one time or another every region of BR has had an allocation of these locomotives and even the Southern Region had some on their books for a short period.

Class '50': English Electric 2,700hp Co-Co diesel-electric
Following the demise of the 'Westerns' and 'Deltics', the Class '50's are now the flagships of BR's passenger locomotive fleet. A total of fifty were built; originally numbered D400 to D449, they now carry numbers between 50001 and 50050.

Left The number two end cab of 50002 prior to it being refurbished. Note the 'marker light' arrangement of the headcode box.

Below The 'A' side of 50002. When refurbished, the right-side body side window was replaced by a ventilation grille.

Right *A close-up view of the end details on a Class '50'. The prominent footplates above the buffer stocks are worthy of note.*

Below *Bogie details and some features of the number two end of a Class '50' in its original form are illustrated here. Note the two lifting brackets on the bottom edge of the bodywork.*

Left *The* Lima *Class '50' is based on the locomotives in their original condition, but it is not difficult to modify it to depict one of the refurbished examples. The first six refurbished members of the class (50006, 50017, 50019, 50001, 50047 and 50013 in that order) returned to service in the overall rail blue livery. The rest, however, were painted in the 'large logo' colour scheme with light grey roof and large bodyside numbers when they returned to traffic after refurbishment.*

Below left *'B' side details on a detailed* Lima *Class '50'. Note the bodyside window above the loco number has been replaced by a grille. The lifting brackets are small pieces of plastic cut to shape, whilst cab footsteps have been fitted to the bogies.*

Top right *Front end details showing the central headlight, indicative of a refurbished member of the class. The lamp is just a disc of plastic with the lens painted on in silver.*

Middle right *The number one end roof details. The engine exhaust outlets have been cut out to give them a greater depth.*

Right *The number two end roof details on a detailed* Lima *Class '50'. Note the additional extractor fan vent in the middle of the roof, and the plated-over former recess which now matches the rest of the roof profile.*

Entering service in October 1967, the Class '50's are another of the types that will be with us for some time to come. However, their future is not totally secure. Already a couple have been withdrawn from service.

There are no really major variations within the class. However their appearance did change slightly after they were refurbished in the early 1980s. All were delivered in rail blue. After refurbishment they received light grey roofs, yellow cab sides, black window surrounds and large BR logos. Recently some have been repainted in 'Network SouthEast' livery.

Initially all were based on the LMR where they worked between Crewe and Glasgow. After electrification of the northern part of the West Coast main line, they were transferred to the WR. Apart from passenger and freight workings on that region, they also operate over the Waterloo to Exeter line. There is a proposal for a freight-only Class '50/1' variant with 50149 (formerly 50049) being the first to be so modified in the middle of 1987.

Class '52': BR 2,700hp C-C diesel-hydraulic

If any class of diesel could be thought beautiful, perhaps the Class '52's might be considered as such. There was something about them that is hard to explain. A certain *je ne sais quoi* which made them stand out from all the others. There was no way in which one could mistake a 'Western' for any other class of locomotive: 74 were constructed, numbered D1000 to D1073.

First appearing in December 1961, the final members of the class were with-

One of the five 'Westerns' fitted with a square ventilation grille on each end was D1071, shown here at Birmingham.

Above *The* Lima *'Western'. The moulded tail lamp on each end has been carved off and new lamp brackets made up from flattened wire. Scale couplings and other bufferbeam details have been added to advantage.*

Below *A side view of the model. Note the red route restriction dot painted on the cabside below the numberplate, and the scribed vertical lines on the body side windows.*

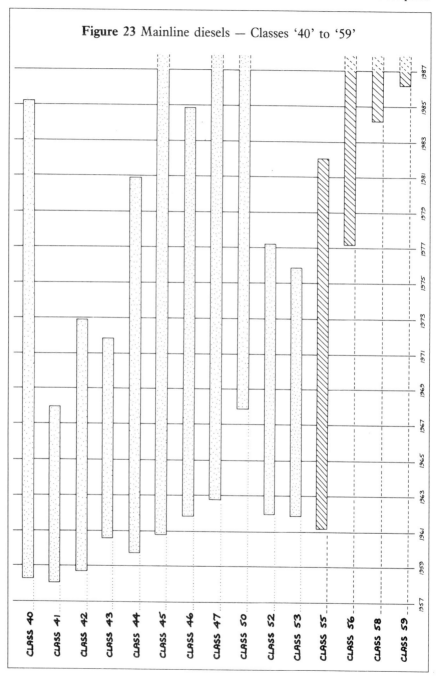

Figure 23 Mainline diesels — Classes '40' to '59'

drawn during February 1977. Again, there were no major external variations within the class. Desert Sand, Golden Ochre, Maroon and Brunswick green were the early liveries applied. Eventually all were repainted in rail blue.

The 'Westerns' were always allocated to the WR. After a brief spell on the former GWR route from London to Wolverhampton, they settled down to hauling the principal services from Paddington to South Wales, Bristol, Plymouth and Penzance.

Class '53': Brush 2,800hp Co-Co diesel-electric

Better known as *Falcon*, this class consisted of just the one locomotive of that name. Initially numbered D0280, it became 1200 after passing into BR ownership in 1970.

Appearing in October 1961, it was finally withdrawn from service fourteen years later in October 1975. No structural alterations were made to *Falcon* during its years of service.

The locomotive carried three different livery styles, reflecting its changing circumstances *vis-à-vis* BR. Until 1965 it was owned and entirely maintained by Brush: during this period the locomotive had a light green/pale brown livery. From 1965 to 1970 the locomotive was on loan to BR: over those years it carried the then standard two-tone Brunswick green and Sherwood green style. After 1970, under BR ownership, it was painted rail blue with full yellow ends.

After trials on the ER, on both passenger and freight trains, *Falcon* moved to the WR. From the mid 1960s to the early '70s it generally worked expresses between Paddington and Bristol. Its final years were spent hauling freight trains in South Wales.

Falcon was one of three prototype locomotives for the second generation of BR Type '4's in the 2,700hp and 2,800hp bracket. The other two, *Lion* and *DP2*, built by the Birmingham Railway Carriage and Wagon Co and English Electric respectively, were never taken into BR ownership.

★ ★ ★

A summary of BR's Type '4' locomotives is given in *Figure 23*. This also covers the final group of diesels to be considered, the top of the range Type '5's.

SEVEN
Mainline diesels: The Type '5's

The high powered elite of the diesel fleet. Four classes come within this category, from the much loved 'Deltics' to the recently introduced American-built Class '59's.

Class '55': English Electric 3,300hp Co-Co diesel-electric
For almost twenty years the 'Deltics' were the lords of the East Coast main line. Their characteristic drone could be heard every day over the 393½ miles between London and Edinburgh: 22 were built, initially numbered D9000 to D9021. With the 1973/74 renumberings they became 55001 to 55022.

Entering service in February 1961, the class was finally withdrawn at the beginning of January 1982.

There were detail differences between individual members of the class, but there were no major structural variations within the 'Deltics'.

All were initially in Brunswick green with a light green skirt and white cab surrounds. Eventually they appeared in overall rail blue with yellow nose ends.

The 'Deltics' seldom wandered from the East Coast route and were rarely seen on anything other than express passenger duties.

Class '56': BR 3,250hp Co-Co diesel-electric
Extensively used on heavy freight work, 135 of these locomotives have been built. They carry the numbers 56001 to 56135.

The class entered service relatively recently, in February 1977, so, as may be expected, none has yet been withdrawn.

There are basically three versions. 56001-56030 were built in Romania and have the early design of cab. 56031-56055 were built by BR and are similar to the first batch but with detail differences. 56056-56135 were also built by BR, but with a redesigned cab front.

The Class '56' locomotives were delivered new in one of three livery styles. Up to and including 56083 appeared in standard overall blue with full yellow ends. 56084 and 56134 were finished with blue body sides, light grey roof, yellow cabs, black window surrounds and large BR logo and numbers. The final member of the class, 56135, was painted in railfreight grey. This railfreight grey livery is now being applied to the rest of the class, though it will be many years before they all receive it.

Allocated to three regions, on the ER and LMR they are usually to be seen at the head of merry-go-round coal trains. On the WR their duties are more varied, covering iron-ore trains in South Wales and heavy stone traffic around the borders of Somerset and Wiltshire.

Class '58': BR 3,300hp Co-Co diesel-electric

Although one might mistake a Class '56' for a Class '47', as they have a similar bodyshell, the shape of a Class '58' is unique. Fifty of these freight locomotives have been constructed, numbered 58001 to 58050.

The class were officially first taken into operating stock in February 1984. However the first Class '58' had been completed by December 1982 whilst others were on revenue-earning work during the latter part of 1983.

There are one or two minor detail differences within the class and we will consider these in chapter 14, but as regards liveries, they are all in railfreight grey. Currently the entire class is based on the LMR though they do work on to other regions. Their main duties are on merry-go-round coal trains.

Class '59': General Motors 3,300hp Co-Co diesel-electric

The four locomotives making up this class, numbered 59001 to 59004, are not owned by BR. Although maintained and operated by BR staff, the Class '59's are the property of the firm of Foster Yeoman.

Built in America by General Motors, the locomotives arrived together in Britain towards the end of January 1986. They entered service during February 1986. These locomotives work on heavy stone trains from Foster Yeoman's quarry complex at Merehead (between Frome and Shepton Mallet in Somerset) and the company's distribution depots located in South-east England.

There are no significant variations between the four class members. They are finished in an attractive silver and blue livery, with black bogies and underframe, and yellow warning panels on each end.

*   *   *

These Class '59's are not the only privately-owned Type '5's to have worked over BR metals. The previous thirty years had seen two high-powered prototypes on the scene. The first of these, *Deltic*, built by English Electric, was a 3,300hp Co-Co diesel-electric and the prototype for the Class '55's. In a bright blue livery with speed whiskers painted on the ends, it was definitely not a style for the faint-hearted. Appearing in October 1955, it first worked over the West Coast route and also undertook trials over the Settle and Carlisle line. At the beginning of 1959 it was transferred across to the East Coast main line where it remained until withdrawn in March 1961, just as the production 'Deltics' were coming on the scene.

HS 4000 *Kestrel* was the most powerful diesel locomotive ever to run in Britain. Built by Brush, it was a Co-Co diesel-electric with a 3,946hp engine. Painted in a two-tone golden yellow and chocolate brown livery, a noteworthy feature of the locomotive was its streamlined front with wrap-round cab windscreens. In January 1968 it was handed over to BR for service trials. May of that year saw it allocated to the ER where it was employed on coal trains from the Mansfield area of Nottinghamshire to Whitemoor marshalling yard at March.

Its use on slow freight work was rather ironic for *Kestrel* was designed for express passenger duties in the 120mph/130mph speed range. One problem was the high axle-loading of the locomotive, so during 1969 it was fitted with lighter Class '47'-type bogies. That autumn it appeared hauling passenger trains on the East Coast main line between Kings Cross and Newcastle. However it did not last very long on top-link work and was soon back hauling freight trains until withdrawal came during April 1971. Subsequently it was sold to the USSR and shipped abroad.

Developments are still continuing in the Type 5 power range on BR. On the drawing board at the moment are plans for a new breed of freight locomotive of some 3,000hp to be known as Class '60'. Tender documents have been sent out to various firms, both at home and abroad, for delivery of up to 100 locos by the early 1990s.

EIGHT
DC Electric locomotives

The DC electric locomotives which survived to be included in BR's numerical classification of the different types, worked on one of two systems. Classes '70' to '74' served on the Southern Region, where the electric supply was 660-750V DC third rail, while Classes '76' and '77' worked on the Eastern and London Midland regions, where the electric supply was 1,500V DC overhead.

Class '70': SR 1,470hp Co-Co electric
Numbered 20001 to 20003, the first two of the three Class '70's were built in Southern Railway days and were originally numbered CC1 and CC2 respectively. Designed for mixed traffic duties, in addition to picking-up the current from the third rail they were each fitted with a pantograph which enabled them to collect current from overhead wires in sidings and goods yards where the live third rail would have endangered the shunting staff.

The first of this trio of early electrics appeared in July 1941. The last members of the class were withdrawn during December 1968.

There were a number of variations between these three locomotives so one has to exercise great care when modelling this class. The last to be built, number 20003, differed from the others in having a more angular cab front and revised arrangement of body side louvres. Steam whistles were originally fitted, located by the side of the front cab windows on 20001 and 20002, and on the roof of 20003. In the mid 1960s twin air horns were mounted on the roofs, replacing the whistles. Other details on the individual locomotives were as follows.

20001 was initially fitted with a two-digit route box located between the cab windows, but lacked front electric lights and headcode discs. However before the BR period, lights and discs were fitted and the route box was blanked off. During the 1960s the route box was brought back into use and the electric lights and discs were removed.

20002 appeared from the start without the central route box but with the electric lights and headcode discs. It was also equipped with a pair of waist-level multiple-unit jumper cables on each end. These jumpers were removed around 1959, whilst a few years later the electric lights and headcode discs were also taken off the ends and replaced by a central two-digit route box.

20003, like 20002, initially lacked the route box but had lights, discs and waist-level jumpers. These features were eventually removed and a route box fitted.

There seems to be an unwritten law which states that the fewer members there are in a class, the more variations there will be. These locomotives prove the point: take the question of liveries that were applied to them. At nationalization 20001 and 20002 (or CC1 and CC2 as they were at the time) were in Southern Railway Malachite green with yellow lining. 20003 was also delivered in this colour but with 'BRITISH RAILWAYS' in full on the body side rather than 'SOUTHERN' as on the other two. The sequence of later liveries applied to each locomotive can be summarized here:

20001: 1 Black with aluminium lining, small BR emblem.
2 BR malachite green with white/red/white lining, BR crest.
3 Unlined multiple-unit green, BR crest.
4 Rail blue, BR logo.
20002: 1 Still as CC2 in an experimental blue with silver lining, 'BRITISH RAILWAYS' in full.
2 Black with aluminium lining,small BR emblem.
3 BR malachite green with white/red/white lining, BR crest.
4 Unlined multiple-unit green, BR crest.
20003: 1 Black with aluminium lining, large BR emblem.
2 BR malachite green with white/red/white lining, BR crest.
3 Unlined multiple-unit green, BR crest.

These locomotives generally worked within the area bounded by London in the north, Portsmouth in the west and Eastbourne in the east. They appeared on both passenger and freight duties, and became particularly associated with the Newhaven boat trains.

Class '71': BR 2,552hp Bo-Bo electric

Twenty-four of these electrics were built and like the previous class they were fitted with a pantograph in addition to their normal third rail pick-up shoes. Initially the class were numbered E5000 to E5023. Towards the end of 1962, E5000 was renumbered E5024. During 1967 and 1968, ten were rebuilt as electro-diesels, later becoming Class '74'. This gave rise to some further renumberings, whilst later they appeared in the 71XXX series:

E5000 to E5024, later to Class '74'.   E5012 to 71012.
E5001 to 71001.   E5013 to 71013.
E5002 to 71002.   E5014 to 71014.
E5003 to Class '74'.   E5015 to Class '74'.
E5004 to 71004.   E5016 to Class '74'.
E5005 to Class '74'.   E5017 to Class '74'.
E5006 to Class '74'.   E5018 to E5003, then 71003.
E5007 to 71007.   E5019 to Class '74'.
E5008 to 71008.   E5020 to E5005, then 71005.
E5009 to 71009.   E5021 to Class '74'.

| E5010 to 71010. | E5022 to E5006, then 71006. |
| E5011 to 71011. | E5023 to Class '74'. |

The first of the Class '71's appeared right at the end of December 1958, though it did not enter service until the following year. They were all withdrawn by November 1977, but had been in store for about a year prior to this.

There were a few modifications applied to the class during their years in service. The first concerned the position of the electric train heating jumper cable. Initially this was located on the front of the locomotive's body, just above the nearside buffer. Soon though it was repositioned lower down at bufferbeam level, alongside the nearside buffer. Rainstrips running the length of the loco-motive at cantrail level were also subsequently added. On at least one member of the class (E5024), the central set of ventilation louvres was blanked off in the mid 1960s.

Initially all were painted in BR Malachite green with white/red/white lining, medium grey roof, black bogies and underframe, and off-white front cab window surrounds. Later they appeared unlined in a different shade of green, similar to that used on multiple units. Their final livery was rail blue with full yellow ends.

The class was designed for two main roles in connection with the electrifica-tion of the Southern Region lines to the Kent Coast: firstly on freight and parcels trains between London and the Channel Ports of Dover and Folkestone; second-ly, on the heavy boat trains such as the 'Golden Arrow' and the 'Night Ferry'.

Class '73': English Electric 1,600hp/600hp Bo-Bo electro-diesel

The most successful and versatile of the Southern Region electrics are these dual-purpose locomotives. As well as picking-up current from the third rail and operating as conventional electrics, they are fitted with a 600hp diesel engine. Hence they can work, albeit at reduced horsepower, on non-electrified lines. A total of 49 were built, numbered E6001 to E6049. The first six were constructed by BR in 1962 and the rest by English Electric between 1965 and 1967. At the beginning of 1974 they were renumbered into the 73XXX series. E6001 to E6006, which differ slightly from the others, became 73001 to 73006, whilst the remainder had their numbers altered as follows: E6007 to E6026 became 73101 to 73120; E6028 to E6049 became 73121 to 73142. E6027 was not renumbered as it had been withdrawn in 1972 due to extensive collision damage.

The first of the BR-built batch of Class '73's appeared in February 1962. Those of English Electric manufacture began to come off the production line during October 1965.

Though length, height and width are the same for all the Class '73's, there are some external differences between the two batches. *Figure 24* outlines these variations, the main ones being at the front end and in the arrangement of the body side grilles. Some modifications to watch out for include the following.

1   E6001 to E6003 of the early batch originally had oval headed buffers whilst E6004 to E6006 had large round ones from the start. Subsequently, during

Figure 24 The Class '73' electro-diesels

FRONT END DETAILS

E6001 — E6006

E6007 — E6049

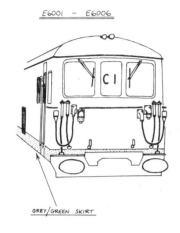

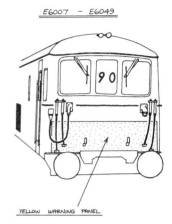

GREY/GREEN SKIRT

YELLOW WARNING PANEL

ARRANGEMENT OF BODYSIDE GRILLES

E6001 — E6006

E6007 — E6049

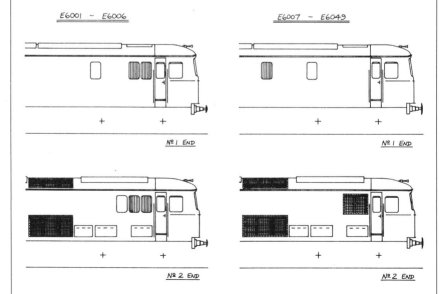

Nº 1 END

Nº 1 END

Nº 2 END

Nº 2 END

A pair of Class '73's standing in the sidings at Clapham Junction.

the early 1970s, the first three also received the large round headed type.

2 The bogie sideframe details on E6001 to E6006 differed slightly from the rest of the class. Initially they were not fitted with sandboxes, but received them in 1963. However, the design of these was different from the sandboxes that were fitted from new to the later members of the class.

3 A more recent modification applied to those numbered between 73101 and 73142 is the fitting of flashguards along the bottom edge of the bogie sideframes. During 1984 these locomotives began operating on the push-pull shuttle trains between London Victoria and Gatwick Airport. After a couple of months, severe arcing problems led to their temporary withdrawal from this service. After some track alterations they were soon back on the scene, but to prevent future damage from arcing, guards were fitted to protect the bogies.

Changes in the liveries carried by the Class '73's, especially in recent years, have resulted in quite a variety of colour schemes. When first in service, the locomotives were painted as follows:

E6001   appeared in BR Malachite green with a medium grey roof, red bufferbeams, and black bogies and underframes. Rectangular yellow warning panels were on each end and the front cab window surrounds were picked out in a very pale grey/off-white shade. Rather than the then-standard BR crest, the circular coaching stock type of crest was applied to the body side.

E6002 to E6006   were also in Malachite green but lacked the yellow warning panels. Instead they had a grey/green skirt band running around the length of the locomotive.

E6007 to E6013   were painted in rail blue, but with a matt rather than a gloss finish. The roof, including that over the cabs, was light grey, whilst around the bottom edge of the body side was a light grey skirt band. White cab window surrounds, yellow warning panels on the ends, and black bufferbeam and bogies completed the livery. Supplies of the BR logo must have been limited when the first few of these were delivered as at least E6007, E6008 and E6009 ran in service without the logo on the side of the body.

E6014 to E6049   were also in matt rail blue but lacked the light grey skirt band.

Eventually the entire class received the standard rail blue gloss finish with full yellow ends. However prior to the general application of the full yellow ends, in 1967 E6018 had the whole of its cab front and sides painted yellow. Things remained constant throughout much of the 1970s, save for the renumbering of the class as mentioned above. The 1980s, however, have seen a more colourful array applied to the Class '73's. The first movement away from overall blue occurred in 1980.

Naming of the locomotives was back in favour, and this included these electro-diesels. The first four named members of the class had their roofs painted a very pale shade of grey, these being numbers 73101, 73121, 73129 and 73142. At around this time, 'overhead live wire' flashes also began to be applied to the class. In 1983 it was decided to paint the '73's in the same style adopted for some of the Class '37's, '47's, '50's and '56's, namely rail blue body sides, light grey roof, yellow cab front and sides, black window surrounds and large BR logo and numbers. This livery has become standard on the Class '73/0's, and was applied to over a dozen of the Class '73/1's (Nos 73104, 73105, 73114, 73126, 73129, 73131, 73132, 73133, 73138, 73139, 73140, 73141, 73142).

However, it was soon realized that the livery did not match up at all well with the colour scheme that BR had applied to the coaches that these locomotives worked with on the 'Gatwick Express' service. Furthermore, at this time the Gatwick push-pulls were transferred from the London & South-East business sector of BR to the Inter-City one. Hence the decision to paint the Class '73/1's in two shades of grey with white and red body side stripes. The first one in this livery appeared in May 1984 for the inauguration of the improved Gatwick trains. This was 73123 and it differed from later members painted in this style in having a light grey roof and large body side numbers.

It was almost a year before another was turned out in this Inter-City livery, this being number 73102. On this, and subsequent repaints in this scheme, the upper dark grey band was extended around the cab front and included the central portion of the roof. The top of the cab roofs were yellow and the locomotive's number was positioned on the cab side in normal size figures. This livery is now the standard for the Class '73/1's though it will be a few years before all are in this style.

Class '73's work throughout the Southern Region, including the formerly restricted Tonbridge to Hastings route. Nowadays their appearances on passenger duties centre mainly on the 'Gatwick Express' service, but in their early days they were regular performers on the Waterloo to Bournemouth line. Freight haulage is an important element of their work, again across the whole of the region. From our viewpoint as modellers they provide the essential character of the Southern scene without the need to equip one's layout with the electrified third rail.

Class '74': BR 2,552hp/650hp Bo-Bo electro-diesel

The ten Class '71's rebuilt as electro-diesels were numbered from E6101 to E6110, and later 74001 to 74010. Fitted with 650hp diesel engines, the conversion altered the appearance of the locomotives quite markedly with a different arrangement of body side grilles and jumper cables on the front ends.

In their rebuilt form, the first of the Class '74's appeared during November 1967. All had been withdrawn by the end of December 1977. There were no external variations between the ten members of the class.

The Class '74's only ever carried one style of livery: overall rail blue with full yellow ends. BR logos were positioned on each of the four cab sides. At least

Deep in Southern territory, one of the Class '74' electro-diesels passes through Eastleigh station.

E6101, E6102 and E6103 initially had 'overhead live wire' flashes attached to plates fitted to the front handrail at the four corners of the locomotive. This was not a very sensible place to locate them and they were soon removed.

Principally the locomotives were used on the line between Waterloo and Bournemouth covering such duties as boat trains from London to Southampton Docks, newspaper and parcels trains, and freight work.

Class '76': BR 1,868hp Bo + Bo electric

The 1,500V DC overhead system on which the Class '76's and '77's worked covered the former Great Central trans-Pennine route from Manchester to Sheffield, together with the branch from Penistone to Wath, six miles south-east of Barnsley in Yorkshire. Fifty-eight Bo + Bo electrics were constructed, largely to work the freight trains over these lines.

The first of the class was built by the LNER and completed during the Second World War whilst the remainder were constructed by BR between 1950 and 1953. The prototype was initially numbered 6701 by the LNER and later 6000. After nationalization it became 26000. The rest of the class were numbered 26001 to 26057 from the start. In the late 1960s all, with the exception of 26035 and 26042, gained an 'E' prefix to their numbers. The early 70s saw the majority

The long-closed Sheffield Victoria station plays host to a Class '76' with a train from Manchester. This locomotive was one of those fitted with a train-heating boiler — note the hose connection on the bufferbeam.

renumbered into the 76XXX series in the same order as their previous numbers, thus 26001 became 76001, 26002 became 76002 and so on.

Eight of the class were withdrawn prior to this and so were not renumbered (these being E26000, E26005, E26017, E26019, E26031, 26035, 26042 and E26045). In 1976, in order to bring those subsequently fitted with air brakes into one series, some further alterations were made to the numbering:

76003 became 76036	76039 became 76048
76018 became 76035	76044 became 76031
76036 became 76003	76048 became 76039
76038 became 76050	76050 became 76038

The LNER-built prototype for the class was completed by April 1942. Its early years were mostly spent in storage before it was loaned to the Netherlands Railways between 1947 and 1952. The first BR-built examples appeared during October 1950 but it was to be some years before they started revenue earning on the routes for which they were designed. The final members of the Class '76's were withdrawn in July 1981 following the closure of most of the 1,500V DC system over which they worked.

There were a number of variations within the class, particularly concerning the front end details, and these are outlined in *Figure 25*. Number 26000 differed from its later-built brothers in having smaller front cab windows, wider cab doors, no cab side windows, slightly modified bogie details and a different arrangement of body side grilles on one side. Up until 1970, some of the locomotives were fitted with train steam-heating boilers. This resulted in the addition of a connection hose on the bufferbeam of 26000, 26020 and 26046 to 26057. Also around 1970, E26006 to E26016 and E26021 to E26030 were fitted with air brakes and equipped for multiple-working operation.

This equipment led to extra jumper cables being positioned on the cab fronts and additional pipes on the bufferbeams. The mid 1970s saw further members of the class, 76031 to 76039, equipped with air brakes and multiple-working equipment fitted, but unlike the others, these had their vacuum brakes removed at the same time.

The initial livery applied to the Class '76's by BR was overall black, relieved by red lining of the body panels and with the bottom of the bodywork picked-out in grey and cream. Cab side numbers, red bufferbeams and a large BR emblem added the finishing touches. Number 26000 differed slightly in having a smaller emblem and its numbers located on the body side. The late 1950s saw the introduction of a more colourful livery scheme. This consisted of Brunswick green bodywork with orange/black/orange lining, a cream painted roof, black bogies, red bufferbeams and the later style of BR crest. Small yellow warning panels were added to each end of the locomotives in the early '60s, but none ever carried 'overhead live wire' flashes.

By 1966 the class was beginning to appear in blue livery. At first they retained the small warning panels on the ends and also the BR crest. Soon though, full yellow ends were applied and the new BR logo replaced the crest. It is almost

Figure 25 Six faces of the Class '76's

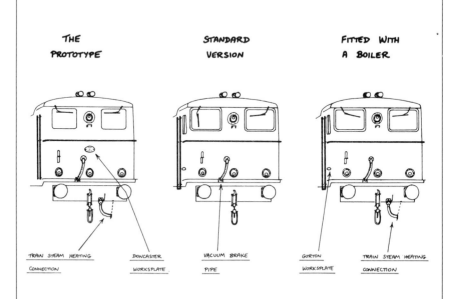

THE PROTOTYPE

STANDARD VERSION

FITTED WITH A BOILER

TRAIN STEAM HEATING CONNECTION

DONCASTER WORKSPLATE

VACUUM BRAKE PIPE

GORTON WORKSPLATE

TRAIN STEAM HEATING CONNECTION

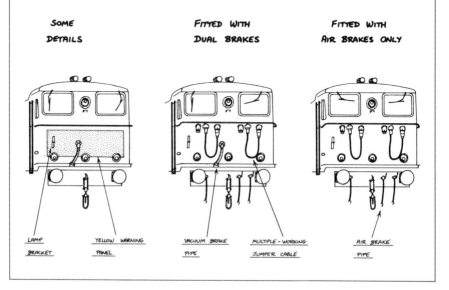

SOME DETAILS

FITTED WITH DUAL BRAKES

FITTED WITH AIR BRAKES ONLY

LAMP BRACKET

YELLOW WARNING PANEL

VACUUM BRAKE PIPE

MULTIPLE-WORKING JUMPER CABLE

AIR BRAKE PIPE

certain that some of the early repaints in blue were in the shade known as 'electric blue', the colour that was originally applied to AC electric locomotives. It is believed that 26015 was the first Class '76' in blue livery, and this was certainly the 'electric blue' shade. Not all survived long enough to receive a blue livery of any description. Numbers E26000, E26005, E26017, 26035 and 26042 ended their days in Brunswick green with small yellow panels. Not every member of the class received the BR logo either; 76022 for example retained its BR crest on the body side right up to its withdrawal in 1981.

Freight traffic over the Manchester, Sheffield and Wath lines was the staple work for the Class '76's. In their early years they could be seen at the head of long strings of short wheelbase wooden-bodied coal wagons. Later they became a familiar sight at the head of rakes of merry-go-round hoppers. Coal haulage was probably their main task but steel, oil, sand, chemicals and more general products all came within their grasp. They also appeared on passenger duties, especially in the late 1960s after the withdrawal of the Class '77's.

Class '77': BR 2,760hp Co-Co electric

Bearing a family likeness to the Class '76's, but being some 9ft longer, a total of seven Class '77' locomotives were constructed with the numbers 27000 to 27006. A year or two before withdrawal, they received an 'E' prefix to their numbers.

The first Class '77' appeared during December 1953. All the locomotives were officially withdrawn from stock in October 1968, though they had been in store since March of that year.

The principal variation was the addition of rotary windscreen wipers to one end of 27002. These circular wipers were fitted to the number one end of the locomotive by the early part of 1964 and it retained them for the rest of its service life.

Initially the class was painted black (including the roof and bogies). Buffer-beams were red, as was the body side lining. Unlike the Class '76's, the bottom edge was not picked out in grey and cream. A large-sized BR emblem was applied to the side of the body. The autumn of 1956 saw the start of painting these locomotives in Brunswick green with orange/black/orange lining and a medium grey roof. The first in green, number 27000, had its bogies painted aluminium. It also retained the BR emblem at first as the new style of crest was in short supply at the time. The majority of the class kept the green livery until withdrawal but with the addition of small yellow warning panels on the ends. However in the autumn of 1963, 27002 appeared in electric blue livery with a light grey roof. Some reports suggest that 27001, 27004 and 27006 were also painted blue but I have not been able to confirm this.

Throughout their careers on BR metals they worked almost exclusively on passenger trains between Manchester and Sheffield. After withdrawal and a long period spent in storage at Bury in Lancashire, they were all sold to the Netherlands Railways and shipped across to Holland in September 1969. One was soon scrapped for spares but the rest were rebuilt and most remained in service until 1986, having had a longer working life on the continent than in Britain.

NINE
AC Electric locomotives

More and more of the BR network is becoming electrified on the 25kV AC overhead system each year. As well as the West Coast main line from Euston to Glasgow which came under the electric wires in the 1960s and early '70s, electrification in East Anglia is now nearing completion and the erection of overhead lines on the East Coast main line is well under way. Soon a new generation of electric locomotives will leave the workshops and enter service on this expanded network. But what of the types currently in use, or the classes already withdrawn? Let's look at these now.

Class '80': Metropolitan-Vickers 2,500hp A1A-A1A electric

This locomotive was rebuilt from the 3,000hp Co-Co gas turbine machine considered earlier (p. 31). Its main role was on crew training prior to the arrival of the production run of electric locomotives. In its new form as an electric, number 18100 was soon to become E1000 and later it was renumbered E2001.

Appearing in October 1958 as an electric locomotive, it was finally withdrawn around April 1968 after lengthy periods in store.

Apart from a lowering of the roof to provide space for a pantograph, the external appearance of the locomotive was remarkably little changed from its gas turbine days. It retained its original black and aluminium livery style right to the end. The only difference was the substitution of the early BR emblem on the body side for the later design of crest.

For the relatively short period that this locomotive operated on driver training duties, it was mostly to be seen on the Crewe to Manchester and Liverpool lines. Its active life was largely confined to the years between 1958 and 1961. After this it was usually kept away from the public eye in storage.

Class '81': British Thomson-Houston/Birmingham Railway Carriage & Wagon 3,200hp Bo-Bo electric

The first batch of electric locomotives for the West Coast main line consisted of 100 machines in five different classes. Whilst broadly of the same appearance, the fact that they were constructed by various manufacturers meant that they did differ in detail. The first to appear were the Class '81's comprising 25 locomotives, initially numbered E3001 to E3023 and E3096 to E3097. The original plan had been to number the final two members of the class as E3301 and E3302, BR's intention at the time being to have two basic categories for AC electrics: Type 'A', numbered in the E30XX series (these were geared for 100mph express passenger duties) and Type 'B', numbered in the E33XX series (these were geared for 80mph freight work).

BR decided not to pursue the idea of differently-geared locomotives for freight or passenger work, but E3096 did actually carry the number E3301 for a few months after it was built. By the mid 1970s the class had been renumbered into the five-digit series from 81001 to 81022.

Having first appeared in November 1959, the class is now getting on in years and hence has only a reasonably short service life ahead of it.

Over the years a number of modifications have been applied to the class. Initially they were equipped with two 'Stone-Faiveley' pantographs, but as the locomotives only picked up power from one at a time, it was decided to remove one of them. Thus by the early 1970s the pantographs at the number one ends of the class were taken off and the resulting space on the roof was used to house three main reservoirs used in connection with air brakes that were fitted to the

Cabside details of a Class '81'. Note the large maker's plate below the number.

class around this time. Underframe details were also slightly altered with modified smoothing chokes on one side.

Initially the class was painted in electric blue livery, with black underframe and bogies, and red bufferbeams. Buffer shanks were black rather than red whilst the cab roof and window surrounds were painted white. A new design of cast alloy crest appeared on the side of the body, with raised metal numerals on the cab sides. Small yellow warning panels were later applied to the ends. Eventually the class appeared in rail blue with full yellow ends and the BR logo rather than the alloy crest.

All manner of traffic has been handled by these locomotives over the whole route from Euston to Glasgow. Nowadays though, whilst they can still be seen on the occasional express passenger working, they are more often to be found at the head of freight trains.

Class '82': Metropolitan-Vickers/Beyer Peacock 3,320hp Bo-Bo electric
A class of ten locomotives, originally numbered E3046 to E3055, eight Class '82's survived to be renumbered into the five-digit series from 82001 to 82008.

The Class '82's first appeared during May 1960. They had been withdrawn from general service by July 1983 after a period in store, but two (82005 and 82008) have been retained for empty coaching stock duties at Euston.

There was a variation in the types of pantograph carried by the class. Whilst the first nine had a pair of the standard Stone-Faiveley make, E3055 had two AEI crossed-arm pantographs: later though it did receive one of the more usual design. Modifications have seen the removal of the number one end pantographs and the fitting of roof mounted air reservoirs. The body side grilles on one side of the locomotive have also been altered, as were some of the underframe details.

From the attractive electric blue livery with white cab roof and window surrounds, the class was repainted in rail blue. Much to everyone's surprise, in 1986 number 82008 appeared in the Inter-City livery of two-tone grey with white and red stripes.

Duties performed by these locomotives were similar to those of the Class '81's; both passenger and freight over the West Coast main line.

Class '83': English Electric 2,950hp Bo-Bo electric
English Electric built fifteen of these locomotives, initially numbered E3024 to E3035 and E3098 to E3100. E3098 and E3099 carried the numbers E3303 and E3304 for their first year in service. Later the class became 83001 to 83015.

July 1960 saw the first of these locomotives in service. They were withdrawn from general use by July 1983: like the class '82's, three (83009, 83012 and 83015) are still at work on empty coaching stock trains out of Euston.

Again, one of the original pair of pantographs was removed and replaced by three air reservoirs on the roof. The body side grilles also received slight modifications.

All the class were in electric blue livery at first, later being repainted in rail blue. In the middle of 1986, 83012 was repainted in the Inter-City colour

Side view of 83007 at Birmingham New Street. The central bodyside louvres above the BR logo were originally a window, like those on the left.

scheme. Both passenger and freight work was undertaken by these locomotives on the electrified lines of the LMR out of Euston.

Class '84': General Electric/North British 3,080hp Bo-Bo electric
Initially numbered E3036 to E3045, the '84's later became 84001 to 84010 respectively. After withdrawal, 84009 was retained for departmental use and re-numbered ADB 968021.

The Class '84's first appeared in March 1960. The last members were withdrawn from service during November 1980.

The removal of one of the pantographs and the slight alteration of the body side grilles also applied to this class.

Initially in electric blue, they were all subsequently to appear in the less glamorous rail blue. ADB 968021 was painted in the red and blue livery used on BR's Research Division locomotives.

Like the previous classes, their duties covered both passenger and freight turns over the West Coast main line.

Class '85': BR 3,200hp Bo-Bo electric
The largest class in the first batch of AC electrics are these forty machines. Numbered E3056 to E3095 in their early days, the mid 1970s saw them become 85001 to 85040.

Appearing in June 1961, the vast majority of the class are still in service.

As on the other early AC electrics, one of the original pair of pantographs was

Stafford station in the late 1960s — E3182 arriving with an up express. Note the white cab roof on this Class '86'.

removed and the resulting space fitted with three main reservoir tanks. Like the Class '81's, modified chokes caused a slight change in the underframe details. However unlike the previous classes, the body side grilles and windows were not subsequently altered. A characteristic feature of the Class '85's in their early years of service were the very deep recesses above the front and side cab windows. These were later filled in and new rain strips fitted over the cab doors. During the mid 1970s at least one of the class, E3063, ran with rotary windscreen wipers of similar design to those on one of the Class '77's.

The initial electric blue livery with white cab roof and window surrounds later gave way to rail blue with full yellow ends.

Yet again, the duties performed by these locomotives have taken in both freight and passenger trains on the West Coast route.

Class '86': BR 3,600hp/4,040hp Bo-Bo electric

The second batch of electric locomotives for the 25kV AC network again consisted of 100 machines, but this time they were in just the one class. After twenty years these Class '86's are still the backbone of the majority of services over the West Coast main line and are now becoming a common sight on the recently electrified lines in East Anglia.

Like the Class '37's, the original numbering of this class was quite straight-forward, but gradually over the years things have become more complex. Initially numbered in the range E3101 to E3200, subsequent modifications applied to the locomotives have seen them renumbered into five separate series:

1   860XX   —   Retained original bogies but were fitted with multiple-working equipment, produced 3,600hp and had a maximum speed of 80mph.

Above left *Cabside details on 86233. The locomotive has the original design of sandbox flap.*

Above right *The* Hornby *Class '86'. On the front end, the headcode characters have been removed and two circular lamps made from slivers of plastic rod have been fitted.*

2 861XX — Fitted with Class '87'-type bogies, were not equipped for multiple-working, produced 5,000hp and had a maximum speed of 110mph.

3 862XX — With modified bogies (resilient wheels, flexicoil springs), were not equipped for multiple-working but produced 4,040hp and gave a maximum speed of 100mph.

4 863XX — Original bogies but fitted with resilient wheels, these were fitted with multiple-working equipment, gave 3,600hp and had a maximum speed of 100mph.

5 864XX — With modified bogies (resilient wheels, flexicoil springs), these locomotives were fitted with multiple-working equipment, gave 3,600hp and a maximum speed of 100mph.

By early 1987 the 860XX and 863XXX number series were made extinct following the completion of the conversion of these two sub-classes to the Class '86/4' variant. Meanwhile, plans are afoot for some of the '86/2's to be fitted with push-pull equipment and renumbered in a new 865XX series.

The Class '86's appeared on the scene beginning in June 1965. Barring accident damage, their future is secure into the next century. After an initial spell in electric blue livery, all the class appeared in the familiar rail blue shade. Now they are being repainted in the Inter-City two-tone grey scheme with white and red stripes. An everyday sight over the whole of the West Coast electrified network, those of the Class '86/2' variety are also to be seen in East Anglia.

Class '87': BR 5,000hp Bo-Bo electric
Thirty-six of these powerful machines are currently in service numbered 87001

87015 at Birmingham, showing the bufferbeam and front end details.

to 87035, and 87101. Appearing after the introduction of the five-digit number-ing system, they have never carried the earlier E3XXX numerals. Development of the Class '87's is not yet at an end for during 1986, well over a decade after the first appeared in service, a further 29 were ordered. The original intention was to number them in the 872XX series, but as they are different from the other Class '87's in several ways, they are now known as Class '90's and numbered in the 90XXX range.

The first Class '87' entered service in June 1973 and they have a long term future on the West Coast route. The first examples of the Class '90' were completed in the latter half of 1987.

Within the Class '87/0's and the '87/1's there are only a few variations.

Originally painted in rail blue, the class is now in the Inter-City two-tone grey livery style.

Like the other AC electric locomotives, the Class '87's appear on both passen-ger and freight work on the West Coast main line.

★　★　★

A summary of the different classes of electrics is shown in *Figure 26*. There are, however, just two more types of electric locomotive worthy of mention, though as I write these words neither is yet in revenue-earning service. First there is the solitary Class '89' numbered 89001. This Co-Co electric of some 5,800hp was to be the prototype for a large class of locomotives to operate over the newly electrified East Coast main line. Such is the pace of progress that even before 89001 emerged from the workshops at Crewe it was perhaps something of a white elephant. However, the performance shown by this loco on its initial road trials suggests that there may well be a future for the Class '89' after all. BR's motive power for the East Coast route will now be in the hands of a fleet of 31 Class '91' 'Electra' locomotives. These will be 6,072hp Bo-Bo's with a potential top speed of 140mph, the first examples being due for delivery early in 1988.

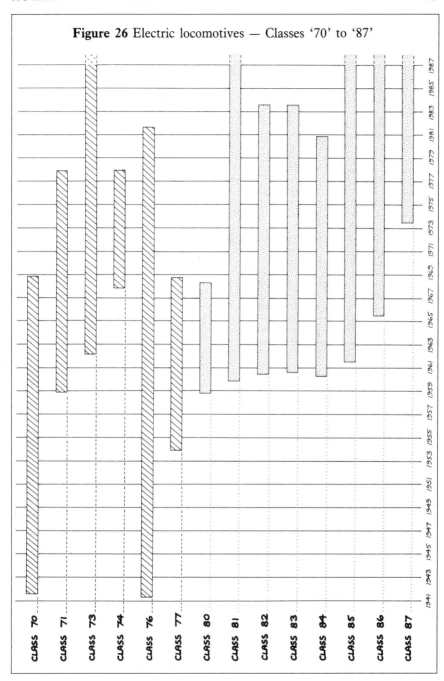

Figure 26 Electric locomotives — Classes '70' to '87'

Above *The BP9-type bogies and underframe details on 87013.*

Below *The* Lima *Class '87', comparing a detailed model on the left and one yet to be modified.*

Above *Painting the roof well light grey, as shown in the top model here, improves the appearance.*

Below *Scraping away the thick chrome windscreen surround really makes the model look more like the real thing. Note the repositioned lamp bracket on the front of the cab.*

SECTION 3
More detail for modellers

TEN
What the model manufacturers provide

The basic building blocks in modelling are the kits and ready-to-run items produced by the model trade. Although, of course, we could ignore completely what has been produced commercially and scratchbuild our models, one needs a great deal of time, patience and, above all, skill to do so successfully. How many of us can take a sheet of metal or plastic and form it into an accurate and realistic locomotive? I am not saying that one shouldn't have a go at building from scratch, far from it, but with the quality and value of ready-to-run equipment, it would be a shame not to consider first that which is readily available.

The model manufacturers have actually provided us with quite a lot, especially as regards the different types of mainline diesel locomotives. However there are some noticeable gaps in the range of electric locomotives and diesel shunters that are available. Much depends on the scale one is working in, so perhaps it is worth pausing here for a moment to consider the main scales and gauges that railway modellers deal with. *Figure 27* gives a comparison between the most common scales used in Britain. The choice of scale in which to model is important and is really dependent on what one wants to achieve in the hobby. If your interests lie in having a collection of highly detailed models of locomotives, then 7mm scale is worth looking at. On the other hand if you want to run full-length trains on the layout and yet have only a limited space, then perhaps 2mm scale is the best bet. No single scale is intrinsically 'better' than any other, but certain scales are better at some things than others so it is a personal choice than has to be made. Here we'll be looking at the offerings from the model trade over the last thirty years or so since many proprietary items, although no longer in production, are fairly readily available second hand. I must stress that the following is not a list

Top right *A comparison of track gauges with, from top to bottom, examples of O gauge, OO gauge and N gauge trackwork.*

Middle right *'Hymeks' in O gauge (7mm/ft) and OO gauge (4mm/ft).*

Right *Second-hand equipment is always worth looking at, though not necessarily worth buying. Here we have a* Trix *'Warship' and 'Western', a* Tri-ang *Class '77' and an old* Airfix *plastic kit of a Class '04' diesel shunter.*

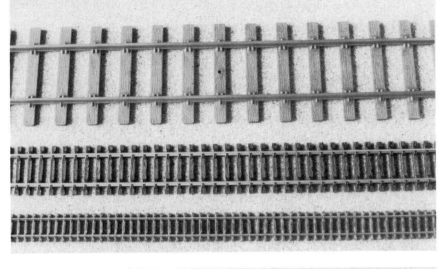

Figure 27 A comparison of scales and gauges

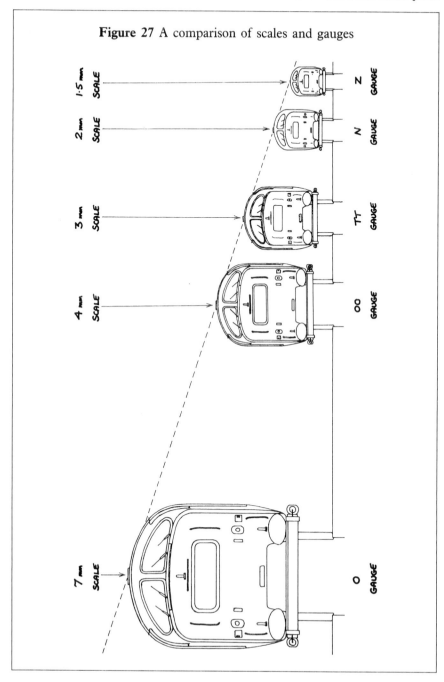

of what is currently available in the market place today. With new models appearing and old ones being deleted, the best way to get the current picture as to what is, and what is not, available is to study the relevant manufacturers' catalogues and look at the advertisements in the monthly model magazines.

Gauge 1 (track gauge = 45mm) — 10mm/ft scale with a ratio of 1:30·5

This is generally regarded as the largest of the scales in which it is possible to build a complete standard gauge layout within anything like a reasonable space. Even so, models of this size are very large and beyond the scope, and the pocket, of most of us. Scratchbuilding or having models made to order is the norm in this scale, with no ready-to-run items of modern motive power having been produced. Working in this size one is approaching the border between general railway modelling and the more specialized realm of model engineering.

Gauge 0 (track gauge = 32mm) — 7mm/ft scale with a ratio of 1:43·5

During the 1920s and '30s this was the most popular scale in Britain. Even into the 1950s many of us began our modelling careers with a circle of 0 gauge tinplate track laid out on the lawn. As the size of houses and gardens became progressively smaller, and technical advances were made in the design of electric motors and other miniature components, attention turned away from 0 gauge to the more space conscious scales of 4mm and 2mm/ft. However in recent years 0 gauge has undergone something of a revival, with interest in the scale growing. Perhaps this is a move away from the more mass produced and packaged 00 and N gauges to something with a little more individuality. There is a certain 'feel' to 0 gauge stock that captures the elusive massiveness of the prototype so well and which tends to be lacking in the smaller scales. Newcomers to this large scale can be handicapped, though, by the lack of many ready-ro-run items of modern stock, or indeed the lack of ready-to-run items in general. To counteract this, there is quite an extensive range of kits featuring modern locomotives of both the diesel and electric variety.

Turning first to ready-to-run items, a very famous name in the model world, *Bassett-Lowke*, introduced in 1958 a model of the prototype 'Deltic'. Constructed of brass, it was fitted with two motor bogies, the central wheels of which were unpowered and flangeless to enable it to negotiate sharp curves.

During 1966 *Tri-ang* brought out a battery-powered Class '35' 'Hymek'. At first sight in its rather garish blue and white livery, and with 'Blue Flier' in raised lettering on the side of the body, it could easily have been mistaken for something of freelance design. This toy image was reinforced by the bright red polypropylene track on which it ran and 'The Big Big Train' tag under which it was marketed. In fact it was an exceedingly accurate 0 gauge model of a 'Hymek' and after a repaint, and the addition of a few extra details, it could stand comparison alongside many more expensive items. In more recent times this plastic-moulded locomotive has been sold under the *Novo* brand label.

The 1970s saw *Lima* enter the field with a fine model of the Class '33'. Again of plastic construction, this one was powered by the more usual electric motor.

An early 0 gauge kit was produced by *Douglass Models* in 1961. This was of the Class '31' and consisted of a plastic moulded 'Bondaglass' bodyshell, with bogie sideframes available as an optional extra. Later, *Jago Model Railways* introduced Class '47' and Class '52' diesels. These were complete kits comprising a reinforced plastic body, cast white metal bogies with etched brass brake gear, wheels, motors and gears.

More recently *Malcolm McGechan* of Edinburgh has produced a moulded Class '42' 'Warship' body featuring glass windows. Also included in the kit are some of the sideframe details, notably the bogie springs.

The Class '04' and Class '08' diesel shunters have been made by *Vulcan Model Engineering*. These kits consist of white metal castings for the bodywork and the footplate, brass main frames and nickel silver coupling rods. Again, the wheels, motor and gears have to be purchased separately to complete the model.

By far the largest group of 0 gauge kits covering modern motive power is that from *Post-War Prototypes*. Amongst the range there are kits for the following classes: '20', '25', '26/27', '31', '33', '37', '40', '42', '45/46', '47', '50', '52', '55', '56', '58', '59', '73', '86', '87'. Also available, as I mentioned earlier, are the former LMS 10000/1 Co-Co diesels. The firm also produces kits to make up into the High Speed Train, both the power cars and the intermediate passenger coaches appearing in their range. All of these kits consist of a mixture of etched brass parts and cast white metal fittings. The etched brass bodyshell is pre-formed to make construction that much easier. Bogie parts are also included but, as in the majority of 0 gauge kits, the wheels, gears and motor have to be bought separately. Whilst not for absolute beginners, with a little skill and patience these kits can be made up into very nice models. Just one final point concerning *Post-War Prototypes* is that when they were initially introduced, they consisted of just the locomotive body superstructure and did not include any bogie parts. Advertisements at the time generally referred to them as *Parkins Diesel Kits*.

Gauge S (track gauge = 22·2mm) 4·76mm/ft scale with a ratio of 1:64

One of the less familiar modelling scales is this 4·76mm/ft. At first sight this seems a very odd and cumbersome number to work with, but in Imperial rather than metric terms it converts to the much more manageable 3/16in/ft. Somewhat of a halfway house between 0 gauge and 00 gauge, there is very little commercial equipment produced. This is the scale for the individual who wants to scratchbuild most of his models and achieve something a little different. As far as I can ascertain, no ready-to-run models or kits of modern motive power have appeared in this scale.

Gauge 00 (track gauge = 16·5mm); Gauge EM (track gauge = 18mm); Gauge P4 (track gauge = 18·83mm) 4mm/ft scale with a ratio of 1:76·2

In Britain the most popular scale to work in is undoubtedly 4mm/ft. However the question of the actual gauge of the track to be used is quite another matter. There are heated discussions is modelling circles over the relative merits of each of the different gauges. For many years, modellers were content to use a track gauge of 16·5mm on which to run their 4mm scale locomotives and rolling stock. A problem, though, is that 16·5mm scaled up becomes 4ft 1½in (against the 4ft 8½in track gauge of the prototype). Moves to greater accuracy during the late 1940s saw the establishment of EM gauge, with the distance between the rails increased to 18mm. This was still slightly narrower than the prototype gauge, but it was a great deal closer to it than 00 track. The inevitable happened during the middle of the 1960s with P4 appearing on the scene. With a gauge of 18·83mm this corresponds exactly to the 4ft 8½in of the prototype.

So one has a choice to make. If one wants to use ready-to-run items straight off the shelf then 00 gauge is the natural choice. For finer scale standards there is EM gauge (now generally quoted as 18·2mm), or for the ultimate is accuracy then there is P4, but please ignore all the hot air and loud noises as people sound off about their gauge being so much better than all the rest. If you want to work to more exacting standards and enjoy what you are doing then that is fine, but using 00 gauge is not going to label you a second class modeller! Personally I am quite content to run my trains on 16·5mm track; it has never worried me in the slightest and I have never lost any sleep over it. After all, although we say that the prototype's track gauge is 4ft 8½in (or 1435mm as BR like to refer to it nowadays), around 1970 BR adopted a gauge of 4ft 8 ⅜in (1432mm) for some of their high speed routes. So if one is modelling the contemporary scene to P4 standards, should the track gauge be 18·79mm rather than 18·83mm? Does it really matter anyway since we make so many other compromises in our modelling? Providing the layout looks right, works reliably and captures the atmosphere of the real thing, what more can one ask?

The range of locomotives available in 4mm scale is very wide. The various kits produced are suitable for whichever track gauge one is working in but ready-to-run items are only made for 00 gauge. Changing the wheelsets, however, can make them suitable for EM and P4.

The *Hornby-Dublo* range of modern motive power covers five different classes. First to appear, towards the end of 1958, was a model of the Class '20'. This was then followed by the Class '08' shunter. Both of these had plastic-moulded bodies with, in the case of the Class '08', a die-cast chassis with dummy outside frames, whilst the Class '20' had die-cast bogies.

The next two diesel outline models released appeared in the shops during 1961. The first was broadly based on the Class '55' 'Deltic', though it was shorter than scale length and differed in some features from the prototype. The other was of the unusual Class '28' Co-Bo. With these two models, *Hornby-*

Dublo reverted to a cast-metal bodyshell rather than the plastic of the previous two types. Finally in 1964 there came the Class '81' electric and back came the plastic body. All of these models were available in either two-rail or three-rail versions, whilst the Class '81' could also collect its current from the overhead wires.

Though *Hornby-Dublo* is no longer with us, the Class '08' and Class '20' are still available under the *Wrenn* label. As well as the normal powered version of the Class '20', this firm also makes an unpowered dummy of this item. Since the Class '20's usually operate coupled together in pairs, the provision of these dummy units by the manufacturers is an excellent idea. As so many classes of diesels, and some electrics too, operate in multiple, it is a shame that other model firms do not imitate this idea and bring out unmotorized dummy units of their ranges.

Hornby-Dublo's great rival of the 1950s and early '60s was *Tri-ang*. A wide variety of modern forms of motive power have emerged from their Margate factory in Kent. These models can be divided into three main groups, relating to the ownership and financial status of the company making them:

1 **Tri-ang** Under this label the following ready-to-run items appeared: an 0-4-0 diesel shunter of vaguely North British design; a Class '08' shunter, but without the characteristic outside frames; a Class '31'; a Class '77' overhead electric; the WR 'Blue Pullman' train.

2 **Tri-ang Hornby** In 1964 the ailing *Hornby-Dublo* was taken under the *Tri-ang* wing. Under the *Tri-ang Hornby* regime there appeared three modern outline models: Class '35' 'Hymek'; Class '37' (on incorrect Class '31'-type bogies); Class '81', derived from the same type of model formerly made by *Hornby-Dublo* but with different bogies and motor.

3 **Hornby Railways** Further money troubles around 1970 saw the firm go into liquidation, to be subsequently resurrected under the banner of *Hornby Railways*. A wide range of modern types have been produced under this label: Classes '21/29'; Class '25'; Class '47'; Class '52' 'Western'; Class '58'; The High Speed Train; The Advanced Passenger Train; Class '86' overhead electric and, most recently, the small Class '06' diesel shunter.

In the 1950s *Kirdon* made a ready-to-run model of the LMS 10000/1. The same firm also produced the small North British 0-4-0 shunter (numbered between D2700 and D2702) and also, for a short period, the Class '08'. Another early example of the Class '08' was made by *Essar* with a die-cast metal body and the correct outside frames. Into the 1960s, excluding *Tri-ang* and *Hornby-Dublo*, only one other manufacturer made any 4mm ready-to-run models. This was *Liliput* which produced a very nice Class '81' in 1960. It was later to be incorporated in the *Trix* range.

The early 1970s was a very quiet period as far as new releases went. The great ship of railway modelling was stuck in the doldrums. However it was far from being on the rocks and the second half of the 1970s saw a resurgence in the 00 gauge ready-to-run market. Four manufacturers appeared on the scene, the majority not new to modelling but new to 4mm scale, who were to improve the detail and running qualities of diesels and electrics.

Jouef made the Class '40' and also some scale length Mark 3 coaches suitable for conversion to High Speed Train trailers. The largest range of modern outline items is made by *Lima* and covers the following classes: '09', '20', '33', '37', '40', '42/43', '47', '50', '52', '55', '73', '87'. The firm also produces the High Speed Train, again with the power cars and intermediate coaches. *Airfix* have produced the Class '31' whilst *Mainline* had Classes '03', '42', '45' and '56' in their range. Most of the *Airfix* and *Mainline* models are nowadays made and sold by *Dapol* though the Class '03' is marketed by *Replica Railways*. A model of the new Class '89' electric is also on the horizon from *Dapol*.

The range of kits available in 4mm scale is quite staggering. The variety of the materials used is also very wide, covering such things as plastic, white metal, etched brass and nickel silver. Leaders in the field are *Modern Traction Kits* with an extremely comprehensive selection of items. Essentially they have a range of two types of kit. In the first, the body structure is made up from white metal castings. Also included are windows, bogie sideframes, motor brackets and other small fittings. The actual motor bogies, though, are not provided in the kit. Amongst the range are the following classes: '03', '04', '14', '17', '22', '24', '25', '26', '27', '33', '40', '41', '42/43', '44', '45/46', '47', '50', '52', '56', '59', ex-LMS 10000/1, '71', '73', '74'. There are also a couple of small diesel shunters based on examples built by Ruston & Hornsby and by North British in this white metal series.

The other type of kit produced by this firm has the superstructure of the locomotive made from etched brass, pre-formed to shape. Again the motor bogie has to be purchased separately, but the kit also contains white metal fittings and other details. Kits of the following classes have been produced so far: '14', '47', '50', '73' (both the early and later designs), '81', '82', '85', ex-LMS 10000/1, ex-SR 10201-10203, ex-SR 20001/2, ex-SR 20003.

Finally, *Modern Traction Kits* have also made examples of Mark 3 coaching stock similar to that used for the High Speed Train. In addition to the first and second class coaches, there are the different types of restaurant and buffet cars in their range. These kits consist of an aluminium bodyshell pre-formed to shape and with the windows cut out. Also included are interior details, glazing and bogies.

Another manufacturer with a wide selection of models is *Q Kits*. The range covers most of the Type '4's which have run on BR together with the more exotic one-off prototypes. Rather than employing white metal or etched brass, the locomotive's body is a one-piece fibreglass shell. Available either just as a body kit or with motor, gears, wheels and chassis parts, the following classes have appeared: '40', '41', '42' (body kit only), '45', '50', '52', '55', '56', ex-LMS 10000/1, ex-SR 10201-10203, *Falcon, Lion*, DP2, *Kestrel*, gas turbine 18100.

A recent recruit to the 4mm scale kit field is *Modern Outline Kits*, with a growing number of models. These include Classes '08/09', '13', '15', '40' and '47', with others to follow. In addition to an etched brass body, nickel silver bogies and cast fittings, the kits come complete with motor, gears and buffers. I am sure that many people are put off buying kits because of all the extras one has to find, so it is nice to be able to report the introduction of a range such as this where the wheels, gears and motor *are* included.

The smaller diesel shunters seem to be gaining in popularity and two firms in particular are catering for this demand. The Class '04' is made by *Vulcan Model Engineering* which, like its 0 gauge cousin, is a cast metal kit with an etched chassis. Alternative cab sides, cowcatchers and side plates are also provided in the kit, though the motor, gears and wheels have to be bought separately.

Kits for the Class '02' and '07' are produced by *Craftsman Models*, these being essentially of etched brass, pre-formed to shape, with white metal fittings. Also included are interior cab details, glazing and dummy brake gear but, as usual, the wheels, gears and motor are an added expense.

In the early 1960s *Airfix* brought out an unmotorized plastic kit of the Class '04'. This has been unobtainable for very many years but it will soon be reintroduced under the *Dapol* banner. Another range of unmotorized plastic kits was made by *Kitmaster*, these first appearing around 1959. They produced three diesel outline models: the Class '08', the prototype 'Deltic' and the LMR version of the 'Blue Pullman'. The demise of this firm was much lamented in the model world and its loss is still felt by many. *Dapol* has, however, come to the rescue with a limited re-run of the prototype 'Deltic' kit.

Other manufacturers in the 4mm field include *Jidenco* with an etched brass superstructure kit for the Class '50', *A 1 Models* with white metal body kits for the prototype 'Deltic' and the Class '23', in either its original or refurbished form. These are designed to fit a proprietary chassis. Class '73' and '74' have also been produced by this firm as etched brass body kits, again for use with a proprietary mechanism. A model of the Class '76' Bo + Bo overhead electric comes from *d.c. kits* and consists of a one-piece moulded resin body with etched brass bogie sideframes. Again, one has to buy the motor, gears and wheels separately. This firm has an expanding range of kits, including the LMS 10000/1, the Class '41' diesel-hydraulic and the Class '77' Co-Co electric. New models are, of course, appearing all the time and recent examples include kits from *ConstructEON Models* for the Class '06' and Class '14', whilst *D. Alexander Models* have a Class '15' and Class '17'. A cast resin bodyshell for the Class '23' has been produced by *Golden Arrow*, whilst from *DJH* there is a very detailed kit of a Class '25'.

Gauge 'Trix' (track gauge = 16·5mm), 3·8mm/ft scale with a ratio of 1:80

The majority of the items that were produced by *Trix* were to the scale of 3·8mm/ft, though running on 00 gauge track. Their first ready-to-run diesel locomotive appeared in 1958 and was based on a Ruston & Hornsby 0-6-0 shunter. With the model came a GWR-style shunter's truck, a nice touch. Next in the range was the Class '76' electric which some advertisements at the time (though not I hasten to add *Trix*'s own) referred to it as the 'new pantograph overhead pick-up diesel'!

Then followed a model of the Class '42' 'Warship'. On all these locomotives the body was of cast metal, though the roof section of the 'Warship' was plastic. In their final diesel, the 'Class '52' 'Western', *Trix* used plastic for the super-structure as a whole, but retained a die-cast chassis. After withdrawal from the market by this firm, the Class '52' later appeared under the *Liliput* label for a short while.

Gauge HO (track gauge = 16·5mm), 3·5mm/ft scale with a ratio of 1:87·1

In North America and on the Continent many modellers use the same 16·5mm gauge track that we have in Britain. However they do not model to 4mm scale but rather to 3·5mm/ft which gives the correct relationship between the scale and the gauge of the track. A number of continental firms have used this HO gauge as a springboard to the British model railway market, but without much success. Whilst there are a number of dedicated British HO modellers, the scale has not really taken off in this country.

Although no kits have been produced to this scale for British outline models, a number of ready-to-run items have appeared over the years. First on the scene in 1961 was *Playcraft*, with their models made by the French firm of *Jouef*. Their initial diesel release was of the Class '21' Bo-Bo with a plastic body and eight-wheel drive. Towards the end of 1963 they also brought out a small diesel shunter based on the North British design numbered between D2703 and D2707.

Whilst the bodywork was reasonably accurate the features below the footplate were some way off the mark in that the prototype had an 0-4-0 wheel arrangement and not the four-wheel type of chassis depicted on the model. In addition to the normal electric-powered version of this shunter, the manufacturers also made one powered by clockwork. The Class '21' was reintroduced in 1975 with a new motor, gearing and chassis, and sold under the *Jouef* brand name .

Next came the West German firm of *Märklin* who in 1967 brought out the Class '42'. The model was an excellent runner though let down by an in-accurately dimensioned body which did not capture the true feel of a 'Warship'. There were actually two versions of this model: that sold under the *Märklin* name was for use on their AC stud contact system, whilst that under the *Hamo* label was for the standard two-rail 12V DC supply. Prior to producing models in 00 gauge, the Italian manufacturers *Lima* tested the water of the British market with a small range of 3·5mm scale models. Amongst these was the Class '33' which appeared in 1974. Perhaps the best ready-to-run British HO gauge locomotive has come from *Fleischmann*, this being yet another model of the Class '42' 'Warship'. Unfortunately, their range was never developed to its full extent, indicative of a lack of general interest by established 00 gauge modellers in changing over to HO. Finally in this scale there is an 0-6-0 diesel shunter from *Roco*. Although the model is of a Netherlands Railways locomotive, the design derives from the ex-LMS 350hp shunters numbered between 12033 and 12138 (BR Class '11'), so only minimal work is required to make it fit for a British style layout.

Gauge TT (track gauge = 12mm), 3mm/ft scale with a ratio of 1:101·6

This 'Table Top' gauge developed rapidly in Britain during the late 1950s and, with equal vigour, declined during the mid '60s. There are still a number of devotees to this scale as it has many attractive qualities, requiring less space than 00 gauge but being significantly larger than N gauge. Hence an interesting layout could be built in a reasonably small area yet the individual items of rolling stock were large enough to be detailed to a high standard. The fortunes of TT gauge were allied closely, and, as it turned out, too closely, to one manufacturer. When they pulled out of this scale, so did the majority of modellers.

The firm concerned was *Tri-ang*. They produced two modern outline locomotives, the first being the Class '08' diesel shunter, albeit without the outside frames, and the second was the Class '31'. Apart from these two ready-to-run items, *Bec* made a white metal body kit of the Class '47' to use with the *Tri-ang* motor bogie.

Gauge N (track gauge = 9mm), 2·06mm/ft scale with a ratio of 1:148

N gauge is probably the second most popular of all the various scales and gauges that are to be found. However there is a slight complication in that models of this general size are constructed to one of three different scales: 2·06mm/ft (1:148); 2mm/ft (1:152·4); 1·91mm/ft (1:160). Continental manufacturers usually work to 1·91mm/ft whilst in Britain 2·06mm/ft is the norm. Some firms, though, interpret these standards rather liberally, even to the extent of having different-sized models in the same range. At least they all run on the same gauge of track!

Leader in the ready-to-run field in Britain is *Graham Farish* with an ever-growing range of models. So far they have produced the following classes: '08', '20', '25', '33', '37', '40', '47', '50', '52', '55'. The High Speed Train also comes from this stable. Meanwhile, *Minitrix* make models of Classes '27', '42' and '47', whilst from *Lima* come the Class '31', Class '55' and Class '86'. The *Lima* models, which were originally sold under the *Wrenn* label, do have some discrepancies in their measurements. In particular they tend to be slightly too high and wide, and this does show when they are compared with correctly proportioned N gauge items. Although virtually unobtainable nowadays, there was another range of N gauge models in the early 1960s. These came from *Lone Star* and their diesel outline locomotives consisted of Classes '23' and '24'.

A varied selection of kits has also appeared. They are of similar construction, consisting of a set of white metal castings which, when assembled, fit on to a proprietary chassis. However, as in the larger scales, a growing number of etched brass body kits are also appearing on the market. Looking first at the white metal kits, *Langley Miniature Models* have produced Classes '21/29', '24', '25' and '37', together with the gas turbine locomotive numbered 18000 and the small Class '04' diesel shunter.

ABS Models have also made a kit for the Class '04' whilst from *Peco* there is a

Class '35' 'Hymek'; *Anbrico* have produced the Class '50' and *Modern Traction Kits* the Class '52', the latter of these being later sold under the *Fleetline* name. *Modern Traction Kits* also introduced the High Speed Train with kits for the power cars and trailer vehicles, whilst *ECM* once sold white metal castings to make up into the High Speed Train power car superstructures. Meanwhile *P & D Marsh* have produced Classes '45/46', '47' and '56' in kit form. In etched brass, *Modern Traction Kits* have brought out a body kit for the Class '73' electro-diesel, whilst the Class '73' and '74' are also available from *A 1 Models*.

Gauge Z (track gauge = 6·5mm), 1·5mm/ft scale with a ratio of 1:220

The smallest of the commercial scales, at 1·5mm/ft, first appeared on the scene in 1972. The driving force behind this was *Märklin*, with a range of Continental and American inspired models. In 1980, using the *Märklin* chassis as a basis, *Ellmar Products* announced an ambitious series of British outline ready-to-run diesels and electrics. The initial range covered Classes '47' and '87' together with the High Speed Train, whilst a Class '55' was also planned for later release. Photographs of mock-ups of the models were published in the railway magazines towards the end of 1980, but it was not until well into 1982 that any items appeared in the shops. As far as I have been able to ascertain, only the Class '47' ever actually entered the market. Developments in British Z gauge look rather bleak at the moment with no sign of any new models on the horizon.

ELEVEN
A look at liveries

Since nationalization there have been many different styles of livery applied to BR stock. Colours have come in and then gone out of favour. The black of the early 1950s gave way to green later in the decade. Overall blue then came into vogue, while at the moment various shades of grey are the favourite choice. On the prototype, the principal reason for painting the vehicles is to protect their surfaces from the elements and hence prevent corrosion. Of course the appearance of the locomotive or coach is important, and BR themselves realize the value of promoting a certain 'image' through the look of their rolling stock.

On model locomotives and stock we are not really concerned about corrosion. Granted, if one has an outdoor layout in the garden then rust may rear its ugly head, but for the majority of layouts situated in the house or in a shed it is not a problem. Dust is our number one enemy and it doesn't matter how many coats of paint are applied, or what shade they are, dust will still be a major problem. From the modelling viewpoint then, it is the appearance of the various styles of livery that concerns us most. *Figures 28* to *31* outline the broad changes in livery that have occurred since the formation of BR, and summarize the various colour schemes that have been applied to the locomotives and express passenger multiple-units. In this chapter we'll be looking in a little more detail at the different styles of livery that have appeared over the years.

Black livery
For the first half of 1948, BR's locomotive fleet continued to be painted in their old colours. A few had their former pre-nationalization markings removed and 'BRITISH RAILWAYS', in various lettering styles, applied in full to the side of the body. Others ran without any insignia pending the design of a new BR symbol. The first style of insignia was unveiled on the tender of an ex-LMS 'Princess Royal' steam locomotive at Marylebone station in London just a few days before Christmas 1948. This new emblem, the top drawing of *Figure 32*, consisted of a lion astride a spoked wheel. The emblem came in for a fair amount of criticism, being variously dubbed as 'the hungry lion', 'the starving lion', 'the bicycling lion', 'the unicyclic lion' or even 'the ferret and dartboard'.

Quite why it came in for so much stick I cannot say, though perhaps it had something to do with the British public's perennial delight in knocking the

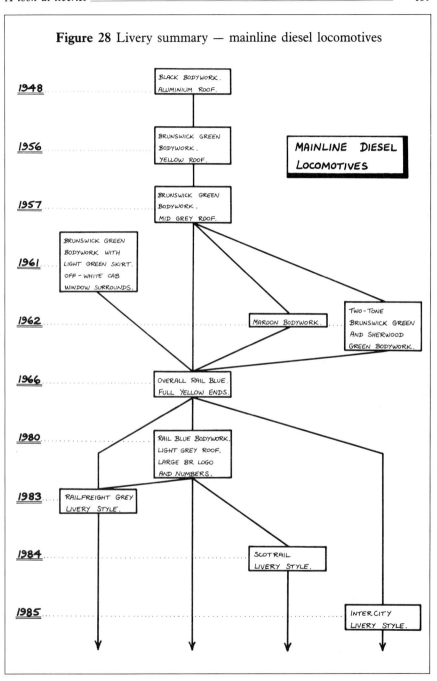

Figure 28 Livery summary — mainline diesel locomotives

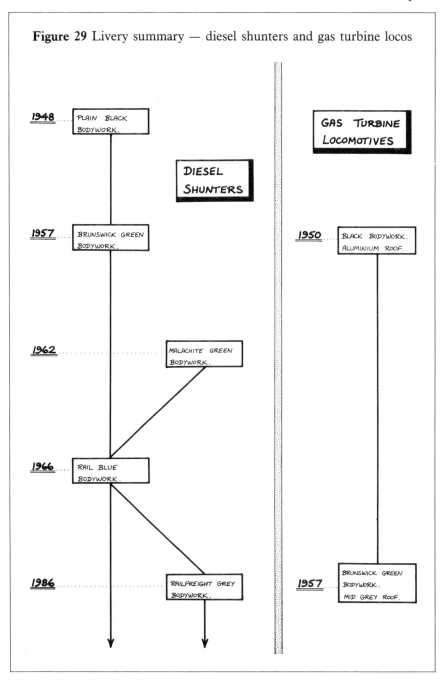

Figure 29 Livery summary — diesel shunters and gas turbine locos

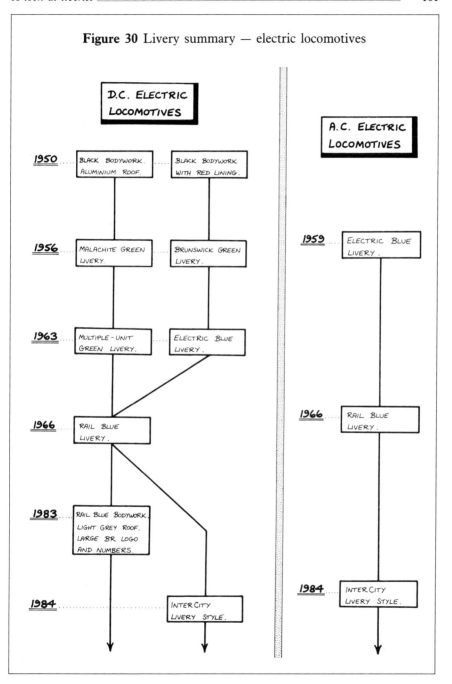

Figure 30 Livery summary — electric locomotives

Figure 31 Livery summary — express passenger multiple units

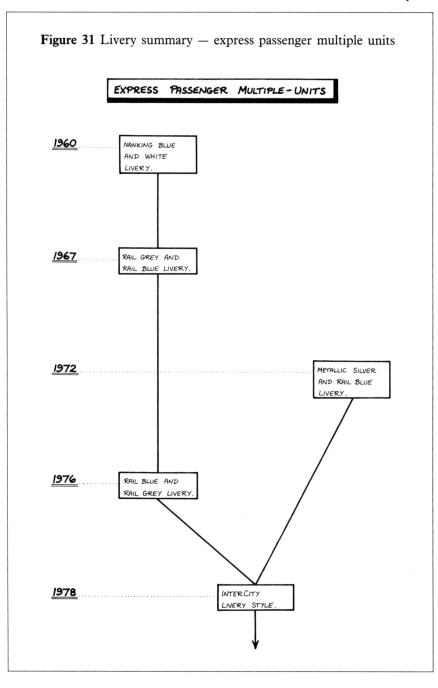

Figure 32 BR insignia — the emblem and crest

— THE BR EMBLEM —

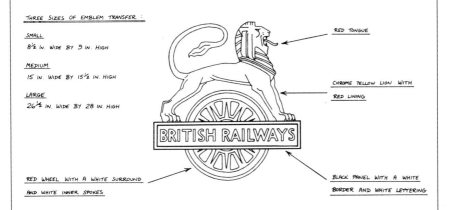

THREE SIZES OF EMBLEM TRANSFER :

SMALL
8½ IN. WIDE BY 9 IN. HIGH

MEDIUM
15 IN. WIDE BY 15½ IN. HIGH

LARGE
26½ IN. WIDE BY 28 IN. HIGH

RED TONGUE

CHROME YELLOW LION WITH
RED LINING

RED WHEEL WITH A WHITE SURROUND
AND WHITE INNER SPOKES

BLACK PANEL WITH A WHITE
BORDER AND WHITE LETTERING

— THE BR CREST —

TRANSPARENT BACKGROUND
TO THE CREST

SILVER WHEEL

RED LION WITH STEEL-COLOURED
TEETH, TONGUE AND CLAWS

BUFF-COLOURED FRAMING
AND LETTERING

BUFF-COLOURED HERALDIC CROWN,
ROSE, THISTLE, LEEKS AND
OAK LEAF

TWO SIZES OF CREST TRANSFER :

SMALL
30¼ IN. WIDE BY 14¾ IN. HIGH

LARGE
43¾ IN. WIDE BY 21¾ IN. HIGH

railways. I must admit to finding this emblem rather attractive, being much more stylish than the later rather fussy crest, or the sterile double arrow logo. Two versions of the emblem transfer were produced, with the lion facing either to the left or to the right, and it was made in three sizes: small (8½in long), medium (15in long), large (26½in long). Because of limited supplies of these emblem transfers they did not come into general use, and hence appear on the side of locomotives, until about the middle of 1949.

The colour schemes for the various classes of locomotive were finalized early in 1949 and they were as follows:

1   Top-link express passenger steam locomotives — medium blue with black and white lining, red bufferbeams and cream numerals.
2   Other express passenger steam locomotives — Brunswick green with black and orange lining, red bufferbeams and cream numerals.
3   Mixed traffic steam locomotives — black with red, cream and grey lining, red bufferbeams and cream numerals.
4   Freight steam locomotives — black without any lining, red bufferbeams and cream numerals.
5   Mainline diesel, electric and gas turbine locomotives — black with aluminium roof, bogies, lining and numerals.
6   Diesel shunting locomotives — black without any lining, red bufferbeams and cream numerals.

The numerals were in Gill Sans medium type as shown in *Figure 33*. This *sans serif* typeface had originally been designed by Eric Gill for the LNER but was adopted by BR because of its clarity and simplicity.

The black livery applied to BR's non-steam locomotives was developed from the glossy black and aluminium colour scheme used by the LMS on their mainline diesels. When clean this was quite an attractive livery, the contrast between the black and aluminium being particularly effective. BR's own instructions regarding the positioning of the numerals and emblem on their diesel and electric locomotives is worth quoting:

> 'Main-line locomotives with cabs at each end; engine numbers to be on each side as near at each end as convenient, with crest in centre.
> Main-line and shunting locomotives with single centre or end cabs; engine number on cab side immediately below windows.
> Crest in centre of bonnet portion.
> "Built" plates below engine numbers, but no cast number plate on front or rear.'

Note how BR refer to their emblem as a 'crest' when it is actually nothing of the sort — being strictly speaking only an insignia or symbol.

With one or two exceptions, the style of painting the diesel shunters was pretty constant. The bodywork and underframe were black, as were the handrails, whilst the bufferbeams and stocks were red. The Gill Sans numerals were 8in high and pale cream in colour, being located on the cab sides. The emblems were of the medium size: on the larger shunters in the 350hp range they were position-ed on the engine compartment doors, but on the 153hp to 204hp shunters the

Figure 33 BR locomotive numbering styles

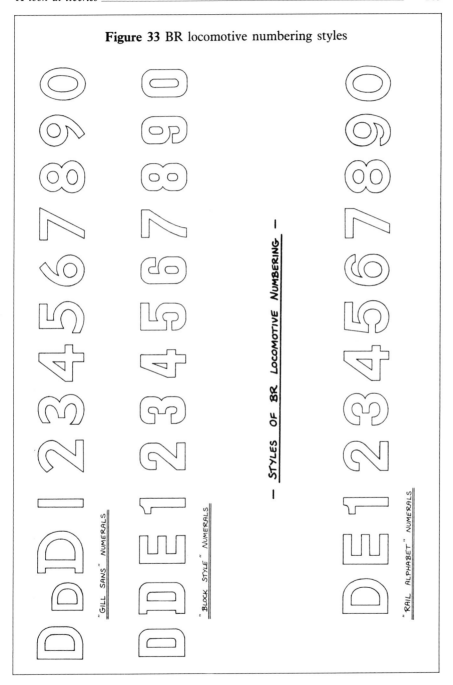

emblems were on the cab sides above the numbers. The lion on the emblem invariably faced towards the front, that is the radiator end, of these diesel shunters. Hence one side of the locomotive had a right-handed emblem whilst on the other side there was a left-hand version. The main exceptions to this, as I have mentioned on pages 17-18, were the large size of emblem on 15107 and the reversed positions of the numbers and emblem on 15000 to 15004. In addition to their cab side numbers, many shunters also had numbers displayed on their front and rear bufferbeams. These were located either directly above the coupling hook or to one side of it.

On the mainline locomotives the style of black livery was a little more varied, with differences between the individual classes. All the following had black bodywork with an aluminium painted roof and bogie sideframes:

10000 and 10001— 12in high raised aluminium numerals, 4in wide raised aluminium waist band, large size emblem (both sides face to left), black bufferbeam and stocks, handrails in bright finished metal.

10201 to 10203 — 10in high raised aluminium numerals, 3in wide raised aluminium waist band, medium size emblem (both sides face to left), red bufferbeam and stocks, handrails in bright finished metal.

10800   — 8in high transfer numerals, no lining, medium size emblem (facing to right on one side and to left on the other), red bufferbeam and stocks, handrails painted black. Remember that the top of the engine compartment on this locomotive was only painted aluminium for a short period.

18000   — 12in high raised aluminium numerals, 4in wide aluminium-painted waist band, large size emblem (both sides face to left), black bufferbeam and stocks, handrails painted black.

18100   — 12in high raised aluminium numerals, 4in wide raised aluminium waist band, large size emblem (both sides face to left), black bufferbeam and stocks, handrails in bright finished metal.

20001 and 20002— 12in high transfer numerals, 4in wide aluminium-painted waist band, medium size emblem (both sides face to left), red bufferbeam and stocks, handrails in bright finished metal.

20003   — 12in high transfer numerals, 4in wide aluminium-painted waist band, large size emblem (both sides face to left), red bufferbeam and stocks, handrails in bright finished metal.

The other types of mainline locomotives were painted black but without the aluminium roof and bogies. The 'Fell' diesel, number 10100, was plain black without any lining and had the medium size of BR emblem. The former North Eastern electrics were in unlined black with red bufferbeams. On the Manchester, Sheffield and Wath line the electric locomotives were in lined black livery with red bufferbeams, the large size of emblem (which always faced to the left) and 8in pale cream numerals. Around the bottom edge of the bodywork on the Class '76's there was a ⅝in wide grey band and above this a ⅛in wide cream band. The bodywork itself was lined with a ¼in wide red line. This red, cream and grey lining was similar to that used on BR's mixed traffic steam locomotives. The Class '77's were also lined out in red but lacked the bottom grey and cream band.

Green livery

In 1956 BR set about brightening up its rolling stock. New regional colours appeared on the coaches: chocolate and cream on the WR, a new shade of Malachite green on the Southern and maroon for the other regions. Rather than the black livery then in current use, it was decided to paint the diesel and electric locomotives green. The majority received a coat of Brunswick green, though the electrics on the Southern were painted a shade of Malachite green.

To accompany these new colour schemes a crest was designed and this was given approval by the College of Arms in England and Wales, and the Lord Lyon Kings-of-Arms in Scotland. The crest, as applied to locomotives, is shown in the bottom drawing of *Figure 32*. In heraldic terms this consisted of a demi-lion rampant, representing the British Lion, holding between its paws a silver locomotive wheel. The lion was issuant from a heraldic crown on which were arranged the rose of England, the thistle of Scotland, the leek of Wales and the oak leaf of Great Britain. Like the previous emblem there were two versions of this crest transfer, with the lion either facing to the left or to the right. For use on locomotives, two sizes of crest were made: small (30¼in long), large (43¾in long). This new crest made its first appearance, again at Marylebone station, in the middle of June 1956 on the tender of a 'Britannia' Pacific steam locomotive. It was to be the following year, though, before the crest started to become a common sight throughout the BR network as stocks of the old emblem were used up.

The initial style of Brunswick green livery on the mainline diesels and electrics was as follows:

Bodywork	— Brunswick green with black and orange lining. This lining was the same as that used on the express passenger steam locomotives, namely an ⅛in wide orange line, then ½in of green, a 1in wide black line in the middle, another ½in of green and ⅛in of orange.
Roof	— Primrose yellow was first specified, but this was soon changed to cream.
Underframe	— Black.
Bufferbeams	— Red.
Bogies	— Black.
Numerals	— Still in Gill Sans type, but yellow rather than pale cream in colour.

On the Southern Region, electric locomotives were turned out in a shade of

Malachite green with a medium grey roof. Along the side of the body at waist height ran a red band approximately 2in wide, bounded on either side by a thin white line, each being ¼in in width. Meanwhile, diesel shunters on all regions began to appear in unlined Brunswick green livery with a black underframe, red bufferbeams and yellow Gill Sans numerals.

The new design of crest generally had the lion facing towards the number one end, that is the radiator end, of the mainline diesel and shunting locomotives. Thus on one side of the locomotive the lion faced to the left whilst on the other side it faced to the right. Usually the small size of crest was used, even on the larger types of diesel.

Towards the latter part of 1956 BR began to devise a new scheme for numbering its diesel fleet. With many new locomotives under construction and countless more on the order books, the five-figure 10,000 series which hitherto had been used, was beginning to become unwieldy. With so many new types the numbering would have had to continue into the 100,000 range which could have led to reporting errors. Also it would have been difficult to allocate consecutive blocks of numbers for the new designs. To overcome these difficulties it was decided to number diesel locomotives in a new series between 1 and 9999 with the prefix 'D' to differentiate them from steam locomotives bearing the same numbers. After a few false starts, the broad categories were finalized for the numbering blocks of the different types of diesels:

    D1-D1999   — Type '4's
    D2000-D2999 — small shunters (153hp to 330hp)
    D3000-D4999 — large shunters (350hp range)
    D5000-D6499 — Type '2's
    D6500-D7499 — Type '3's
    D7500-D7999 — Type '2's
    D8000-D8999 — Type '1's
    D9000-D9499 — Type '5's
    D9500-D9999 — Type '1's.

The mainline diesels already in service were not covered by this system and retained their original numbers. Most of the diesel shunters were, however, re-numbered; the exceptions being those of pre-nationalization design which were unchanged. Soon the electric locomotives were to have their numbering, too, in a more logical sequence:

    E2001 upwards — AC electrics (2,000hp range)
    E3001 upwards — AC electrics (3,000hp range)
    E5001 upwards — DC electrics
    E6001 upwards — Electro-diesels.

Again, the pre-nationalization types, including the Class '76's and '77's, kept their old numbers.

Coupled with these changes in locomotive numbering came a new style of numerals. Out went the attractive Gills Sans type, to be replaced by numerals in a block style as shown in *Figure 33*. These appeared during 1957 on the first of the new classes of diesel that had been ordered under the 1955 Modernization Plan. The new numerals were shorter than the Gill Sans previously employed, being 6in high. The colour was also different, not pale cream or yellow, but white. The Gill Sans type, however, continued to be used on diesel shunters for a few more years. Indeed as late as 1961 some newly-built shunters were being turned out with Gill Sans numerals. By then though, the 'D' prefix had been introduced and so this appeared on the cab side in front of the number. The style of the 'D' varied; on some locomotives it was 8 in high, on others it was shorter. Some were in the correct *sans serif* type whilst others had a serifed 'D'.

With the block style numbers of 1957 there came a slight alteration in the Brunswick green livery:

Bodywork	— Still Brunswick green but without the black and orange lining. Instead, there were lining bands of pale grey or off-white. These varied in size, shape and positioning between the different classes of locomotive.
Roof	— Out went the cream-coloured roof to be replaced by a more durable medium grey shade. The Class '76' and '77' electrics, however, retained their cream roofs and also, by the way, the orange and black lining.
Underframe	— Black.
Bufferbeams	— Red.
Bogies	— Black.
Numerals	— Block style, white in colour. Initially the 'D' prefix was in *sans serif* style but soon, for greater clarity, serifs were added to the 'D'. The following classes, or at least the early members of them, had the 'D' without any serifs at first: '15', '16', '20', '24', '26', '28', '31', '40', '41', '42'. The Class '02' and North British 330hp 0-4-0 shunters also lacked the serifs to the 'D'.

As mentioned above, the crest was produced in two versions with the lion facing either to the right or to the left. By 1959 BR realized that it only had heraldic approval for the crest with the lion facing to the left, so henceforth it used only that type. However some early locomotives, including members of Classes '16', '20', '26' and '28', carried both versions of the BR crest: on one side it faced to the left and on the other the right.

During 1961, as a variation from the rather plain Brunswick green, a couple of classes appeared in a brighter livery scheme. On the 'Hymeks' and 'Deltics', the Brunswick green, while still the basic colour, was enlivened by a broad waist band of a light green shade usually referred to as 'green yellow'. The cab window surrounds were also picked out in off-white which made a nice contrast with the green. The following year saw the start of a more comprehensive scheme to improve the Brunswick green livery. A new colour known as Sherwood green made its appearance, being lighter than the Brunswick green but darker than the 'green yellow'. A two-tone combination of Brunswick green and Sherwood green livery was applied to many, and in some cases all, members of Classes '14', '17', '25', '29', '47' and '53', and isolated examples from Classes '24' and '27'.

Over the years there have been some detail changes in the green livery. During 1959, after experiments the previous year, black and yellow diagonal stripes began to be painted on the ends of the diesel shunters. This was as a safety measure to make the locomotives more conspicuous to railway staff in goods yards and at the trackside. At about the same time the handrails were also picked out in white, again to make them more visible. 1960 saw the introduction of 'overhead live wire' flashes and gradually these began to appear on both diesel shunters and the mainline locomotives. The flashes, white rectangular plates 8in by 5in in size with a red arrow pointing upwards and the wording 'Danger, overhead live wires' in red, were fitted to various points on the locomotives' superstructure. Finally, from 1962 onwards yellow warning panels were applied to the ends of the mainline locomotive fleet, again as a safety measure to warn permanent way men working on the line of the approach of a train. The size of these panels varied between the different classes but generally they were rect-angular in shape.

Maroon livery

Apart from the introduction of the two-tone green livery, 1962 also saw the emergence of a new colour scheme that was subsequently to be applied to some of the Type '4' diesels. The Western Region, not noted for following the party line, decided that it wanted something a little different for its top-link express diesel-hydraulics. The Brunswick green, a colour once synonymous with the GWR, was abandoned in favour of maroon which was, if anything, a shade asso-ciated more with their rivals, the LMS. Quite what the former Great Western diehards at Swindon thought about painting some of their own products in maroon is perhaps best left to the imagination.

The shade of maroon chosen was the same as that then being applied to BR's coaching stock. Rather than using the more usual crest as seen on the majority of the locomotive fleet, the circular coaching stock crest was applied instead. This crest (the bottom drawing of *Figure 34*) had originally been introduced at the same time as the other BR crest in 1956 and had also been produced intially in both left hand and right hand versions. However by 1962 when it first made its appearance on locomotives, only the version with the lion facing to the left was used.

Only three classes received the maroon livery: the Class '52' 'Westerns' and many, but not all, of the Class '42' and '43' 'Warships'. Details of the maroon colour scheme are as follows:

Bodywork	— Maroon without any lining whatsoever. On the 'Westerns' the cab window surrounds were picked out in off-white.
Roof	— Dark grey roof panels. These soon weathered giving the appearance of being black.

Figure 34 BR insigia — the alloy crest and coaching stock crest

— THE BR CAST ALLOY CREST —

THE CASTING IS SECURED TO
THE BODYSIDE BY FOUR
COUNTERSUNK BOLTS

SIZE OF THE CASTING :

18 IN. SQUARE

ONE-PIECE CAST ALLOY CREST

— THE BR COACHING STOCK CREST —

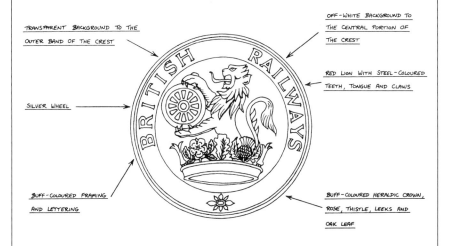

TRANSPARENT BACKGROUND TO THE
OUTER BAND OF THE CREST

OFF-WHITE BACKGROUND TO
THE CENTRAL PORTION OF
THE CREST

RED LION WITH STEEL-COLOURED
TEETH, TONGUE AND CLAWS

SILVER WHEEL

BUFF-COLOURED FRAMING
AND LETTERING

BUFF-COLOURED HERALDIC CROWN,
ROSE, THISTLE, LEEKS AND
OAK LEAF

SIZE OF THE TRANSFER :

16½ IN. DIAMETER

Underframe	— Maroon.
Bufferbeams	— Black. On the first few 'Westerns' these were painted yellow prior to the application of the rectangular warnings panels.
Bogies	— Black.
Numerals	— Block style, white in colour. The 'Westerns' again differed in having metal numberplates instead of the usual transfers.

Blue livery

For twenty years now, the overall rail blue livery scheme has been a very familiar sight throughout the whole of the BR system but other shades of blue have also been seen. For the AC electric locomotives working on the LMR, a very striking shade known as electric blue was adopted in 1959. This was an exciting and vibrant colour which exactly matched the clean lines and quiet power of these locomotives. To accompany the electric blue a new design of cast alloy crest appeared (as shown in the top drawing of *Figure 34*) instead of the standard BR crest. Of all the embellishments to be carried on BR locomotives, this alloy crest was surely one of the most attractive and it is a pity that it did not have a wider application. The electric blue livery style was as follows:

Bodywork	— Electric blue. The cab window surrounds were off-white or possibly a very pale shade of grey. The top of the cab roofs were painted white.
Roof	— Grey.
Underframe	— Black.
Bufferbeams	— Red, with black buffer stocks.
Bogies	— Black.
Numerals	— These were in a modified Gill Sans style with a serifed '1' and a straight topped '3'. On the majority of the electric classes the numerals were made of aluminium, but on the Class '81's they were fabricated from stainless steel sheet.

Another shade of blue was the principal colour used on the aptly named 'Blue Pullman' luxury express passenger multiple-units that were introduced on the LMR and WR in 1960. This was Nanking blue, a shade with the same intensity as electric blue but a fraction darker. Complementing the blue was a broad panel of white around the window areas and a medium grey roof, whilst the buffer stocks were red and the bogies black.

In 1964 a newly built Class '47', D1733, was experimentally painted in a overall blue livery with a new design of BR symbol. This symbol was no fussy crest or badge but the later familiar double arrow logo design. On the locomotive, rather than a black underframe and bogies, these items were painted a chocolate brown colour. The shade of blue was turquoise, a lighter colour than the rail blue which was later adopted as standard. The brown underframes were designed to disguise the colour disfiguration that black bogies received from the brownish stains caused by dust from the brake shoes.

After some deliberation, a slightly modified form of this livery was announced to the public early in 1965 as being the future standard for all of BR's locomotives. So it came to pass that blue became the prominent colour associated with our railway system for the next twenty years. As applied to locomotives, the overall blue style was as follows:

Bodywork	— Rail blue with full yellow ends. Initially, though, some of the early blue repaints had only small warning panels rather than the full yellow ends.
Roof	— Rail blue.
Underframe	— Black.
Bufferbeams	— Black.
Bogies	— Black.
Numerals	— As part of its new corporate image a standard *sans serif* alphabet was introduced. These 'Rail Alphabet' numerals are shown in *Figure 33*: they are normally 6in high and white in colour.

Probably the most controversial element in this new livery was the design of the BR logo. The insignia, shown in *Figure 35*, was officially described as 'two-way traffic arrows on parallel lines representing tracks'. It came in for a fair amount of criticism at the time it was introduced but over the years it has appeared on virtually every item associated with BR, from station buildings to street hoardings, rolling stock to television advertisements and road vehicles to pocket timetables. It has come to symbolize the British railway network. Whether one likes it or not, the BR logo will no doubt still be with us well into the next century though perhaps not as extensively used as at present.

Whilst a few electric locomotives were painted in the rail blue during 1965, though without the new BR logo, it was not until the following year that rail blue began to appear on other classes. On the majority of locomotives the logo was a white-coloured transfer usually 2ft 6in long, although a smaller size was also available. For Classes '81' to '86' a cast alloy version of the logo was introduced, replacing the alloy crest previously carried by these locomotives. On the 'Blue Pullman' multiple-units the attractive Nanking blue livery gave way to a rail grey and rail blue colour scheme that was then being applied to other Pullman stock on BR. The first 'Blue Pullman' turned out in this grey and blue style appeared in 1967.

The prototype High Speed Train of the early 1970s was painted in a similar colour scheme but the experimental Advanced Passenger Train of 1972 received rather different treatment. Whilst at first glance it appeared the same as the prototype HST in grey and blue, these colours actually had a metallic sheen, making the grey more of a silver colour. On the first production HST sets, entering service in 1976, the standard rail blue and grey livery was used rather than any special colour scheme.

Figure 35 BR insignia — the logo

— THE BR LOGO —

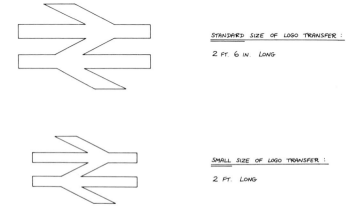

STANDARD SIZE OF LOGO TRANSFER :

2 FT. 6 IN. LONG

SMALL SIZE OF LOGO TRANSFER :

2 FT. LONG

— THE BR CAST ALLOY LOGO —

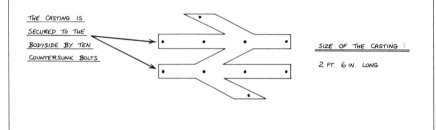

THE CASTING IS
SECURED TO THE
BODYSIDE BY TEN
COUNTERSUNK BOLTS

SIZE OF THE CASTING :

2 FT. 6 IN. LONG

Towards the end of the 1970s it was felt that the livery on the locomotive fleet needed brightening up a little. Hence in 1978 a Class '56', No 56036, was given a special repaint to assess a possible new standard livery. Rail blue was retained for the body sides, as was black for the underframe and bogies, the ends remaining yellow. The roof, however, was painted pale grey and the cab windows were given black surrounds. The most remarkable features of this new livery though, were the extremely large logos and numbers. The logo was the full height of the body side whilst the numbers were 420mm high (by this time BR were quoting their dimensions in metric measurements). This style was adopted as standard for Classes '50' and '56' in 1980 and has subsequently appeared also on members of the Class '37's, '47's and '73's.

Grey livery

When the prototype Advanced Passenger Train was unveiled to the press in 1978 there was no sign of the ubiquitous rail blue paint to be seen anywhere. Instead, the sleek lines of the APT were enhanced by shades of light and dark grey, separated by bands of red and white. Whilst this 'Inter-City' livery style, as it came to be known, did not help the fortunes of the APT itself, it was felt to be sufficiently attractive and durable to have a wider application. In September 1983 a Western Region HST set was painted in this grey colour scheme as part of BR's relaunch of its Inter-City business services. Since then this 'Inter-City' livery has become the norm for the entire HST fleet.

Some classes of locomotive have also appeared in a variation of this 'Inter-City' livery style. In 1984 it became the standard for the Class '86' and '87' electrics, and has also been applied to some Class '47's and '73's. In Scotland a modified version of this livery has appeared on their Class '47' push-pull fleet: instead of the 180mm wide red body side stripe usually associated with the 'Inter-City' style, these 'ScotRail' examples have a light blue band along the side of the body.

Another shade of grey is steadily becoming more familiar as the standard livery for 'Railfreight' locomotives. Appearing first on the new Class '58' heavy freight machines, it has now been extended to selected members of Classes '08', '20', '26', '31', '37', '47' and '56'. Livery development is still continuing on BR, of course, and a recent example is that to be found on the Network South East. This is the brand name for rail services in the London and South East area of England, launched in the middle of 1986. Although predominantly applied to multiple-units, a number of Class '47's and '50's have been turned out in this new red, white and blue colour scheme.

Locomotive names

The nameplates that adorn a growing number of locomotives and power cars are an important aspect of liveries. On the prototype a named locomotive is always the centre of attraction. Even travellers not particularly interested in railways will sometimes look up from their book or newspaper as a named train enters the station. The same is true of models too: a locomotive with a name has more appeal that one with just a plain number. Indeed, the name carried is often the main reason why we model a particular locomotive in the first place. In Appendix 2 I have listed all the official names carried by BR's diesel and electric fleet, and the HST power cars. This is correct to the autumn of 1987, though obviously by the time you read these words there will have been further namings. The list shows the year in which the locomotive received its nameplates, although some types, especially Class '40', '44' and '76', had their plates removed many years before they were withdrawn.

The majority of the nameplates seen on BR are aluminium alloy castings, though on the Class '76's and '77's they were cast in brass. Some of the early named Class '47's and all the Class '52' 'Westerns', however, had fabricated nameplates with aluminium cast letters and beading fitted to a steel backplate. The background colour of the plates has changed over the years, dependent on the livery carried by the locomotive as is indicated by the table below.

Background colour of locomotive nameplates

Class	Green livery	Maroon livery	Blue livery (pre 1977)	Blue livery (post 1977)	Grey livery
08	—	—	—	Black	—
31	—	—	—	—	Red
33	—	—	—	Red	—
37	—	—	—	Red	Red
40	Red	—	Red	—	—
41	Red	—	Black	—	—
42	Red	Black	Black	—	—
43	Red	Black	Black	—	—
44	Green	—	Blue	—	—
45	Red	—	Red	Red	—
46	Red	—	Red	Red	—
47	Black	—	Black	Red	Red
50	—	—	—	Red	—
52	Red	Black	Black	—	—
55	Red	—	Red	Red	—
56	—	—	—	Red	Red
58	—	—	—	—	Red
73	—	—	—	Red	Red
76	Red	—	Red	—	—
77	Red	—	—	—	—
86	—	—	—	Red	Red
87	—	—	—	Red	Red
HST	—	—	—	Red	Red
APT	—	—	—	—	Red

Model nameplates are produced by a number of firms. Amongst the first in the field was the 'Kings Cross' range of ready coloured engraved plates made by the *Model Railway (Mfg) Company*. A wide range of names in 4mm scale are available together with a more limited selection in 2mm, 3mm and 7mm. These nameplates, however, do have to be cut to shape. Small nail scissors are used to cut away most of the excess metal whilst a file gets down to the final shape. Cutting and shaping one's first plate can be a little daunting, but it is not difficult providing one does not rush it.

Pre-cut and etched to shape nameplates are also available from a number of manufacturers, including *C.G.W.*, *Jackson-Evans* and *LFC*. These are generally to 4mm scale but *Post-War Prototypes* also produce their range in 2mm and 7mm scales. If you do not want to bother with etched plates (though I feel that the effort and expense of them is well worthwhile) then *S.M.S. Model Products* have a range of waterslide nameplate transfers.

Paint specifications

To conclude our look at liveries, a brief mention must be made about paint specifications. I have talked glibly about Brunswick green, Sherwood green, different hues of blue and shades of grey. Colours can be rather subjective. We do not, for example, all perceive a certain shade of red in the same way, but the railways have to be more objective. Hence BR have a list of paint specifications which cover many different aspects of their business. Some of the specifications seem to belong to a different age. Spec 23A dealing with 'marking enamels and paints for use on parcel bags, hampers, cartage and wagon sheets' seems to have a curiously historic air about it. Others such as Spec 44A ('undercoating and enamel for renovation of stove enamelled and plastics panelling') and Spec 50 ('self-adhesive preformed protective tape and surface preparatory materials for the protection of steel surfaces') have little relevance to our railway modelling. We are more interested in the shades of paint applied to locomotives and these are covered by Spec 30A, Spec 53, Spec 71 and Spec 81. Some of the main colours from each of these BR specifications are as follows:

Spec 30A (the 'Green Era')

Item 9	Red	for bufferbeams and buffer stocks.
Item 34	Locomotive Green	this is the 'Brunswick green' for the locomotive's superstructure
Item 36	Locomotive Black	for underframe and bogies.
Item 40	Black Lacquer	for wheels, axles and bogie framing.
Item 43	Grey	for roof areas.
Item 50	Electric Blue	for AC electric locomotives.
Item 58	Sherwood Green	intermediate body colour for diesel locomotives

Spec 53 (airless spray paints for initial blue/grey livery)

Item 13	Rail Blue	for the locomotive's superstructure.
Item 16	Black	for underframe and bogies.
Item 17	Yellow	for warning panels and ends.

Spec 71 (later gloss paints for blue/grey livery)

Item 28	Rail White	for handrails and other details.
Item 31	Warning Yellow	for locomotive ends.
Item 33	Rail Red	for background to nameplates.

Item 37	Rail Grey	for HST window surround areas.
Item 37A	Executive Light Grey	for APT bodysides.
Item 37B	Executive Dark Grey	for APT window surround areas.
Item 39	Black	for bufferbeams and other details.
Item 40	Rail Blue	for locomotive superstructures and HST body sides.
Item 50	Underframe Black	for underframe and bogies.

Spec 81 (the current specification for BR finishing paints; all are Gloss Finish unless otherwise specified)

Item 200	Executive Light Grey	the light grey shade of the 'Inter-City' livery style.
Item 201	Executive Dark Grey	the dark grey shade of the 'Inter-City' livery style.
Item 202	Warning Yellow	used for locomotive ends and on HST power cars.
Item 203	Rail White	the white body side stripe of the 'Inter-City' livery style.
Item 204	Rail Red	the red body side stripe of the 'Inter-City' livery style; also the red shade of the 'Railfreight' livery style.
Item 205	Black	used for bufferbeams, HST roofs and ends, and on underframes.
Item 206	Rail Grey	diesel locomotive roofs and other details.
Item 207	Rail Blue	the familiar shade of blue for locomotive superstructures.
Item 208	Provincial Light Blue	the light blue body side stripe of the 'ScotRail' livery style.
Item 210	Yellow Uroalkyd	used for road vehicles but now obsolete; item 202 used instead.
Item 215	Black Semi-Gloss	used for cab window surrounds.
Item 226	Rail Freight Grey	the grey shade of the 'Railfreight' livery style.
Item 229	Dark Brunswick Green	used on a few Class '47's and a '50'.
Item 291	Underframe Black	a slightly lower gloss than item 205, its use on underframes has declined.
Item 500	Orange Band	used for body side safety lines.

As modellers we are fortunate in there being a number of paint manufacturers who include BR colours in their range. Firms such as *Humbrol, Precision Paints, Gloy, D.B.I.* and *Rail Repaints* all have a selection of railway shades in their collections. There is also a large range of transfers of the BR insignia and locomotive numbers. The traditional waterslide transfers are produced by *S.M.S.* and *Kemco*, whilst the dry print variety come from the *Model Railway (Mfg)*

Company with their 'Kingsprint' range. *Howes* market a range of rub-on transfers in 2mm, 4mm and 7mm scales, whilst *P.C.Models* produce two types of transfer. Their 'Pressfix' series are applied dry, pressed into position and then the carrier tissue is removed with water. This method leaves only a very small varnish surround to the transfer and their 'Methfix' range leave no varnish surround at all. These are applied, as the name suggests, with a solution of methylated spirit and water. After positioning and leaving to dry for a few minutes, the carrier tissue is again removed with a little water. Although it sounds rather messy using meths, the results are excellent and long lasting, and well worth the effort. *Woodhead Models* also produce a range of 'Pressfix' transfers. *Replica Railways* have a wide selection of transfers in 2mm, 4mm and 7mm scales, whilst *FMR* also have an expanding range.

One could devote a whole book to the subject of BR liveries but the above notes should give a broad outline of the styles of painting and the variety of colours used.

We live in a very exciting time as far as BR liveries go, with new colour schemes on the horizon. Keep your eyes open for the stylish swallow emblem that has appeared on some HST power cars and watch out for the striking new two-tone grey Railfreight livery. It is quite a sight, incorporating as it does some rather flashy new body side markings and insignia.

TWELVE
Modelling techniques and tools for the job

Having looked at the prototype from a number of different angles our thoughts can now turn towards modelling some of these modern forms of motive power. Techniques used in modelling are largely a matter of common sense and railway modelling is no different in this respect. Whilst one can learn quite a lot by reading the articles that appear each month in the model magazines, there is no substitute for having a go oneself. There may be disasters along the way but in the end you will triumph. There is little point in me going over ground which is already in print. A comprehensive bibliography at the rear outlines books which may be useful and magazine articles that have appeared over the years covering various aspects of modelling diesel and electric locomotives. But don't just read; I am firmly convinced that actually doing the modelling is the best way to go forward and achieve something worthwhile. Reading might provide some inspiration but it does not give tangible results. Give some thought to modelling by all means, but do not spend all the time pipe-dreaming. After all, railway modelling is a hobby which requires some active participation. If we want to sit back and just absorb rather than create, then there is always that rectangular box in the corner of the living room to turn to!

Tools

In detailing proprietary models, and here we shall be concentrating on the plastic-bodied mass produced examples, very few tools are required. No need for that well-equipped workshop with a lathe, machine tools and so on: just a few simple hand tools are quite sufficient. Indeed it can be an advantage not to be encumbered with too much equipment. For example, have you noticed photographers at the lineside with all their different cameras, lenses, tripods and other gadgets? Along comes a train and by the time they have decided which lens to use, checked the aperture and shutter speed, it is half a mile down the line and out of range. On the other hand, those with just a simple camera do not have to worry about their equipment and have time to compose an attractive picture. The same applies to tools, for they are only an aid to our modelling. The important thing is that they are effective for the task in hand. Whilst there is no hard and fast rule as to which tools to use, some are obviously of greater value than others for any particular job. Here are some of the basic ones I use in my modelling:

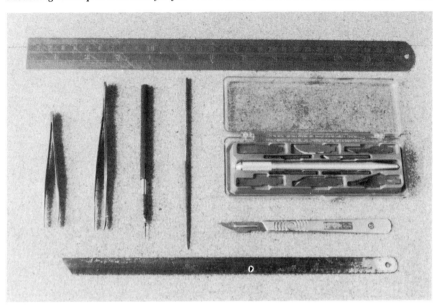

Above *A range of simple tools is all that is required to modify proprietary ready-to-run models.*

Below *A soldering iron and some other tools are also useful.*

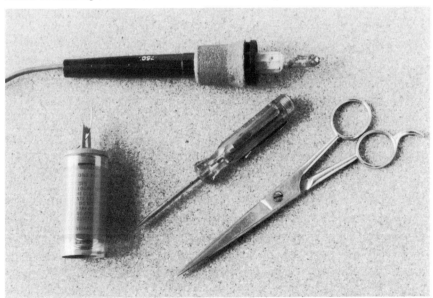

Craft knives When dealing with plastics, top of the list of tools must come the craft knives. One becomes attached to these in a way that one does not with any other tool. They almost become an extension of oneself. The knife has to be light and comfortable, and I prefer the slim surgical type for the majority of tasks. They are nicely balanced and the sharp surgical blades easily slice through the plastic, though they are quite delicate and the pointed tip can sometimes snap off. Therefore a medium-duty type of knife is useful for more onerous work, together with a selection of differently shaped blades to reach into awkward corners.

Steel rule A metal straight edge is essential for the accurate cutting of plastic card, paper and other materials. The best buy is a 12in long stainless steel ruler marked in both metric and imperial measurements.

Razor saw Modifying plastic-bodied locomotives often entails cutting through the superstructure to alter various features. The best tool for this job is a razor saw; a saw with a thin narrow blade having very fine teeth. Although this is a useful piece of equipment, I must confess to not actually owning one myself. For cutting plastic bodies I use an old hacksaw blade, maybe not as elegant as a razor saw but almost as effective. This does illustrate, however, that one is not bound to a strict list of mandatory tools for modelling. On occasion one can use something that purists might reject!

Needle files A range of miniature needle files is a valuable addition to the work box. In particular, the flat and half round shaped files are especially useful for various smoothing jobs.

Tweezers These are always handy for holding and positioning small or delicate items. A pair with serrated points is to be recommended for extra grip.

A metal point Holes for handrails, bufferbeam pipework and so forth, can be made in the plastic locomotive bodyshell by a number of different methods. Probably the most professional way is with a pin chuck and a fine drill bit. However I prefer to use a needle mounted in a handle, heating it and then melting a hole through the plastic. Again, maybe not the orthodox method but one I find effective. If it works, what is wrong with that?

Scissors For cutting paper and thin card a pair of scissors is required. The types used by hairdressers are the best for they have nice long sharp points for accurate work. There is a great temptation to also use them for cutting pieces of wire, but do try to resist this for the blades of the scissors will soon become blunt. Pliers having a wire-cutting surface are the right tools for that job.

Screwdriver Dismantling the model locomotive into its component parts often requires the use of a screwdriver: the small plastic-handled variety is quite sufficient for our needs.

Soldering iron Finally there comes the inevitable soldering iron. Whilst its use when detailing plastic locomotive bodies is rather limited, it comes into its own when, for example, one is fitting extra pick-ups to a bogie and wires need to be soldered.

These, then, are the basic tools used in detailing proprietary ready-to-run models. I think you will agree that there is nothing here in the way of specialized or expensive equipment. The most important tool is a good quality craft knife with a supply of sharp blades.

Materials

As with tools, the list of materials contains nothing really out of the ordinary. The choice of which material to use for a particular job is largely one of personal preference.

Plastic card When talking about plastic card one immediately thinks of the 'Plastikard' sheets produced by *Slater's*. Available in a variety of thicknesses, this is a very versatile material which can be easily cut and filed to shape and then glued into position. A transparent version is also made for use as a glazing material, but a cheaper option is to use a clear plastic one finds supporting collars in shirt boxes. The motto, of course, is to keep an eye out for suitable modelling materials and never throw anything away.

Ordinary card In our haste to use new materials let us not forget that old faithful — card. Although plastic card has taken over many of its former roles, card still has an important part to play in modelling. Indeed it sometimes has the edge when it comes to curved surfaces. Card and plastic are perfectly compatible and there are no problems using the two materials together. The only thing to watch when using card is to take care when cutting it. It is easy to produce a ragged edge which spoils the appearance, so use a sharp blade or scissors when cutting out pieces.

Paper Good quality paper is also a handy modelling material. Thin strips can be used for the beading around windows and grilles, whilst larger pieces can simulate roof hatches and other panelling on the bodywork.

Wire Various thicknesses of wire are used to fabricate some of the smaller details found on the locomotive superstructure. Handrails, underframe pipework and windscreen wipers can all be formed from different lengths of wire bent to shape.

Odds and ends Other bits and pieces are also useful when detailing and improving proprietary models. It is amazing what one collects over the years and puts into the scrapbox. It may look like a load of old junk, but eventually a use will be found for the majority of items. Discarded pieces from old plastic kits can often find a new life when fashioned into a different shape and attached to another model, old strips of foam rubber can be glued inside locomotive body-shells to help deaden the noise of the motor, press studs from the sewing basket can be made into handbrake wheels and other household items can be used to advantage. Really it is a matter of keeping one's eyes open and using a little imagination.

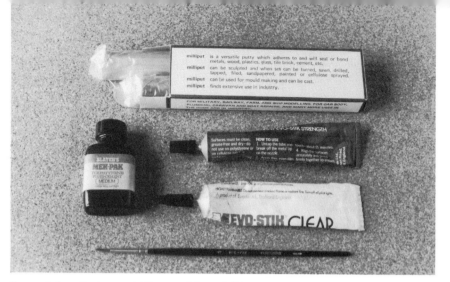

Some of the adhesives and fillers used in modelling.

Adhesives and fillers

The range and variety of glues available is at times most bewildering, with claims and counter claims made about the merits of each. For most purposes I have found that three types of adhesive are sufficient.

Liquid polystyrene cement This is used for bonding the 'Plastikard' type of material. The adhesive is applied with a fine sable paint-brush and moves by capillary action in and around the plastic pieces, eventually setting and forming a strong joint. However since the liquid cement has no body to it, the pieces to be joined must be accurately aligned to ensure a good bond.

Normal polystyrene cement The normal type of polystyrene adhesive, the kind one buys in a tube, covers the majority of our model detailing tasks. As well as sticking plastic together, it is also suitable for card and paper.

Impact adhesive Where metal parts such as couplings and handrails have to be glued into place, it is best to use an impact adhesive. Check, though, that the glue does not affect the plastic as some brands do have a tendency to soften and distort some types of material. The key is not to spread the adhesive too thickly; a thin, even film of cement on each of the surfaces to be bonded is all that is required.

The main thing to remember about all adhesives is that they work best, and hence give the maximum amount of strength to a joint, when the surfaces they are bonding are clean, dry and free from grease. It is important too, to follow the instructions on the packet or tube for optimum results. If it says coat each surface and leave for fifteen minutes until dry to the touch, then take note of this advice. It is easy to be impatient and try to rush things, only to become unstuck (both literally and metaphorically) later on.

I have made no mention of the cyanoacrylate 'superglues' or epoxy resins. The superglues tend to be somewhat overrated, so why pay more when a conventional adhesive works just as well? As most of our detailing and conversion work is concerned with plastic and card, polystyrene cements are generally quite adequate. However if you feel at home with either of these adhesives then by all means use them.

Filler A good body filler is essential for much of the conversion and detailing work undertaken on plastic locomotive superstructures. For filling in gaps, building up areas, covering over unsightly marks and smoothing out joins it has no equal. Like adhesives, there are several brands of filler on the market. Some are sold in tubes and others in tins. I prefer the two-part epoxy type of putty which comes in stick form. Equal amounts of the two sticks provided are mixed together until a uniform consistency is achieved, then it is ready to use. An advantage of this filler is that the individual sticks have an indefinite shelf life and only become active when mixed together. Sometimes the filler in tins can get hard and a proportion of it has to be wasted. A disadvantage of the two-part filler, however, is that it is slightly more messy to use than the already mixed varieties.

Whichever type of filler one uses, it is necessary to remove the excess and leave a smooth finish. Carve away any large chunks of filler with a knife and then file down to the rough shape required. Finally use wet-and-dry paper, well lubricated with water, to achieve that smooth surface ready for painting.

Painting

The main question here is whether to use an airbrush for painting or the more traditional sable paint-brushes. Again this is largely a matter of personal preference. I like to completely finish my models before painting them and hence tend to brush paint rather than use a spray. On the other hand, if you paint the individual pieces prior to assembly or mask over certain parts of the bodywork, then you may feel like using an airbrush. The choice is yours.

As with adhesives, the important thing about painting is cleanliness. Before starting, make sure that the bodywork and bogies of the locomotive are clean and free from dust and grease. If any etched brass pieces have been used then remember that they will need a coat of self-etch primer so that the metal will accept the paint. The environment too, must be clean. It is no good trying to paint in a room with people walking to and fro as the air will be disturbed too much. Also watch what you are wearing yourself. That woolly jumper may look very nice but the fibres will get onto the surface of the model and spoil the finish. If using a brush then work at a steady pace with the paint not too thick. Do not scratch along but use fairly broad strokes in a single direction. Try to cover at least one side of the body in a single go; if you have missed any bits you can always go over them again with a second coat. Finally put the model under a shoebox or clean biscuit tin and leave it to dry thoroughly. Resist the temptation to lift the lid or touch the model until the paint has hardened properly, otherwise it is back to square one.

★ ★ ★

Right then — let us put some of these words and thoughts into practice and look in more detail at a selection of some of my favourite types of modern motive power.

The following series of photographs illustrates some of the stages in detailing a Mainline Class '45'. I wanted to convert it into a Class '46', so some further alterations were also required. The first step is to unclip the body from the chassis, an easy enough job, then, unscrew the tension lock couplings and the pivoting wheel-sets within the bogies. The couplings extend too far out on the model and look unsightly, so cut 4mm from the flat area on which the coupling rests. Remove the hook and spring from the coupling, and cut off the spring housing. Drill a new hole into the flat area and screw the now modified coupling back into place.

Cut off each of the buffer-beams from the locomotive's bodyshell and glue these, with a contact adhesive, to the front of the bogies above the couplings.

Adding details to the bodywork; they are simply made up from off-cuts of paper and card.

'A' side details added to the model are shown in white. The roof hatches and body-side footsteps have been plated over with thin card. The additional side grille has been cut into the body and the resulting aperture filled with a piece of card that has been scribed to represent the new louvres.

Further work being undertaken on the model in the shape of adding strips of paper to the bogie side-frames.

'B' side details at the number one end of the model. Note the speedometer cable on the bogie made from a piece of wire. The Class '46's have a different design of battery box cover so the details on the Mainline model were filed off and replaced by rectangular flat pieces of card.

Above *'B' side details at the number two end of the model. Note the altered rainstrip, most of the upper one at cantrail level having been carved off with a sharp knife.*

Below *Almost ready for the paint shops. Front end details have been filed off to create the later style of nose section without the headcode boxes. The two circular lamps are just the heads cut from a couple of pins and glued into position. The front cab windows have been flush-glazed and, as you can see, the windscreen wipers are being added.*

THIRTEEN
High Speed Trains

When the last HST opens up its engines, spews its exhaust over the concourse at Paddington and heads west into the setting sun, there will be a large group of enthusiasts watching its final departure from the London terminus, standing at the end of platform 8. Today the trainspotters there seldom give the HSTs a second glance. I suppose this is understandable as one can go to Paddington, St Pancras and Kings Cross at any time and see a never ending procession of HSTs. This will not last forever, though. In a few years, with electrification of the East Coast main line, HSTs at Kings Cross will be just a memory like the 'Deltics', 'A3's and 'A4's, and the Stirling 'Singles' before them. Eventually they will be displaced from the other routes too, such is the rapid march of progress.

The Blue Pullmans — *'Précurseurs du HST'*
The French railway magazine *La Vie du Rail* once described the Blue Pullman trains as *'précurseurs du HST'* — the forerunners of the HST. Mechanically perhaps not, but as the concept of a dedicated express diesel passenger unit, then they had much in common with the HSTs that appeared over ten years later.

Six different types of vehicle were built by Metropolitan-Cammell in Birmingham, to make up the Blue Pullman trains:

M60090-M60093	Driving motor brake first
W60094-W60099	Driving motor brake second
W60644-W60649	Intermediate motor parlour second
M60730-M60733	Intermediate motor kitchen first
W60734-W60739	Trailer kitchen first
M60740-M60743 W60744-W60749 }	Trailer parlour first

These vehicles were formed into five Blue Pullman trains; two six-car sets and three eight-car sets. The two six-car sets entered service in July 1960 on the former Midland line from Manchester Central through the Peak District to London St Pancras. Only one of the sets was used at a time, the other being kept spare. The eight-car sets began working a few months later in September 1960; one from Wolverhampton via Birmingham Snow Hill to Paddington ('The Birmingham Pullman') and the other from Bristol to Paddington ('The Bristol

One of the 8-car Blue Pullman sets at Cardiff in 1973. The unit is in the later rail grey and blue livery with yellow ends.

Pullman'). The third set was initially kept as a spare but from the following September was used for 'The South Wales Pullman'.

Electrification from Euston to Manchester and Liverpool, and the introduction of new Pullman services on this route, made 'The Midland Pullman' redundant from April 1966 but the sets used on this route were eventually transferred to the Western Region to join the other Blue Pullmans there. Early in 1967 these two six-car sets were fitted with multiple-working jumper cables so that they could operate as a single twelve-car train if required: details are shown in *Figure 36*. Some of the acommodation was also altered so that they could cater for both first and second class Pullman clientele since originally the six-car sets were first class only. Further electrification in the West Midlands saw the demise of 'The Birmingham Pullman' in March 1967 and a general rearrangement of Western Region Pullman services.

Livery changes were also made to these trains around this period. Towards the end of 1966 the front ends of the units began to receive a coat of yellow paint. From a safety viewpoint this may have been all very well, but aesthetically it was a disaster. The following year saw the beginning of the end for the attractive Nanking blue and white colour scheme when one of the sets was turned out in rail grey and blue livery. Soon all the units were repainted like this: not a patch on the original style.

Services to Bristol and South Wales continued until May 1973. Then, with the introduction of new air-conditioned coaches on these routes the Blue Pullmans were sold for scrap and all were cut up.

Although it is many years since either *Tri-ang* or *Kitmaster* made their 00 gauge models of the Blue Pullman, a surprising number crop up on the secondhand market. Between them, these two firms made all the vehicles for both the six-car

Figure 36 The Blue Pullman - front end details

ORIGINAL   CONDITION

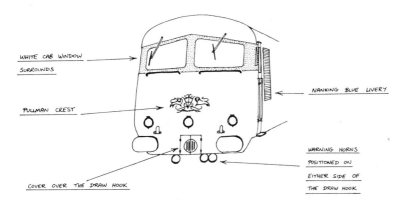

WHITE CAB WINDOW
SURROUNDS

NANKING BLUE LIVERY

PULLMAN CREST

WARNING HORNS
POSITIONED ON
EITHER SIDE OF
THE DRAW HOOK

COVER OVER THE DRAW HOOK

AS FITTED WITH MULTIPLE - WORKING JUMPERS

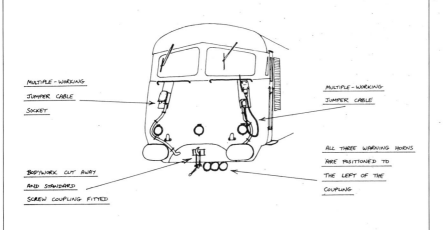

MULTIPLE - WORKING
JUMPER CABLE
SOCKET

MULTIPLE - WORKING
JUMPER CABLE

BODYWORK CUT AWAY
AND STANDARD
SCREW COUPLING FITTED

ALL THREE WARNING HORNS
ARE POSITIONED TO
THE LEFT OF THE
COUPLING

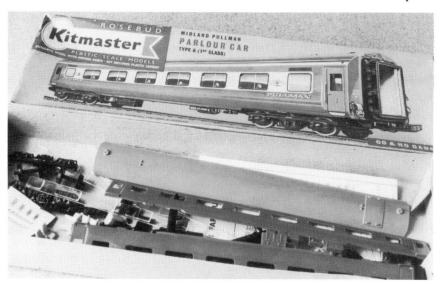

Above *An unmade* Kitmaster *trailer parlour first kit. These kits were well thought of by most modellers, but are exceedingly hard to find nowadays.*

Below *One of the earlier* Tri-ang *Blue Pullman vehicles with the separate flush-glazed window strip. This particular model is being converted into a kitchen car. The seating has been reduced in length and a card partition will be made to serve as the kitchen area. Compare the two bogies. The one on the right is as yet unmodified whilst the other has had most of the details filed off to make it look more like the prototype.*

and eight-car versions of the train, with the exception of the parlour second. The chief failing of the ready-to-run *Tri-ang* models lies in the bogies which look nothing like the prototype. Their appearance can be improved however by filing off all the details from the bogie sideframes and fabricating parts from plastic card that look more like the original features. Alternatively remove the entire bogie and replace it with the *Kitmaster* version which is more accurate.

The best way to produce the unavailable parlour second is to modify the *Tri-ang* parlour first. *Tri-ang*'s early production of these vehicles had the window strips as a separate push-fit moulding into the body side, giving an effective flush-glazed look. Later batches of their models had the more conventional body with the windows cut through the side with a glazing strip stuck behind. The early batch are the easier to alter for all one does is remove the entire window strip and make a new one out of thin plastic card with the required number of windows: the parlour second has seven large side windows as against the six of the parlour first. This method can also be used to produce the kitchen car, although, of course, this has a different window arrangement. Finally remember to paint the interior seating as this gives depth to the model.

The prototype HST

The initial concept of the HST envisaged a set of Mark 3 air-conditioned coaches sandwiched between single-ended locomotives at each end of the rake. The locomotives were given the class number '41', vacant since the withdrawal of the original 'Warships' at the end of 1967. The coaches had the usual couplings and side buffers, and were wired to the standard 1,000V single-phase AC/DC system. Indeed the intention was to number them in the same series as other loco-hauled coaches with the first class vehicles in the range 3217 to 3220 and the second class 5805 to 5808. Thus there is a gap in the numbering of the Mark 2 coaches. However before they were delivered, a new number series was allocated to cover the Mark 3 stock.

The prototype high speed locomotives and Mark 3 coaches consisted of twelve vehicles:

Class '41' 2,250hp Bo-Bo diesel-electric 41001, 41002.
Mark 3 restaurant second buffet   E10000.
Mark 3 restaurant unclassified kitchen   E10100.
Mark 3 first class open   E11000, E11001, E11002, M11003.
Mark 3 second class open   E12000, E12001, E12002, M12003.

All these vehicles were built in 1972 apart from the two catering coaches which were not completed until the middle of 1973. Meanwhile the other vehicles were formed into the prototype HST set.

By the autumn of 1974 the HST was regarded as a multiple-unit of Class '252'. Why '252'? If the Blue Pullmans had lasted beyond 1973 the six-car set would have been Class '250' and the eight-car Class '251'. Hence the next express passenger diesel-electric multiple-unit train became the Class '252' and it just

happened to be the prototype HST. The vehicles were also renumbered at this time into the coaching stock series as follows:

W43000	(ex 41001)	Driving motor brake (DMB)
W43001	(ex 41002)	Driving motor brake (DMB)
W40000	(ex E10000)	Trailer restaurant second buffet (TRSB)
W40500	(ex E10100)	Trailer restaurant unclassified kitchen (TRUK)
W41000	(ex E11000)	Trailer first (TF)
W41001	(ex E11002)	Trailer first (TF)
W41002	(ex M11003)	Trailer first (TF)
W42000	(ex E12000)	Trailer second (TS)
W42001	(ex E12002)	Trailer second (TS)
W42002	(ex M12003)	Trailer second (TS)

With this stock the prototype HST set was generally formed as follows (the asterisk indicates the kitchen or buffet end of the coach): DMB, TF, TF, *TRUK, TS, TRSB*, TS, TS, DMB. The remaining trailer first was kept as a spare. The other two Mark 3 coaches (E11001 and E12001) were later rebuilt in 1977 for use in the Royal Train.

The prototype HST, or set 252001 as it was now known, entered revenue-earning service for the first time on 5 May 1975. Its initial duties were on the Paddington to Bristol and Weston-super-Mare route, though it later also worked between Paddington and Swansea. Even after the introduction of the production HST sets into service in 1976, 252001 was still used on passenger duties until it was finally taken off these during November 1976.

The late 1970s found the two power cars of HST 252001 still gainfully employed hauling various APT vehicles on lines around the Derby area or along the West Coast main line. In the middle of 1979 W41000 was taken into

Left *The prototype HST approaching Bristol during its first week of revenue-earning service in May 1975.*

Right *A front view of one of the prototype HST power cars. Note that, unlike the production sets, these have standard buffers on each end of the vehicles.*

Below *Side view of a prototype HST power car. It has additional body side louvres compared to the later production build.*

departmental stock and renumbered ADB 975814. Known as Test Car 10, it was repainted in the blue and red colour scheme used on vehicles owned by the Research and the Mechanical & Electrical Engineering departments. Later, W43000 and W43001 became ADB 975812 and ADB 975813 respectively, though they retained their original Pullman-style rail grey and blue livery. ADB 975812 was extracted from store and spruced up for the GWR 150 celebrations of 1985. It now resides at the National Railway Museum in York carrying its original number, 41001. W40000 and W40500 entered departmental stock in

1982 as RDB 975984 and 977089 respectively, the latter subsequently being used as the guinea-pig for the 'Inter-City' livery style of dark and light grey now familiar on the HST fleet. The remaining five vehicles from 252001 are still in everyday use, having been modified in 1982 into standard trailer firsts numbered W41170 to W41174. By its very nature the prototype HST was a unique train, but it did operate for varying periods of time on four of the five regions of BR, thus having a wider use than might at first be imagined. In model form it would make something a little different from the usual HSTs one sees on layouts. There are problems though, in that there are many detail differences between the prototype and production units to the extent that a convincing train would be difficult to achieve without very drastic plastic surgery on the proprietary models. On the trailer vehicles the doors, bogies, roof details and the position of some of the windows on the catering cars all differ from the production batches. In the smaller scales one could probably get away with just repainting the coaches, but it is the power cars which cause the most trouble. The cab front is completely different in terms of window arrangement, length and curvature, as are the position and style of the side louvres. Scratchbuilding a new cab front would appear to be the only answer but would be a difficult operation due to the shape involved. In N gauge, however, it should be possible to carve a new front out of something like balsa wood. I have not tried this myself but it should work: why not have a go yourself and try to recreate this interesting and important train?

The production HST sets

Monday 4 October 1976 was an historic day for the British railway system. Did the entire Southern Region run without any cancellations on that day? Was it the day that the Stranraer to Euston through train actually reached its destination within ten minutes of the advertised time? Or was it the start of the week in which there were no locomotive failures on the Waterloo to Exeter line? No. Rather it was the day which saw the inauguration of 125mph HST services on BR. It was more than just the train itself which makes this day so significant: it is the complete package of train, track, signalling, speed, safety, comfort and the marketability of the whole service that is important. That autumn morning of 1976 brought a new confidence to the rail network and whilst some of the initial magic may have now gone, I for one still find the HSTs fascinating. To see them streaking through the countryside, to lie in bed and hear their characteristic sound penetrate the still night air, or even to stand by a dead power car and watch it slide silently out of the station as the rear one which is doing all the work gets ever louder before it screams past is far from being a dull and boring experience!

The original intention with the production HSTs was to have sets with the same formation and vehicle type on each of the regions they operated on but changing catering requirements soon saw these plans altered, with the cancellation of most of the order for TRUKs and the design of a new vehicle — the TRUB (trailer restaurant unclassified buffet). To provide better accommodation for the guard and increase the available luggage space, a further type appeared — the

Above *The combination of* Hornby *power cars and* Jouef *trailer vehicles can make an attractive model of the production HST sets.*

Below *The clean lines of the power cars are well illustrated in this view of E43098. Note the absence of an underframe tank directly to the left of the bogie. Originally W43002 to W43037 were fitted with a secondary fuel tank in this position, but they tended to cause instability in the vehicles and so were later isolated. Power cars from W43038 onwards were never fitted with this tank.*

Left *A HST set arrives back at Derby Litchurch Lane works after a test run to Darlington. Note the lack of a roof-mounted exhaust deflector on the power car.*

Right *Later batches of the power cars were fitted with the exhaust deflector plates from the start, as shown by E43117 here.*

Below right Hornby *HST power cars. The modified one on the left has been fitted with an exhaust deflector on the roof made from plastic card.*

TGS (trailer guard second). Later changes on the catering front resulted in the modification of further vehicles to take into account new ideas and differing demand for full meals or light refreshments on board trains. This gave rise to new types such as the TLUK (trailer lounge unclassified kitchen), the TRB (trailer restaurant buffet), the TRFB (trailer restaurant first buffet) and the TRFK (trailer restaurant first kitchen). It is worth looking at the different vehicles which go to make up the production HST sets in a little more detail.

Driving motor brake (DMB)

These are the power cars at each end of the rake of HST trailers. A total of 197 were built by British Rail Engineering at Crewe between 1976 and 1982, being numbered from 43002 to 43198. Originally these power car numbers were prefixed with the letters 'W', 'E' or 'SC' depending on the region they were allocated to. Since then, some of the power cars have been moved between the regions and a prefix is no longer carried before their number.

Visually, the most obvious variation within the HST power cars concerns the presence or absence of the body side windows behind the luggage space doors. Accommodation for the guard was initially provided in a compartment at the rear end of the power car, but with the introduction of the TGS vehicle in 1980, this was omitted on the later batches. Thus 43002 to 43152 have these rear windows, whilst the later-built 43153 to 43198 do not. Of the ready-to-run models available, the 00 gauge *Hornby* and the N gauge *Graham Farish* items are based on the earlier power cars with the guard's accommodation, whilst the 00 gauge *Lima* model is of the later style without the windows.

Figure 37 HST power car details

REAR END DETAILS

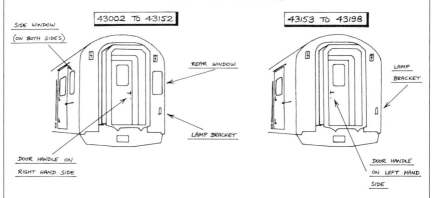

ROOF - MOUNTED COOLING UNIT GRILLES

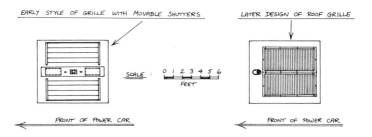

ROOF - MOUNTED EXHAUST DEFLECTOR

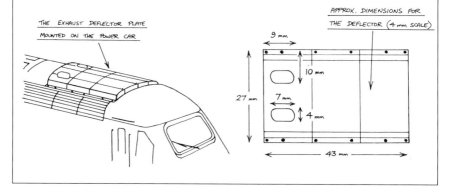

The design of the roof-mounted cooling unit grilles also varies. These are situated between the engine compartment doors and the rear luggage space, and are usually of two types. The early design has movable shutters while the later type has a closer-mesh style of grille. It would appear that the early design is fitted to 43002 to 43152 and the later type on the other power cars. It is difficult to be categoric on this since checking HST roof details is not the easiest thing in the world to do. Drawings of these roof grilles and other power car details are shown in *Figure 37*.

After a new train has been in service for a while, modifications are often found to be necessary to improve the performance or reliability of certain features of the design. The production HST sets have been no different. Externally, the most noticeable change to the power cars has been the fitting of deflector plates on the roofs. Exhaust fumes tended to be sucked down over the trailing cab when the train was travelling at speed, leaving a dirty deposit on the windscreen. As an experiment, W43013 was fitted with a deflector plate in August 1977 to alter the flow of air along the roof and thus minimize the pollution of the cab ends. The favourable results achieved led to all new power cars from E43114 onwards being fitted with these plates. Earlier members were equipped retrospectively and this included W43120 and W43121 which had been built earlier out of sequence and hence initially lacked this feature. Another modification that appeared during the early 1980s was the addition of a water strip below the front windscreen;

The rear of the Hornby *power cars. On the modified one (left) the gangway door has been painted yellow and the overhead live wire flashes picked out in white.*

details of these features and other front end details of the HSTs are outlined in *Figure 38*.

The *Hornby* model was the first ready-to-run one of the HST power car. Although it is a very accurate representation of the original, there are a few things that can be done to improve its appearance and performance. Extra ballast weights can be added to the underframe of the chassis if desired and there is plenty of room for this. The driver's desk controls can be picked out in a little

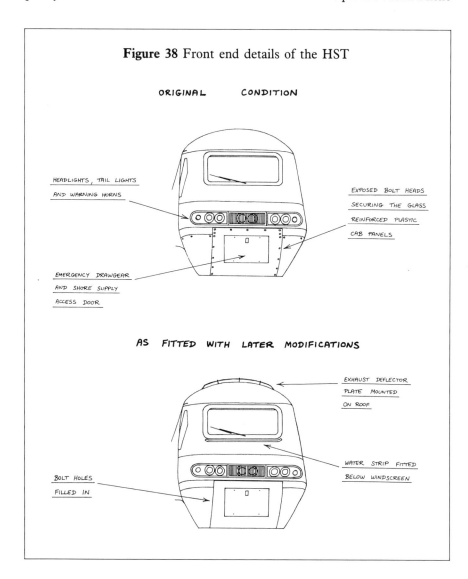

Figure 38 Front end details of the HST

colour and the seats painted black. A driver can be glued in place to add to the effect. Usually one paints the side of the wheels on models in black to tone them down but on the HST this is not necessary as they are equipped with disc brakes, so leave the wheel sides bright and unpainted.

With the body, the first thing is to decide which variant of power car one intends to model. If one of the later batches is being tackled, then file off the earlier style of roof-mounted shutters and fabricate a new one from plastic card scribed with the later grille design. The guard's compartment window is also filled in. Use a rectangle of plastic card to fill the aperture and finally smooth over with modelling putty. The roof-mounted exhaust deflector plate can be made from a thin piece of plastic card, lightly scored so that it can be bent easily to fit the curved contours of the roof, and glued in position.

More general improvements for the power cars as a whole include removing the moulded glazing units and flush glazing all the windows. I find this the most difficult and frustrating part of all the modelling I do, but the results are worthwhile. Cut pieces of transparent plastic material so that they fit exactly into the window aperture without any distortion. If the glazing bends it spoils the whole effect, so it is better to have the glazing a fraction too small rather than too large. Finally glue it into position: I find that the impact type of adhesive is best for this job as it has sufficient 'body' to help hold the glazing in place.

The front headlight and horn cover moulding is a rather poor fit on the model. However the judicious use of a file will make it a much better flush fit into the bodyshell. Other excess mouldings on the bodywork which need to be removed are the dummy jumper cables on the rear end, the paint guide lines along the side and flash marks around the cab doors.

On the plus side, do not forget to add the bogie damper brackets which are a prominent feature of the bottom edge of the body.

Using modelling putty, fill in and smooth over the unprototypical notches below the cab doors and in the middle of the body. Leave enough space behind though, so that the body can still clip onto the underframe securing tabs. If the guard's compartment is being retained then a floor and partition made from card can be stuck into place.

To help deaden noise, some strips of plastic foam can be glued inside the sides and roof of the body, but make sure they do not impede the rotation of the bogies. Finally before reassembling the model, check that none of the wiring has been disturbed or come adrift.

Trailer first (TF)
The first class accommodation in the HST is provided by these trailer firsts. Like all the trailer vehicles, they were built at the Derby Litchurch Lane works of British Rail Engineering, entering service between 1976 and 1982 and numbered from 41003 to 41169. In addition to these TFs, five of the surplus Class '252' cars were modified to this configuration in 1982, becoming 41170 to 41174. The number series was further extended from 41175 to 41177 in 1983 with the conversion of three trailer seconds to carry first class passengers. However in the

following year 41177 reverted to its original second class status.

Unlike the power cars, the HST trailer vehicles still generally carry a regional prefix letter before their number. The initial allocations were as follows:

W41003-W41056	E41057-E41086	E41175-E41177
W41121-W41174	E41097-E41120	SC41087-SC41096

Again, inter-regional transfers have altered the position somewhat, especially in respect of some WR coaches moving to the ER.

A number of manufacturers have made models of the HST trailer vehicles. In the ready-to-run field, *Graham Farish* cater for the N gauge followers whilst in 00 gauge there are models from *Hornby* and *Lima*. The *Hornby* ones are very much under scale length and also incorrect in a number of details, so must really be discounted as the amount of work needed to get them up to an acceptable standard is not worth the effort. To be fair to *Hornby* though, their HST coaches are really aimed more at the toy train market where sharp radius curves and limited clearances abound. Furthermore not everyone has the room for full length HST coaches on their layouts, so they can be used as a compromise.

Another firm that made the Mark 3 coaches on which the HST trailers are based was *Jouef*. Because these 00 gauge models are of the Mark 3 coach rather than the HST cars there are some minor differences. However these can be easily rectified. HSTs have a slightly different arrangement of air extractors on the roof from the loco-hauled Mark 3 stock. Carve off the two outer extractors at each end of the coach and cover the central ones with a rectangular piece of plastic card 7mm by 6mm. The paint used on the roof of the *Jouef* model tends to wear off the ridges, not adhering too well to the type of plastic used. Give the inside of the roof a coat of black paint, then if the paint does wear off it will not show.

On the interior, decide which colour scheme to paint the seats. If the exterior of the coach is to be in the original rail blue and grey livery, then the seats should be a rather bilious shade of orange with white antimacassars and black armrests.

Right *Removing the two outer extractors on each end of the coach roof with a sharp knife.*

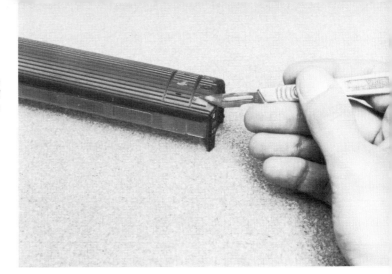

Right *Shaving off the raised moulded line on the bodyside of the coach.*

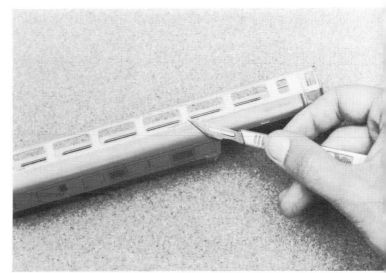

Right *Two rectangular pieces of plastic card are glued to the underside of the coach at one end, on each side of the bogie pivot, to stop the vehicle rocking.*

Left *The Jouef Mark 3 coach in its component parts.*

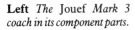

Orange table tops, a deep maroon carpet and cream curtains complete the picture. If the livery of the coach is to be in the 'Inter-City' light and dark grey colour scheme, then the seats are a deep pink colour with white antimacassars and black armrests. The table tops are white whilst the carpet and curtains are deep pink. Before fixing back the roof, do not forget to paint little blue squares below the top edge on the inside of the windows to represent the first class accommodation stickers. Also beside them, on one half of the coach, paint red dots to signify the 'No smoking' section. Some model figures can also be fitted inside the vehicle if desired: have a few sitting down and others walking about.

One of the characteristics of Mark 3 and HST stock is the smooth transition from body to roof. With the roof securely in place, carefully fill in the join along the length of the model with body putty and after it has set, smooth over with wet and dry paper. A raised moulding line on the model separates the blue from the grey of the colour scheme and this can be gently shaved off with the point of a sharp blade if desired.

Before refitting the end gangways (removed in order to lift the roof) pull out the buffers and cut off the buffer stocks. Smooth over the resulting holes in the bufferbeam with filler. Just behind the bufferbeams at each corner, glue short pieces of matchstick to represent the inter-vehicle connecting sockets, and paint them orange.

Finally we come to the bogies, which are really super little mouldings in their own right. To stop the coach rocking, a common fault of many ready-to-run models, glue two rectangular pieces of plastic card either side of the pivot at one end only. These form rubbing plates on which the bogie will rest. Choose the more true-running bogie of the pair and fit it at this end. Do not make any rubbing plates for the other end of the model, just refit the bogie. The idea behind the rubbing plates at one end only is that it forms a stable base for the coach body to rest on whilst the unmodified end allows the vehicle to overcome any track irregularities.

Trailer second (TS)

These are the most numerous type of HST trailer and entered stock between 1976 and 1985. There is not space here to give a full description of their entry into service but since the bodyshell of the trailer second is identical to the trailer first, the same modelling notes apply. However the seating and interior colour scheme is different. For the original blue and grey livery, the seats are a greenish-blue with black armrests; the table tops are also this green-blue shade whilst the carpet is dark blue. No antimacassars or curtains are provided in this second class accommodation. For the refurbished coaches in the 'Inter-City' grey livery the seats are bright red , again with black armrests. Table tops are cream and the carpet is red.

Some of the TS carriages have had their seating altered to increase the capacity from 72 to 76, resulting in more face-to-back seats and fewer tables. The top diagram of *Figure 39* shows this modified arrangement. If modelling one of the vehicles in this condition, then make a false floor to cover the recess between the

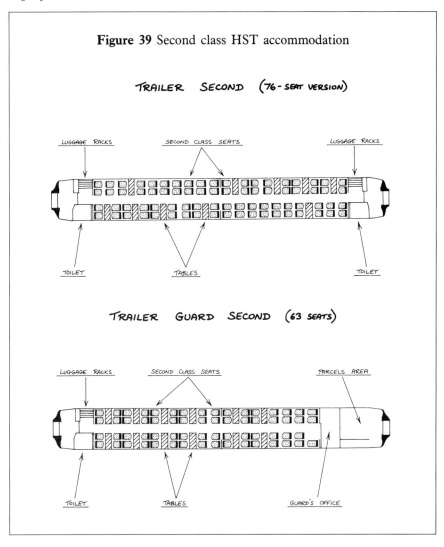

Figure 39 Second class HST accommodation

TRAILER   SECOND   (76-SEAT VERSION)

LUGGAGE RACKS   SECOND CLASS SEATS   LUGGAGE RACKS

TOILET   TABLES   TOILET

TRAILER   GUARD   SECOND   (63 SEATS)

LUGGAGE RACKS   SECOND CLASS SEATS   PARCELS AREA

TOILET   TABLES   GUARD'S OFFICE

bogie pivots and after cutting the *Jouef* interior into individual seats, glue them into their new positions. The four additional seats required can either be cut from another interior strip, perhaps from one used when modelling the trailer guard second, or fabricated up from pieces of plastic card.

Trailer guard second (TGS)
These vehicles were a later addition to the HST building programme, following complaints about the standard of accommodation provided for the guard in the

rear compartment of the power cars. The original intention was to classify these as GTS (guard trailer second), indeed on at least the first of these vehicles the end data panel on the coach had on it the code 'GTS'. Soon though, they were coded TGS, entering stock between 1980 and 1982.

In 00 gauge, *Lima* produce a ready made example of the TGS. However it is quite easy to make one of these vehicles using the *Jouef* trailer second as the basis. The roof details on the TGS differ slightly from the TS in that there is no toilet at the guard's end of the coach and hence no water tank in the roof. Inside the vehicle, the seating can be rearranged to the layout shown in the bottom diagram of *Figure 39*. Additional doors at the guard's end of the body are scribed into the plastic and a recess for the door handle is gouged out. The stepboard beneath these doors can be extended using a small piece of plastic card. The beading around the window at the guard's end is removed with a sharp knife and the small end window, and part of the larger one, is filled in with body putty and smoothed over when set. New beading, from a thin strip of plastic, can then be fixed around the newly formed window.

Trailer restaurant second buffet (TRSB)
The early plans for the production HST sets envisaged just two types of catering car: the TRSB and the TRUK.

Above left *The trailer guard second vehicle can be readily converted from a* Jouef *Mark 3 as illustrated here. The small end window and part of the adjoining one are filled in with body putty and smoothed over when set with wet-and-dry paper. On the bogie, notice that the coil springs have been painted yellow.*

Left *A completed* Jouef *Mark 3 coach modified into a HST trailer second. Note the revised arrangement of details on the end of the roof.*

Right *Bodyside and roof details of TRSB E40020. Note the smooth transition from body to roof with no visible join. This vehicle is now numbered 40420.*

Unfortunately, of the four ready-to-run models of HST catering cars, none are of the TRSB, or indeed the TRUK either. The models, one in N gauge and three in 00 gauge, are all based on the TRUB vehicle. It is a pity about this duplication, particularly in 00 gauge. Fortunately *Modern Traction Kits* have produced 4mm scale kits for the TRSB, and also the TRUK. So whilst it is possible to convert the *Jouef* TRUB into the other types of catering car by cutting out some of the windows and filling in others, it is probably not worth the time or effort. However with the short *Hornby* model it is easy to produce the various catering vehicles by simply painting the new window shapes on the flush glazing strip. Use the eight-window TF or TS for this though, rather than their TRUB.

Trailer restaurant buffet (TRB) and Trailer restaurant unclassified kitchen (TRUK)

To provide more comprehensive catering facilities for WR internal services, ten of their TRSBs were converted to TRBs in late 1984 and early 1985. Numbered 40204 to 40213, this modification resulted in their seating being reduced from the 35 of the TRSB to 23 first class-style seats, for unclassified use.

The other initial type of catering car on the production HST sets was the TRUK. The full kitchen facilities provided in the TRUKs were soon found to be too generous for the level of demand, so in 1981 almost half of them were withdrawn from regular use. One, 40515, was converted for use as part of the Royal Train, whilst two others (40519 and 40520) were altered into modular catering cars for the West Coast main line. Another, 40513, was converted into the 'Executive Saloon' for charter use. In the spring of 1985 the remaining TRUKs were withdrawn from service. Three were reclassified as trailer restaurant first kitchens (TRFK) for use on East Coast Pullman workings whilst the rest were stored for later conversion into further loco-hauled modular catering cars, eventually appearing in their new form in the middle of 1987. During 1985 and 1986 though, some were still to be seen in the formations of HST sets to cover for a shortage of catering vehicles.

Trailer lounge unclassified kitchen (TLUK)

The solitary TLUK, or 'Executive Saloon' as it is better known, was converted from 40513 towards the end of 1983, and retains this number. Designed as a mobile luxury conference room with seating for eight people, when on hire to a party or group it is marshalled in a suitable HST set between the power car and the front trailer first.

Trailer restaurant first kitchen (TRFK)

During 1985 three of the surplus TRUKs, numbers 40501, 40505 and 40511, were refurbished for use on the two East Coast Pullman services introduced in that year: namely 'The Yorkshire Pullman' and 'The Tees-Tyne Pullman'.

Trailer restaurant unclassified buffet (TRUB)

The TRUB is probably the most familiar of all the HST catering vehicles. All the

The seating arrangement in a TRUB or TRFB. It is an easy matter to cut the Jouef *1st Class seating strip with a saw and rearranging the seats into their correct positions. The partition around the buffet and kitchen section of the vehicle is made up from card.*

ready-to-run models of HST catering cars are of the TRUB. Similar modelling notes apply to these vehicles as to the other HST cars. The seats in the *Jouef* 00 gauge model can be located in their correct positions by again making a false floor, cutting out the individual seats and sticking them in place.

Trailer restaurant first buffet (TRFB)
These are exactly the same as the TRUB but with the seating classified for first class passengers.

Trailer restaurant first (TRF)
The final type of HST trailer is the TRF. Again, these are former TRUB vehicles, but equipped for the 'modular' concept of on-train catering.

Table to show the various types of HST catering cars and their seating capacities

	1st class seats	Unclassified seats (1st class style)	2nd class seats
TRSB	—	—	35
TRB	—	23	—
TRUK	—	24	—
TLUK	—	8	—
TRFK	24	—	—
TRUB	—	17	—
TRFB	17	—	—

HST set formations

The routes over which HSTs operate can be broadly divided into four groups. There are the internal WR services from London Paddington to Bristol, South Wales and the West of England. Then there are the cross-country trains linking the industrial centres of Newcastle, Leeds, Sheffield, Liverpool and Manchester with South Wales and the West Country via Birmingham. Next come those operating over the East Coast main line out of Kings Cross to Edinburgh, and beyond to Aberdeen and Inverness. Also in this group are the trains from London to West Yorkshire, Humberside and Teeside. Finally there are the HSTs working out of St Pancras to the East Midlands and South Yorkshire on the Midland main line. The characteristics of these differing routes and levels of demand is reflected in the formation of the HST sets operating the services over these lines.

Few of us have room for a full HST set on the layout. If I put a full length eight-car rake on my layout it would not fit the platform and would completely dominate the scene and look out of all proportion to other items. So we need to strike a balance between what is correct with regard to the prototype and what looks right on the layout. By reducing the number of trailers in the rake by about a half, some extremely effective formations can be produced:

DMB, TF, *TRSB, TS, TS, DMB.
DMB, TF, TRUB*, TS, TS, DMB.
DMB, TF, *TRUK, TRSB*, TS, DMB.
DMB, TF, *TRSB, TS, TGS, DMB.
DMB, TF, TRUB*, TS, TGS, DMB.
DMB, TF, TRFB*, TS, TGS, DMB.

Even if a train of this length is too great then you surely have the space to run two power cars coupled back-to-back. They can be seen running like this on test after overhaul. Nowadays even single power cars can be occasionally seen wending their solitary way along the main line on a trial run. Hence there is no excuse not to have at least one HST vehicle running on the layout.

Liveries

The liveries carried by the production HST sets are reasonably straightforward although there are one or two points to look out for. With one exception, all the power cars and trailers were initially in the standard rail blue and grey colour scheme. The one departure from this was TS 42335 to 42341 which were delivered new in the 'Inter-City' light and dark grey livery. Currently after overhaul, all the HST vehicles are being repainted into this new colour scheme. Soon the blue and grey livery will be a memory, indeed all of the power cars have already been painted in the new style.

Blue and grey livery: Originally the power cars were to be painted with the front portion black rather than the standard rail blue that was later used. Early examples were actually completed in this livery but were quickly repainted before entering service (these being 43002 to 43005, 43007 and 43008). Although this was a very short-lived style there was a tell-tale effect which lasted for some while on these six power cars in that the 'Inter-City 125' lettering on the body side was infilled with black instead of the usual blue.

The brandings on the trailer vehicles began to be altered in the middle of 1978 to incorporate the figures '125' in the legend. This resulted in the following changes:

Vehicle	Original legend	Later branding
TF	Inter-City	Inter-City 125
TS	Inter-City	Inter-City 125
TGS	—	Inter-City 125
TRSB	Buffet	Buffet-Bar 125
TRUK	Restaurant	Restaurant 125
TRUB	Buffet	Restaurant-Buffet 125

The catering cars have a bold red stripe above the windows at the kitchen or buffet end of the vehicle. Some of the TRUKs and the TRUBs (reclassified as TRFBs) later received a yellow cantrail stripe at the other end of the coach, like that on the TFs. On the power cars an orange safety line has been applied subsequently at cantrail level.

Unlike the prototype HST which had its bogies painted in a chocolate brown shade, those of the production sets are black. Note that the springs and dampers are painted different colours on some of the vehicles:

Vehicle	Dampers	Coil springs
DMB	Medium grey	Black
TF	Blue	Yellow
TS	Blue	Yellow
TGS	Blue	Yellow
TRSB	Blue	Yellow
TRUK	Blue	Yellow (Green at the kitchen end)
TRUB	Blue	Yellow (Green at the buffet end)

Dimensions of the lettering, numbering and lining of these HST vehicles (to the nearest 5mm) are as follows:

The white lining dividing the rail blue and rail grey is 20mm wide.
The orange safety line is 20mm wide.
The red catering or yellow first class cantrail bands are 200mm wide.
The large 'Inter-City' lettering on the power cars is 390mm high for the upper case figures and 300mm for the lower case ones.
The branding on the trailers has 200mm high upper case letters with 150mm lower case ones.
The figure '1' on the first class doors is 200mm high.
The HST vehicle numbers on the side are 100mm high.

The 'Guard' lettering on the rear power car doors has 40mm upper and 30mm lower case letters.

The 'load evenly distributed' legend has 25mm upper and 20mm lower case letters.

Depot allocation stickers are 100mm by 75mm.

The unit numbers on the front of the power cars are 125mm high.

'Inter-City' livery: Towards the end of July 1983, power cars 43125 and 43126 entered Derby Locomotive Works for their classified intermediate overhaul. They emerged early in September painted in a new light and dark grey colour scheme, similar to that previously seen on the APT. Meanwhile across the main line and over the London Road at the Litchurch Lane Works, diesel shunter 08103 was busy marshalling a rake of trailer vehicles also painted in this new livery. There was a major difference in the lettering applied to some power cars. On 43125, 43126 and 43151 the same outline-style of lettering was used as on the earlier blue and grey livery, though the 'InterCity' lacked a hyphen. With 43129 and 43130, solid white lettering was used but this time with a hyphen between the words 'Inter-City'.

It was not until early in 1985 that further HSTs were painted in the 'Inter-City' colour scheme. A revised style was applied to the power cars and this is shown in *Figure 40*. The light grey and yellow colours were kept away from the body side louvres as these areas tended to attract dirt and hence disfigure the initial 'Inter-City' livery. The light grey cantrail band on the power cars and trailers was also reduced in depth as compared with the earlier 'Inter-City' style.

The dimensions of the lettering and numbering of this livery are the same as those used on the blue and grey colour scheme. However the widths of the body side bands are different:

The rail red band is 180mm wide.

The rail white band is 100mm wide.

The light grey, red or yellow cantrail bands are 120mm wide.

During April 1987, a slightly modified version of this 'Inter-City' livery appeared. Initially applied to power cars 43051 and 43072, the red and white bands were extended around the front end whilst the light grey on the lower body side also reached the cabside. This reduced the amount of yellow on the vehicles to just the cab roof and lower nose ends. The lettering was also altered to a new 'INTERCITY' style and the BR logo was replaced by a graceful swallow emblem.

The Advanced Passenger Train — 'If only. . .'

To conclude our look at high speed trains on BR, mention must be made about the Advanced Passenger Train, or APT for short. The fate of this bold project is too well known to need repeating here. Anyone who watched the television news broadcasts during the summer of 1986 will have seen contractors smashing up the interior and windows of APT vehicles in a South Yorkshire scrapyard. A sad end indeed for a remarkable train.

Figure 40 HST power car liveries

ORIGINAL BLUE AND GREY LIVERY

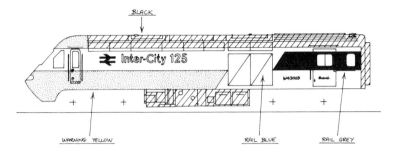

INITIAL "INTER-CITY" STYLE OF LIVERY

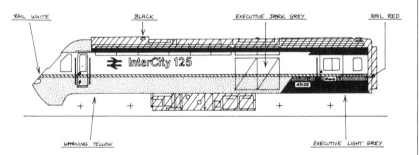

CURRENT "INTER-CITY" LIVERY

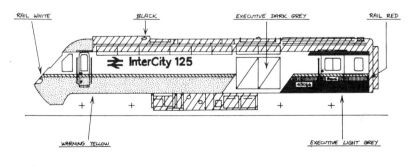

Left *A head-on view of the experimental gas turbine APT-E unit.*

Right *City of Derby leaving the city of Derby. The solitary named APT power car Sc49003 heads away from Derby on a trial run hauled by one of the prototype HST power cars.*

The experimental APT: APT-E

The origins of the APT stretched back to the late 1960s and pre-dated work on the HST. It was developed as a response to the need for reduced journey times on many of BR's sinuous routes, in particular the West Coast main line from London Euston to Glasgow. The APT-E was a gas turbine-driven four-car unit, a mobile test bed for the new technology designed to negotiate these routes. Its test programme lasted from June 1972 until April 1976. Much of the time it worked on the Old Dalby test track near Melton Mowbray in Leicestershire, but also ventured over the main line between Derby and St Pancras, and on the WR in the Swindon and Didcot areas.

In model terms this train in its metallic silver and blue livery would be something really special. However one would have to scratchbuild it: not an easy task with the awkward body curves and profiles involved. I have never seen a working model of the APT-E and doubt if one exists. Why not prove me wrong and have a go at building a model of this train? In 4mm scale and above, plastic card would seem to be the best medium using a wooden former to the shape of the vehicle. In 2mm scale it would probably be better to carve the body out of a solid piece of balsa wood.

The prototype APT: APT-P

Thanks to *Hornby* there is a model of the APT-P available in 00 gauge or at least some of the vehicles making up the complete train. It was a bold step by *Hornby* to introduce their model even before the prototype entered service, so let us hope it paid off for them. The shortest formation possible for an APT would be: DTS (Driving trailer second), TBF (Trailer brake first), M (Motor), TBF, DTS and this is the form in which the *Hornby* model is produced: unfortunately none of the intermediate trailers was made. When the prototype APT entered revenue-earning service for an all too brief spell in December 1981 it was formed: DTS, TS, TRSB*, TU (Trailer unclassified), TF, TBF, M, M, TBF, DTS.

The worst December weather for thirty years with heavy falls of snow and freezing temperatures over the West Coast route from Glasgow to Euston was undoubtedly a contributing factor to the failure of the APT project. It was a severe body blow from which the APT never fully recovered.

The livery carried by the prototype APT sets used exactly the same colours that we are now familiar with on the HSTs, although over the years of testing a couple of modifications were applied. On the power cars, large 'InterCity APT' lettering was added to one side on the body with a BR logo symbol on the other side. In the middle of 1980 the cab window surrounds on the driving trailers were

The standard formation of a 6-car trailer rake of APT vehicles. Note the raised nose section on the leading vehicle, exposing the buffers and coupling.

painted black with the 'InterCity APT' below, on the nose. Whilst black window surrounds are all very well, I feel that those on the front of the APT were not a visual improvement. The interior colour scheme of the train uses a tartan upholstery. In the first class this is predominantly a blue/grey shade with red and green stripes, the second class seating being bright red with medium green stripes. Table tops in the first class section are blue and in the second class, cream.

The *Hornby* model is a fine representation of the prototype and captures well its clean lines and sleek appearance. Especially worthy of mention are the bogies on the power car which really look the part. The model also operates well and actually tilts around curves, though they have to be quite sharp to really see the effect. There are just a few jobs to do to make it that bit more realistic. The colour of the interior seating is a little insipid so it is worth dismantling the body (which is a clip fit) and giving the inside a repaint. Do not bother trying to recreate the tartan pattern of the actual upholstery as it can hardly be seen, but more vivid colours for the seating do show up well. The front ends of the driving trailers can do with a little attention. *Figure 41* outlines the main details here; note in particular the grille and exhaust opening on the roof which *Hornby* have omitted from their model. Rather than cutting out openings in the roof, the grille and exhaust outlet can be drawn with a fine ink pen on a piece of paper and glued into position.

Figure 41 Front end details of the APT-P

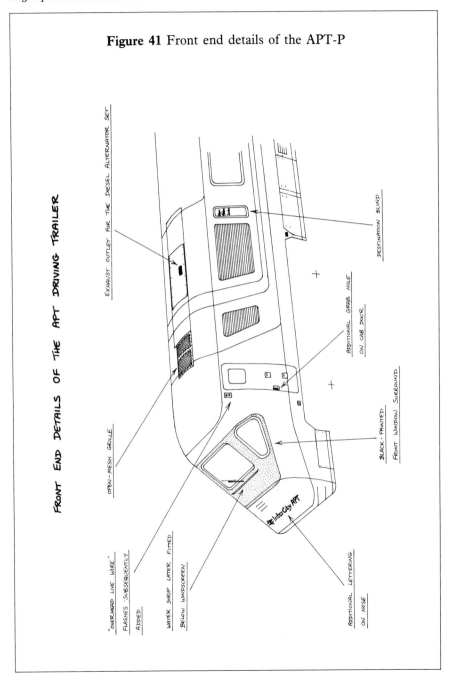

FRONT END DETAILS OF THE APT DRIVING TRAILER

"OVERHEAD LIVE WIRE" FLASHES SUBSEQUENTLY ADDED

WATER STRIP LATER FITTED BELOW WINDSCREEN

ADDITIONAL LETTERING ON NOSE

OPEN-MESH GRILLE

EXHAUST OUTLET FOR THE DIESEL ALTERNATOR SET

ADDITIONAL GRAB HOLE ON CAB DOOR

BLACK-PAINTED FRONT WINDOW SURROUND

DESTINATION BLIND

FOURTEEN
Racehorses, regiments and the heavy brigade

The glamorous, powerful and controversial always attract attention. As it is in everyday life, so it is with railway locomotives. The 'Deltics', one of the classes that we will look at in this chapter, definitely fall into this category. Throughout the 1960s and most of the '70s they hauled the most prestigious passenger trains in Britain, including the internationally famous 'Flying Scotsman'. During the same period they were the most powerful diesels on BR, despite the controversy about their appearance when they were first introduced. It was not until the late 1970s that the 'Deltics' were joined by other locomotives in the 3,000-plus horse-power range, and these were all designed for heavy freight haulage. First there were the Class '56's, then into the '80s with the Class '58's and more recently the privately-owned Class '59's. Through a detailed modelling study of these classes I hope to show what can be achieved with any of the locomotives discussed in Chapters 3-9.

Class '55'

It is a hot summer afternoon in deepest Lincolnshire with not a breath of wind to stir the ripening corn standing erect in the fields. Only the grasshoppers in the undergrowth disturb this tranquil scene. Suddenly the signalman in High Dyke box moves into action and a signal arm swings skyward. The still air is punctuated by a faint drone which gets louder with every passing moment. We recognize the characteristic sound and our expectations rise. Soon, from behind a row of trees on the horizon, the familiar yet welcome sight of a 'Deltic' at the head of a rake of coaches comes into view. The train approaches round the sweeping curve, a quick blast on the locomotive's horn and it disappears into the blackness of Stoke Tunnel. A minute of silence before it emerges from the southern portal and we hear it begin the long descent past Burton Coggles and Swayfield, next stop Kings Cross.

We all treasure our own memories of times and scenes no longer with us. The 'Deltics', a classic locomotive type from the day they were introduced, often kindle such thoughts. No excuse is required to have at least one of these handsome machines on a layout. The routes over which these locomotives worked is known well enough, so their reign on the East Coast main line can be summarized by the following depot allocation periods:

Finsbury Park (London)   February 1961 to May 1981
Haymarket (Edinburgh)   February 1961 to May 1979
Gateshead   March 1961 to May 1979
York   May 1979 to January 1982

Liveries

All the class were originally in a two-tone green livery, with Brunswick green being the main body colour relieved by a light green skirt band and a medium grey roof. With the exception of D9020 and D9021, no yellow warning panels were initially applied to the ends. D9020 and D9021 had them from the start and the rest of the class received them during 1962. As Appendix 2 shows, the 'Deltics' received their names over the period 1961 to 1965. Only D9007, D9009, D9012, D9015, D9018 and D9020 carried nameplates from the outset, the remainder initially had a large-sized BR crest on the centre of the bodyside. When the nameplates were fitted these large crests were removed and replaced by smaller ones positioned beneath the cab side numbers.

The overall rail blue livery with full yellow nose ends first appeared on the class in the autumn of 1966 with D9002 the initial recipient. It took three years to

With the characteristic exhaust plume, Tulyar *eases out of Kings Cross with a northbound express. Note the superb external condition of the locomotive and the white cab window surrounds.*

paint the whole class in blue as the following list shows:

Autumn 1966	D9002 (first in blue livery)
Winter 1966/67	—
Spring 1967	—
Summer 1967	D9008
Autumn 1967	D9000, D9007, D9016, D9019
Winter 1967/68	D9003, D9004, D9010, D9013, D9020, D9021
Spring 1968	D9012, D9015
Summer 1968	D9009, D9011
Autumn 1968	—
Winter 1968/69	—
Spring 1969	D9018
Summer 1969	D9001, D9005, D9006
Autumn 1969	D9014 (last in green livery), D9017

Late 1973, early 1974 saw the class being renumbered into the 55XXX series, D9000 to D9021 becoming 55022 and 55001 to 55021 respectively. Around 1975 the familiar overhead live wire flashes appeared on the nose ends of the locomotives. This was rather later than on other classes for it was not until the late 1970s that the 'Deltics' worked under the wires following the electrification of the Kings Cross suburban services.

Figure 42 outlines the main livery styles carried by the 'Deltics' whilst *Figure 43* shows the front end details and some of the typical headcodes displayed on the class over the years. White cab surrounds reappeared on 55003, 55007, 55009, 55012, 55015 and 55018 in 1979 and these six members of the class, together with 55019, also had double body side numbers. Finally in December 1980, 55002 was repainted in the original two-tone green colour scheme, albeit with full yellow ends and the 55XXX series numbering.

Detail variations and modifications

Whilst differences within the class are apparently slight and of a minor nature, they are worth mentioning for it is these very things which add character and realism to a model. However one should check with photographs for all the details on a specific member of the class. I have said this before and you are probably thinking, 'Oh, it's all right for him, but photographs of the particular locomotive I want to model are hard to come by!' Perhaps this is true for some classes but certainly not the 'Deltics' which have been extensively covered in numerous books and magazine articles. Here then, are some of the details to look out for when modelling a particular 'Deltic':

Headlights and marker lights —At an early date D9000 was fitted with a
flashing warning light in the centre of the nose just above the buffer-beam. This was soon removed but it left its mark on that particular locomotive which always had a more angular inset step above the coupling hook compared with the rest of the class. In the autumn of 1972 D9009 had its headcode box modified to form a marker light

Figure 42 'Deltic' livery variations

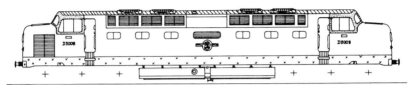

GREEN LIVERY : INITIAL STYLE

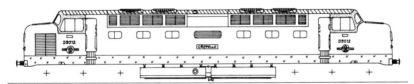

GREEN LIVERY : LATER STYLE

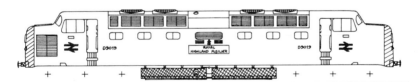

BLUE LIVERY : INITIAL STYLE

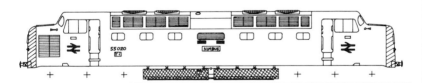

BLUE LIVERY : LATER STYLE

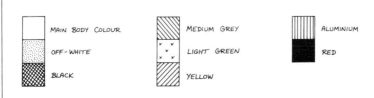

MAIN BODY COLOUR	
OFF-WHITE	
BLACK	
MEDIUM GREY	
LIGHT GREEN	
YELLOW	
ALUMINIUM	
RED	

Figure 43 Front end livery details of the 'Deltics'

[1A16] — No Warning Panel
[1A35] — Small Warning Panel
[1A06] — Full Yellow Front

GREEN LIVERY

[1S17] — Full Yellow Front
With Marker Lights
With Headlights

BLUE LIVERY

Main Body Colour	Off-White
Black	Light Green
Yellow	Red

SOME TYPICAL HEADCODES DISPLAYED ON THE DELTICS :

— THE GREEN ERA —

1A12	Down	"Elizabethan"
1A16	Down	"Flying Scotsman"
1A23	Up	"Talisman"
1A33	Up	"Elizabethan"
1A35	Up	"Flying Scotsman"
1A46	Down	"Talisman"
1E14	Up	"Queen of Scots"
1N24	Down	"Yorkshire Pullman"

— THE BLUE ERA —

1A15	Up	"Tees-Tyne Pullman"
1E05	Up	"Flying Scotsman"
1L22	15.55	King's Cross – Leeds
1N10	11.00	King's Cross – Newcastle
1S16	08.00	King's Cross – Edinburgh
1S17	Down	"Flying Scotsman"
1S32	Down	"Aberdonian"
1S42	Down	"Talisman"

Above *The marker light arrangement of the headcode box with two white circles on a black background. This 'Deltic' is also fitted with the later type of single windscreen wiper blades.*

Right *The headlight arrangement of the headcode box, with the aperture plated over and two lenses fitted to make a more permanent feature. Note that this particular locomotive retains the original twin wiper blades on each windscreen.*

Far left *The additional bodyside louvres to provide more ventilation for the batteries. The Green Howards was the last member of the class to retain its regimental crest above the nameplate.*

Left *Bogie and cabside details of one of the 'Deltics'.*

Below left *Another view of the two additional louvres. The four bodyside holes indicate that this locomotive also once had a regimental crest over its name.*

Right *The modified cabside window showing the plated-over quarter-lights.*

arrangement of two white circles on a black background, illuminated by the light bulbs behind. By the time the display of train headcodes was abandoned in 1976, most of the class had these marker lights. Later all the 'Deltics' except 55008, 55020 and 55022 had the headcode boxes plated over to create a more permanent headlight type feature on the front ends.

Roof details — Like most other diesels, the 'Deltics' suffered from problems with their train steam-heating boilers. Initially there was only one exhaust outlet for this on the roof and it was situated next to one of the engine exhausts. By the mid 1960s the original boiler exhaust was plated over and two new outlets cut in the roof, more towards the centre.

Body side louvres — To provide more ventilation for the locomotive's batteries, additional louvres appeared on the body side just above the nameplates in 1966/67.

Warning horns — D9000 to D9018 originally had their horns situated beneath the bufferbeams whilst D9019 to D9021 had them mounted on the roof. Experiments in the mid 1960s saw D9007 have its horns fitted inside the nose ends. Subsequently it was decided to mount the horns on each side of the bonnet nose and soon all the class had them in this position.

Air brakes and electric train heating — The 'Deltics' were fitted with air

This hinged plate covered the brake exhausters that were situated only in the nose of the number one end of the locomotive on the 'A' side.

brakes during 1967 and 1968, whilst electric train heating equipment appeared on the locomotives between 1970 and 1971. These additions resulted in an extra pipe on the bufferbeam and a hose connection on the nose end.

Sanding gear — This began to be removed from the class in 1976 and entailed plating over the body side sandbox fillers and taking out the flexible hoses that distributed the sand on the rails.

Cabside windows — Also in 1976, the cabside quarter-light windows began to be plated over in an attempt to reduce draughts and the entry of water into the cab. All the class except 55020 eventually received this modification.

Windscreen wipers — A very characteristic feature of the 'Deltics' were the twin wipers on each of the windscreens. From about 1977 single wiper blades were substituted for the twin type, around half the class receiving them. These detail differences are outlined in *Figure 44* and *Figure 45*.

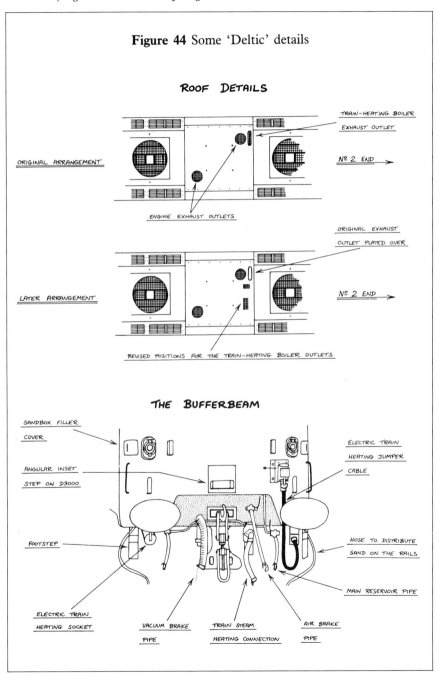

Figure 44 Some 'Deltic' details

ROOF DETAILS

TRAIN-HEATING BOILER
EXHAUST OUTLET

ORIGINAL ARRANGEMENT

Nº 2 END

ENGINE EXHAUST OUTLETS

ORIGINAL EXHAUST
OUTLET PLATED OVER

LATER ARRANGEMENT

Nº 2 END

REVISED POSITIONS FOR THE TRAIN-HEATING BOILER OUTLETS

THE BUFFERBEAM

SANDBOX FILLER
COVER

ANGULAR INSET
STEP ON D9000

FOOTSTEP

ELECTRIC TRAIN
HEATING SOCKET

VACUUM BRAKE
PIPE

TRAIN STEAM
HEATING CONNECTION

AIR BRAKE
PIPE

ELECTRIC TRAIN
HEATING JUMPER
CABLE

HOSE TO DISTRIBUTE
SAND ON THE RAILS

MAIN RESERVOIR PIPE

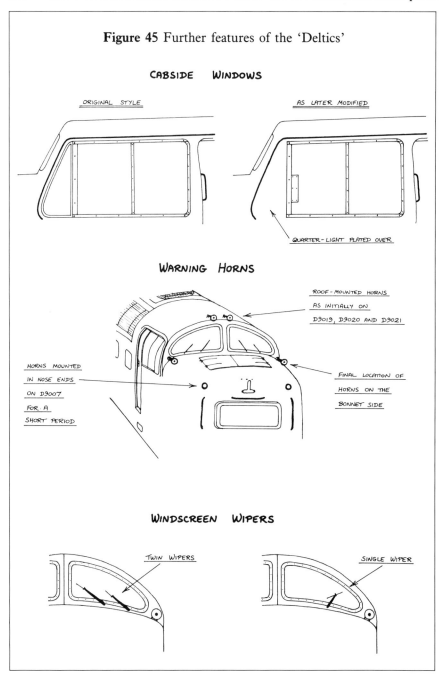

Figure 45 Further features of the 'Deltics'

CABSIDE WINDOWS

ORIGINAL STYLE

AS LATER MODIFIED

QUARTER-LIGHT PLATED OVER

WARNING HORNS

ROOF-MOUNTED HORNS
AS INITIALLY ON
D9019, D9020 AND D9021

HORNS MOUNTED
IN NOSE ENDS
ON D9007
FOR A
SHORT PERIOD

FINAL LOCATION OF
HORNS ON THE
BONNET SIDE

WINDSCREEN WIPERS

TWIN WIPERS

SINGLE WIPER

The models

At first sight the *Lima* 00 gauge model of the 'Deltic' does not look very promising. It is about a scale 2ft underlength whilst the bogie wheelbase is around 1ft short, discrepancies that cannot really be overcome without drastic surgery. Although these errors sound rather bad, the model does look surprisingly like the real thing and with a few additional improvements it can be made even better. What really lifts the model out of the toy category and into something worth having is flush-glazing of the cab and body side windows. The 'Deltic' is probably the most difficult of all the models to flush-glaze with its complex window shapes and curvature. There are kits on the market of preformed clear plastic pieces to fit directly into the window frames, but why not try glazing the windows yourself? The cabside windows are a little tricky because of their convex shape. For these, the simplest method is to use the original *Lima* glazing material. Remove the two vertical window frames and cut the curved glazing so that it fits snugly into the aperture. The vertical frames can then be reinstated by carefully painting them on to the new windows. Normal thin plastic sheet can be used for the other windows. After glazing the body side windows, stick some black card behind them so that one cannot see straight through the model and hence spoil the whole effect.

Although not dimensionally spot on, the Lima *'Deltic' has the potential to be made into a very attractive model.*

Above *Flush-glazing the cab and body side windows on this model is definitely worth doing in order to capture the character of the prototype.*

Below *A head-on view of the model showing the flush-glazing of the windscreen. Note too the wire handrails and the electric train heating connection on the front of the locomotive.*

Above *Roof details on the* Lima *model. Note the two engine exhaust outlets and the position of the train-heating boiler vents.*

Below *A side view of the model which shows to advantage the rectangular plate at the number one end covering the exhausters. This is represented by simply sticking a piece of paper on to the side of the nose.*

Other detailing depends on the period one is modelling. For a 'Deltic' in the early two-tone green livery:
1   Carve off the moulded warning horns on the bonnet nose. For D9019 to D9021 in their original condition, horns shaped from plastic rod can be positioned on the cab roof.
2   With body putty, fill in the two small rectangular body side louvres above the nameplates.
3   On the nose ends remove the moulded handrails and replace with wire ones. Also carve off the electric train heating connection on the nose.
4   Twin wipers, made from pieces of wire, can be added to the windscreens.

With a 'Deltic' in the later rail blue colour scheme:
1   Plate over the original train-heating boiler exhaust with a thin piece of card and form two new outlets on the roof from strips of plastic.
2   Remove the moulded handrails from the nose ends and fashion new ones from wire.
3   The electric train heating connections on the nose ends are rather puny and so larger ones cut from plastic strip can be glued in position.
4   The sandbox covers on the nose can be carved off if desired, whilst those on the body side can be smoothed over with filler.
5   The cabside quarter-lights are plated over with thin card.
6   The headcode boxes can also be plated over with rectangular pieces of plastic card, with two white circles painted on them to represent the headlights.

Class '56'
Amongst the forefront of BR's freight locomotive fleet are the 135 members of the Class '56'. When the price of oil went through the roof in the early 1970s the demand for coal rose in consequence. More locomotives were required to haul the increasing number of coal trains between the colleries and the power stations. Hence the appearance of the Class '56'. In September 1974 BR ordered sixty of the class: thirty from Brush Electrical Machines at Loughborough and thirty from British Rail Engineering Limited at Doncaster. Brush sub-contracted its order to the Romanian locomotive builders, Electroputere, at their works in Craiova in the south west of the country. More orders followed, though these were all for British-built locomotives. Construction details for the class as a whole are as follows:

Numbers	Built	Introduced	Notes
56001-56030	Electroputere	1977	—
56031-56055	BREL (Doncaster)	1977-1979	Early design
56056-56115	BREL (Doncaster)	1979-1983	Later design
56116-56135	BREL (Crewe)	1983-1984	Later design

Only six depots have had an allocation of Class '56's, though currently just four have some on their books:

Tinsley (Sheffield)   February 1977 to January 1987

Class '56's can be clean! This view of 56044, one of the early batch built by BREL, was taken in May 1978 when the locomotive was only a few days old.

Toton	May 1977 to date
Canton (Cardiff)	July 1979 to date
Healey Mills (Wakefield)	May 1980 to May 1983
Gateshead	November 1981 to date
Bath Road (Bristol)	September 1982 to date

The vast majority of the class are employed hauling the merry-go-round coal trains for which they were originally designed. This is especially true of those at Toton and Gateshead where they are seldom seen on anything but coal trains. Those based in South Wales work on the bulk iron-ore trains between Port Talbot and the steelworks at Llanwern, and also some Freightliner turns. Outstationed at Westbury, the Bristol allocation are mainly to be seen on the stone trains which emanate from that district.

Liveries
56001 to 56083 were all delivered in the then standard overall rail blue with full yellow ends. In August 1978 one of the class was repainted in a new livery style. This was 56036, the first in a long line of locomotives to appear in what was later

The first locomotive on BR in the 'large logo' livery was 56036, seen here passing Toton yard with northbound coal empties.

to be known as the 'large logo' blue livery. The body sides were still rail blue but the roof and the tops of the cabs were painted light grey . The cab fronts and sides up to and including the doors were yellow, whilst the window surrounds were black. This livery was subsequently adopted for the class as a whole, with 56084 to 56134 being in this style from the beginning. A few of the earlier locomotives were repainted in this large logo livery, but the final Class '56' appeared in Railfreight grey livery. Whilst the cabs were again yellow and had black window surrounds, the bufferbeams and side framing were painted bright red. This Railfreight grey has now replaced the large logo blue style as the standard livery for the Class '56's and so eventually all the locomotives will be in this colour scheme.

Taking the class as a whole there are some detail differences to watch out for with respect to certain aspects of the livery.

Overhead live wire flashes — These were not originally fitted to the batch of thirty built by Electroputere, though the rest of the class had them from the start. Eventually 56001 to 56030 did have these flashes applied in the same positions as the remainder of the class.

Handrails — Again those built by Electroputere differ from the rest in not having their handrails painted; they have a polished metal finish. On the other Class '56's the handrails are painted white.

Tail light and marker light surrounds — These are painted white on those locomotives built by Electroputere and the batch built by BREL at Doncaster. On those members of the class constructed at Crewe, the surrounds are yellow.

Coupling code symbol — The Class '56's can work in multiple with other locomotives with similar control systems, such as the Class '58's, that have a red diamond coupling symbol. The symbol is painted on the cab front and appeared on 56060 to 56115 from the start. Earlier members of the class have subsequently had them applied, though rather surprisingly the Crewe-built locomotives lacked them initially.

Body side grilles — On 56001 to 56115 these were painted rail blue to match the rest of the superstructure. On the Crewe-built 56116 to 56134 they were picked out in the same shade of light grey that the roof was painted in. On 56135 they were, of course, painted in the Railfreight shade of grey.

Cantrail stripe — 56135, the first member of the class in the Railfreight grey livery, was turned out without any coloured stripe running along the top edge of the body side. Initial repaints in this livery had a white cantrail stripe along the body: later this was changed to the now standard orange.

Detail variations and modifications

Externally the Class '56's can be divided into three basic groups. *Figure 46* outlines the first two of these: those built in Romania by Electroputere and the early BREL production. The third group, the late BREL production, is shown in *Figure 47*.

1 **Built by Electroputere (56001-56030)** These are a fairly homogeneous group of locomotives with, when they were first constructed, no differences between them. They have rubber surrounds to the front and side cab windows, kick-plates below the cab doors and round-headed buffers. The bufferbeam surround extended down the side by the front sandboxes.

   Following accident damage, some of these early locomotives have been fitted with the later style of cab at one end. Those with the new replacement cabs include 56004, 56014, 56029 and 56030. Some also now have oval-headed buffers, whilst a more recent development is the fitting of circular roof vents similar to those of 56063 to 56135.

2 **Early BREL production (56031-56055)** These retain the rubber window surrounds, though only on the front cab windows. 56031 and 56032 have a full bufferbeam surround like the Romanian-built examples, but the rest of

Figure 46 The early batches of Class '56's

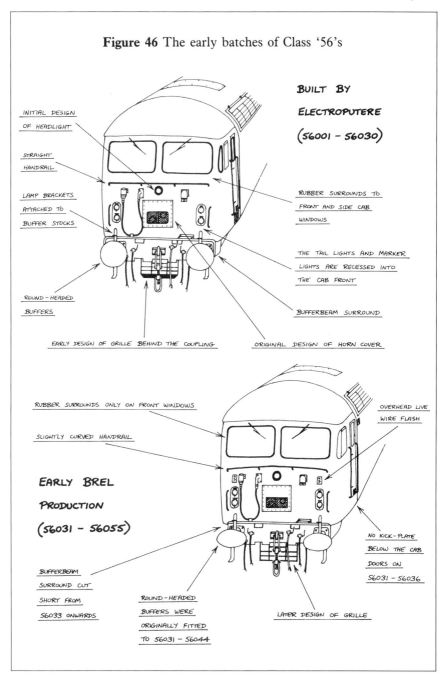

BUILT BY
ELECTROPUTERE
(56001 – 56030)

INITIAL DESIGN
OF HEADLIGHT

STRAIGHT
HANDRAIL

LAMP BRACKETS
ATTACHED TO
BUFFER STOCKS

RUBBER SURROUNDS TO
FRONT AND SIDE CAB
WINDOWS

THE TAIL LIGHTS AND MARKER
LIGHTS ARE RECESSED INTO
THE CAB FRONT

ROUND – HEADED
BUFFERS

BUFFERBEAM SURROUND

EARLY DESIGN OF GRILLE BEHIND THE COUPLING

ORIGINAL DESIGN OF HORN COVER

RUBBER SURROUNDS ONLY ON FRONT WINDOWS

OVERHEAD LIVE
WIRE FLASH

SLIGHTLY CURVED HANDRAIL

EARLY BREL
PRODUCTION
(56031 – 56055)

NO KICK-PLATE
BELOW THE CAB
DOORS ON
56031 – 56036

BUFFERBEAM
SURROUND CUT
SHORT FROM
56033 ONWARDS

ROUND – HEADED
BUFFERS WERE
ORIGINALLY FITTED
TO 56031 – 56044

LATER DESIGN OF GRILLE

Figure 47 The later batches of Class '56's

LATE BREL
PRODUCTION
(56056 - 56135)

ENLARGED HEADLIGHT FITTED FROM
56061 ONWARDS

MODIFIED STYLE OF
CAB DOOR HANDRAILS

ALUMINIUM CAB
WINDOW SURROUNDS

TAIL LIGHTS AND
MARKER LIGHTS
ARE NO LONGER
RECESSED

RED DIAMOND
COUPLING SYMBOL

MORE PROMINENT DESIGN
OF HORN COVER

NO BUFFERBEAM
SURROUND

LAMP BRACKETS ARE
ATTACHED TO THE
CAB FRONT

LATER MEMBERS OF
THE CLASS OMIT
THE GRILLE BEHIND
THE COUPLING; THAT IS
FROM 56091 ONWARDS

AIR BRAKE
PIPE

ENGINE CONTROL
PIPE

MAIN RESERVOIR
PIPE

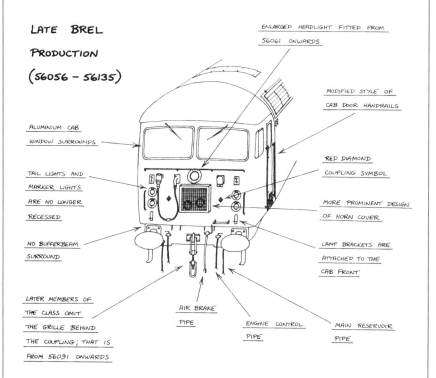

ROOF DETAILS

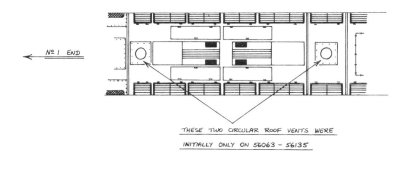

N° 1 END

THESE TWO CIRCULAR ROOF VENTS WERE
INITIALLY ONLY ON 56063 - 56135

this batch from 56033 onwards only have the surround along the top edge of the bufferbeam. Kick-plates were not originally fitted to the first six of this batch but appeared from 56037 to 56055. Round-headed buffers were initially fitted on 56031 to 56044 with the rest of this batch having oval ones. Most of those with the round buffers have subsequently been fitted with the oval-headed type. Again, like the Romanian batch of Class '56's these early BREL examples did not have the circular vents on the roof, though they are now being fitted.

56042 differs from all the other Class '56's in that it has a unique design of bogie. It runs on the CP1 type of bogie, a type which looks similar to that used on the Class '58's though it works on a different principle.

3   **Late BREL production (56056-56135)** A new design of steel cab was introduced from 56056 onwards, resulting in further changes to the external appearance of the class. Aluminium window frames were fitted instead of the rubber surrounds hitherto used. Unfortunately paint, in particular the semi-gloss black used for the cab window surrounds, does not adhere well to this metal. Hence after a short time in service the paint begins to flake off these frames, giving a very tatty appearance to the front ends. The bufferbeam surround was done away with altogether and all this batch have the oval type of buffer. Initially the small type of headlight was retained on 56056 to 56060, but from 56061 an enlarged pattern was used. 56063 onwards had the circular roof vents from the outset, whilst the large metal grille beneath the bufferbeam was dispensed with on 56091 to 56135. Finally, 56073 and 56074 are fitted with flashing light equipment on each of the cab roofs as part of experiments in connection with remote train control.

The models

Only one ready-to-run model of the Class '56' has yet appeared and that is in 00 gauge. Originally sold under the *Mainline* label, it is now made by *Dapol*. The model depicts one of the later batch produced by BREL, specifically one with the circular roof vents and the below bufferbeam grille, that is one from the series between 56063 and 56090. This is another of the models where the quality and performance are so good that one is hard pressed to know what extra details to add to it. The finish is also so good that it does not even require a repaint, except perhaps for the front ends where an additional coat of yellow paint is judicious. Because of the tension lock couplings, there is no space for the actual grille beneath the bufferbeams. If you are fitting scale screw couplings to one or both ends of the model then this grille can be reproduced from strips of plastic card stuck to a backing piece of the same material. The various hoses and brake pipes can be fabricated from different thicknesses of wire. No kick-plates are provided on the model below the cab doors, though by painting this area with silver or aluminium, it gives an effective representation of them. To my eyes the circular roof vents are too obtrusive and do not look quite right. They can be cut off with a sharp knife and replaced by circles of thin plastic or card stamped out from an office punch. If modelling 56056 to 56062 then omit these vents and fill in the

Above *The* Mainline/Dapol *Class '56' is another of those ready-to-run models that requires only a little attention before it can be put to work on the layout. To bring out the exquisite bogie details, the sideframes have been painted a very matt brown colour.*

Below *The* Hornby *Class '47' can be converted into a reasonable model of one of the Romanian or early BREL members of the Class '56's. Whether it is worth the effort, though, is another matter.*

Above *Another view of the two Class '56's. The* Mainline *model already has flush-glazing, but this needs to be fitted to the* Hornby *conversion as seen here.*

Below *The Class '56' in its element, hauling merry-go-round coal hoppers.*

resulting holes in the roof with body putty and smooth over to give a neat finish. The windscreen wipers are moulded on to the windows of the model and so can be picked out in black; similarly the handles on the cab doors can be brought to life with a touch of silver paint. The vertical division on the side cab windows is also moulded on to the glazing and so needs to be picked out in either yellow or black, depending on the livery style one is painting the model. One final point regarding these later Class '56' locomotives (56091 to 56135) — stick a thin strip of plastic card along the bottom edge of the bufferbeam to remove the castellated effect that the earlier examples have.

What about the Class '56's with the earlier design of cab, or those built in Romania? The *Mainline/Dapol* model can be used as the basis for producing one of these, though the work is quite involved. Articles in the model press have covered these alterations in a comprehensive manner and references to these will be found in the bibliography at the rear of the book. Long before the *Mainline* model was produced, I once converted the *Hornby* Class '47' into one of the Romanian-built versions of the Class '56'. It was not too difficult to do and resulted in a reasonable model, at least a little different from everyone else's Class '56'. Although I have not tried it, it might be possible to create one of the early batches of the class by marrying the *Mainline* chassis with an altered *Hornby* Class '47' body. This may be easier than trying to convert the *Mainline* Class '56' superstructure. Anyway, it is a thought perhaps worth pursuing.

The backbone of BR's heavy coal-hauling fleet; Classes '47', '56' and '58'. These three are all based on Hornby *models, with the Class '58' on the left yet to be detailed.*

A side view of the detailed Hornby *Class '58'. Note the engine exhaust outlets on the roof.*

Class '58'

Increasing construction costs for the Class '56', the need to improve reliability and cut down on maintenance time, and the desire to create a locomotive suitable for export markets led to the appearance of the Class '58'. With a twelve-cylinder diesel engine as opposed to a sixteen-cylinder one on the Class '56', and built on the modular principle with the various components bolted into place on a rigid frame, it is both cheaper to build and easier to maintain than its predecessor. Though not as stylish as some of the previous types we have looked at, the Class '58's are a very distinctive design. Whilst it is very easy to mistake a Class '56' for a Class '47', no such error can be made with a Class '58'.

All the class are allocated to Toton depot, situated midway between Nottingham and Derby. Generally they will be seen at the head of a rake of merry-go-round coal hoppers, of both the HAA/HDA and HEA variety. Hauling trains of fly-ash wagons from the power stations or bulk stone trains from some of the East Midland quarries also comes within their sphere of influence. Sometimes at weekends they are employed hauling dead electric locomotives and their trains when the power is off for overhead line maintenance. During the 1984 coal dispute they also appeared on freightliner container trains and lesser ballast workings. Their duties are not just confined to the LMR for they regularly appear on three other regions. On the ER they work around Shirebrook on the Nottinghamshire/Derbyshire border, or across to Peterborough on the fly-ash trains. Over on the WR they can be seen heading coal trains bound for Didcot power station, whilst on the Southern they arrive at Northfleet in Kent, again on merry-go-round coal workings.

Liveries

Railfreight grey livery was applied to this class from the outset, with the main-frame solebars painted bright red, the cabs yellow and the window surrounds black. There is, though, one variation to look out for. 58001 to 58034 have a white stripe running along the upper edge of the body side. From 58035 this is altered to an orange coloured stripe which extends around the entire upper bodywork, including the sides and front of the cabs.

Due to their bonnet-style design it is exceedingly difficult to keep the body-work of the Class '58's in a presentable state. Little is achieved in putting them through an automatic washing machine since the revolving brushes cannot reach the side panels on the locomotive. Hence the dirt builds up and the grey paint-work quickly fades to a very dull shade. The red solebars, in particular, come in for harsh treatment with the paint flaking off and so leading to a very tatty appearance. After only a few months in service the external condition of some members of the class is appalling and not a very good advertisement for Railfreight. Indeed the Railfreight Sector seem to have dissociated themselves from at least one member of the class, for 58004 has run for many years without the Railfreight emblem on the number one end cab side.

Detail variations and modifications

Although there are no really major external differences within the Class '58's, there are some subtle variations between individual members. *Figure 48* outlines the front end details: note that 58001 to 58003 initially lacked the footstep situated on the bufferbeam. By the middle of 1984 58001 had been fitted with them, but at the time of writing the other two locomotives are still without these steps. *Figure 49* illustrates the arrangement of body side grilles, louvres and access doors. Later batches of the class, that is 58015 to 58050, have additional handles fitted to the middle of the engine room and electrical compartment access doors. Other features of the class are shown in *Figure 50*. Three style of cab side can be detected:

1	Initial design	— This applies to the first three members of the class; 58001 and 58003. In the bottom right hand corner, note the straight diagonal edge to the cab side where it meets the mainframe.
2	Intermediate design	— On 58004 to 58035 this diagonal edge is shorter where the cab abuts the mainframe.
3	Final design	— The remaining locomotives, 58036 to 58050,

are similar to the intermediate design. However, in addition they have a rather prominent rectangular ventilation grille in the top left hand corner of each of the cab sides.

When it first appeared, 58001 had a three-rung footstep on the bogie beneath each of the cab doors. Before it entered service it received a larger four-rung type, the design subsequently used on all the rest of the class. From 58036 sand boxes appeared on each corner of the bogies. Finally, on later members of the class from around 58031 onwards, a metal screen was fitted adjacent to the handrails by the cab doors.

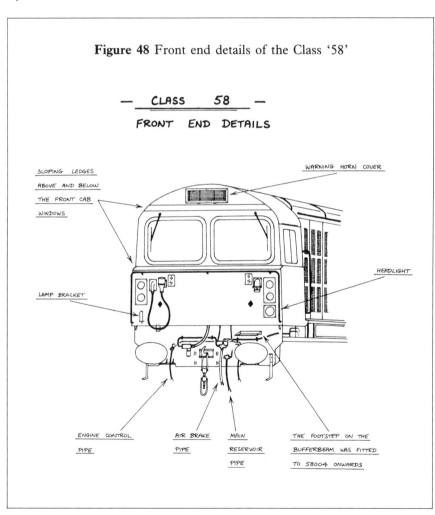

Figure 48 Front end details of the Class '58'

— CLASS   58 —

FRONT END DETAILS

SLOPING LEDGES
ABOVE AND BELOW
THE FRONT CAB
WINDOWS

WARNING HORN COVER

HEADLIGHT

LAMP BRACKET

ENGINE CONTROL
PIPE

AIR BRAKE
PIPE

MAIN
RESERVOIR
PIPE

THE FOOTSTEP ON THE
BUFFERBEAM WAS FITTED
TO 58004 ONWARDS

Figure 49 Class '58' body side grilles and louvres

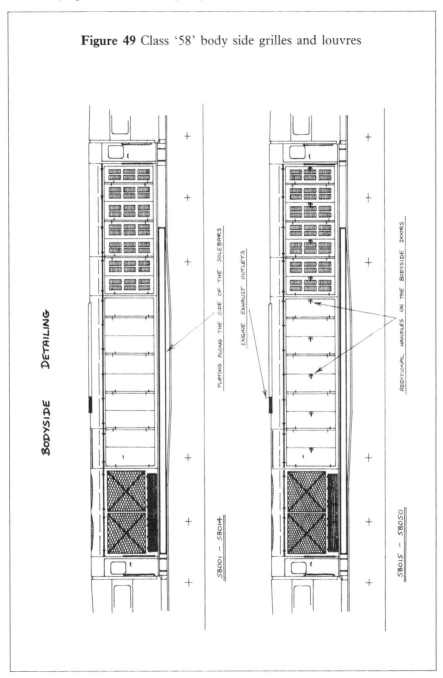

Figure 50 Some features of the Class '58's

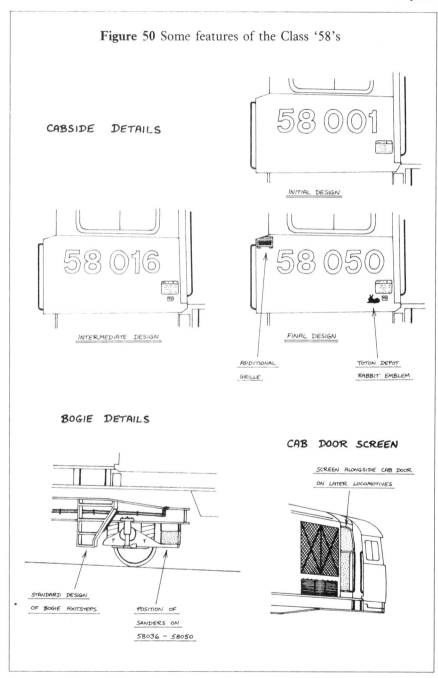

The models

So far only one ready-to-run model of the 'Class '58' has been introduced and that is by *Hornby* in 00 gauge. However there is a kit for 0 gauge modellers made by *Post-War Prototypes*, but as yet nothing for those working in N gauge.

The *Hornby* model is one of their best yet, though let down by some minor inaccuracies which are fairly easy to rectify. It appeared on the market exactly the same month that the prototype rolled off the production line at Doncaster works, so obviously the model makers were working from drawings without the aid of seeing the real thing. This has led to some errors, though commendably few in number. However one must congratulate *Hornby* on their foresight and enterprise in bringing out a model of the Class '58' so quickly. It is rather a strange feeling to have a model on one's layout that is actually older than the prototype which it depicts. What a pity that the firm missed the boat by not making a model of the American-built Class '59'.

The first step in detailing the *Hornby* model is to separate the bogies from the underframe. A great advantage of the form of construction on this model is that the bogies can be easily unclipped from the underframe by using the blade of a screwdriver to prise the rear lugs away from the frame. Disconnect the wiring and put the two bogies to one side. It is possible to unclip the two cabs from the bonnet section of the bodywork, but they are quite a tight fit and unless one wants to add a crew inside one of them, they can be left in place. The following steps can now be undertaken:

1   The two engine exhaust outlets on the roof can be represented by cutting two rectangular notches, 7mm by 3mm, in the raised silencer section.
2   The prototype has sloping ledges above and below the front cab windows whereas the model shows these areas as at right angles to the windscreen. The top ledge can be represented by either a narrow strip of plastic card glued into place, or by filling in the area to create a slope with body putty. The bottom ledge is made by filing the right angle edge below the windscreen until a slope is formed. These alterations really improve the front end appearance of the model.
3   The handrails on the inner facing side of the cab doors are shown almost flush with the body side when in fact they protrude noticeable away from the bonnets. On the model these wire handrails are secured into position through two small holes and folded back at the rear. By unfolding them, pushing them forward so they extend further from the body side and gluing in place, they look much more effective.
4   The louvres on the electrical compartment bonnet doors are slightly wrong on the model. They should be in six sections on each of the doors, not the three depicted. This can be remedied easily by sticking strips of paper measuring 19mm by 1mm down the centre of the louvres to create six sections, painting in Railfreight grey to match the rest of the bodywork.
5   The multiple-working jumper cables on the front ends hang down beyond the bottom edge of the cabs. Carve off the mouldings and replace with wire.

Left *The number one end of the Class '58'. Note the extra details added to the bogies.*

Below left *The number two end of the Class '58'. Note the modified louvres on the electrical compartment bonnet doors. On this side of the locomotive, the valance runs the whole length of the solebar.*

Right *Front-end details on the model. Note the sloping ledges above and below the front windscreen, the black painted window frames and the additional footstep on the bufferbeam. The valance on this side of the locomotive does not extend the entire length of the solebar. Also notice the modified cab door handrails.*

Below *Perhaps a rather too clean Class '58' hauling some merry-go-round hoppers on the layout.*

The plastic moulded handrails can also be replaced by ones bent from wire if desired.

6 The most noticeable omissions from the model are the valances running the length of the solebars. These are easily made from plastic card: on one side the valance, in model form, measures 169mm by 3mm. The other one is shorter, being only 141mm long.

7 On the model, some of the wiring and pipework on the bogie sideframes is missing. Plastic rod can be used to advantage here.

Just one or two points relating to the livery on the *Hornby* model. The large BR logo should really be positioned in the centre of the bonnet, but unless one decides to repaint the entire locomotive it is probably best to leave it where it is. The white (or orange) cantrail stripe extends over the cab doors and does not stop short of them as on the *Hornby* model. Finally, the cab window frames and windscreen wipers should be painted black to match the cab surround.

Class '59'

To end this chapter on the most powerful diesel types on BR, brief mention must be made of the Class '59's. The four locomotives making up this class were built in the United States during 1985 by the Electro-Motive Division of the General Motors Corporation at La Grange in Illinois. After landing in this country during January 1986 and paying a brief visit to the Railway Technical Centre in Derby, they were soon at work hauling the stone trains for which they were purchased by Foster Yeoman Limited.

Based at Merehead quarry in Somerset, they work to the following destinations on heavy stone trains: Brentford, in Middlesex; Botley, in Hampshire; Eastleigh, in Hampshire; Purfleet, in Essex; Theale, in Berkshire.

The quartet were named at the end of June 1986 with the first of the class, 59001, carrying a bell at the number one end above the front cab windows. Such is the success of these locomotives that other firms including the Amey Roadstone Corporation and British Petroleum are considering a small fleet of diesels to haul their trains over BR tracks. Whether they will be like the Class '59's, or purchased from some other manufacturer, only time will tell.

Index

Of further interest

The Professional Approach to Model Railways

John Wylie. The first book to really show in close-up detail, with unique graphics and photography, how any modeller with a modicum of skill and patience, can achieve a 'professional' looking railway layout. Lavishly illustrated with top-quality plans, sketches and colour photographs.

PSL Complete Guide to Model Railways

Michael Andress. Over 500 pages with more than 700 illustrations covering every conceivable aspect of railway modelling including: baseboards, track and electrification, layout planning, structure modelling, scenery, operation, branch line layouts, modern railways and narrow gauge systems. Destined to become the railway modellers' bible.

A Modeller's Guide to the LNER

David Adair. For the first time, a single volume detailing the locomotives, goods, passenger rolling stock, buildings (including stations) signals and track used on the London and North Eastern Railway. Gives scale plans and diagrams; construction details; photographs of the author's own models; and numerous information-packed appendices.